Learn German with Adventure Stories
Bombs on Monte Carlo

HypLern Interlinear Project
www.hyplern.com

First edition: 2025, June

Author: Fritz Reck-Mallaczewen
Translation: Kees van den End
Foreword: Camilo Andrés Bonilla Carvajal PhD

ISBN: 978-1-989643-31-0

kees@hyplern.com
www.hyplern.com

Learn German with Adventure Stories Bombs on Monte Carlo

Interlinear German to English

Author
Fritz Reck-Mallaczewen

Translation
Kees van den End

HypLern Interlinear Project
www.hyplern.com

The HypLern Method

Learning a foreign language should not mean leafing through page after page in a bilingual dictionary until one's fingertips begin to hurt. Quite the contrary, through everyday language use, friendly reading, and direct exposure to the language we can get well on our way towards mastery of the vocabulary and grammar needed to read native texts. In this manner, learners can be successful in the foreign language without too much study of grammar paradigms or rules. Indeed, Seneca expresses in his sixth epistle that "Longum iter est per praecepta, breve et efficax per exempla[1]."

The HypLern series constitutes an effort to provide a highly effective tool for experiential foreign language learning. Those who are genuinely interested in utilizing original literary works to learn a foreign language do not have to use conventional graded texts or adapted versions for novice readers. The former only distort the actual essence of literary works, while the latter are highly reduced in vocabulary and relevant content. This collection aims to bring the lively experience of reading stories as directly told by their very authors to foreign language learners.

Most excited adult language learners will at some point seek their teachers' guidance on the process of learning to read in the foreign language rather than seeking out external opinions. However, both teachers and learners lack a general reading technique or strategy. Oftentimes, students undertake the reading task equipped with nothing more than a bilingual dictionary, a grammar book, and lots of courage. These efforts often end in frustration as the student builds mis-constructed nonsensical sentences after many hours spent on an aimless translation drill.

Consequently, we have decided to develop this series of interlinear translations intended to afford a comprehensive edition of unabridged texts. These texts are presented as they were originally written with no changes in word choice or order. As a result, we have a translated piece conveying the true meaning under every word from the original work. Our readers receive then two books in just one volume: the original version and its translation.

The reading task is no longer a laborious exercise of patiently decoding unclear and seemingly complex paragraphs. What's more, reading becomes an enjoyable and meaningful process of cultural, philosophical and linguistic learning. Independent learners can then acquire expressions and vocabulary while understanding pragmatic and socio-cultural dimensions of the target language by reading in it rather than reading about it.

Our proposal, however, does not claim to be a novelty. Interlinear translation is as old as the Spanish tongue, e.g. "glosses of [Saint] Emilianus", interlinear bibles in Old German, and of course James Hamilton's work in the 1800s. About the latter, we remind the readers, that as a revolutionary freethinker he promoted the publication of Greco-Roman classic works and further pieces in diverse languages. His effort, such as ours, sought to lighten the exhausting task of looking words up in large glossaries as an educational practice: "if there is any thing which fills reflecting men with melancholy and regret, it is the waste of mortal time, parental money, and puerile happiness, in the present method of pursuing Latin and Greek[2]".

Additionally, another influential figure in the same line of thought as Hamilton was John Locke. Locke was also the philosopher and translator of the Fabulae AEsopi in an interlinear plan. In 1600, he was already suggesting that interlinear texts, everyday communication, and use of the target language could be the most appropriate ways to achieve language learning:

> ...the true and genuine Way, and that which I would propose, not only as the easiest and best, wherein a Child might, without pains or Chiding, get a Language which others are wont to be whipt for at School six or seven Years together...[3]

---

1 "The journey is long through precepts, but brief and effective through examples". Seneca, Lucius Annaeus. (1961) Ad Lucilium Epistulae Morales, vol. I. London: W. Heinemann.

2 In: Hamilton, James (1829?) History, principles, practice and results of the Hamiltonian system, with answers to the Edinburgh and Westminster reviews; A lecture delivered at Liverpool; and instructions for the use of the books published on the system. Londres: W. Aylott and Co., 8, Pater Noster Row. p. 29.

3 In: Locke, John. (1693) Some thoughts concerning education. Londres: A. and J. Churchill. pp. 196-7.

Who can benefit from this edition?

We identify three kinds of readers, namely, those who take this work as a search tool, those who want to learn a language by reading authentic materials, and those attempting to read writers in their original language. The HypLern collection constitutes a very effective instrument for all of them.

1. For the first target audience, this edition represents a search tool to connect their mother tongue with that of the writer's. Therefore, they have the opportunity to read over an original literary work in an enriching and certain manner.
2. For the second group, reading every word or idiomatic expression in its actual context of use will yield a strong association between the form, the collocation, and the context. This will have a direct impact on long term learning of passive vocabulary, gradually building genuine reading ability in the original language. This book is an ideal companion not only to independent learners but also to those who take lessons with a teacher. At the same time, the continuous feeling of achievement produced during the process of reading original authors both stimulates and empowers the learner to study[1].
3. Finally, the third kind of reader will notice the same benefits as the previous ones. The proximity of a word and its translation in our interlinear texts is a step further from other collections, such as the Loeb Classical Library. Although their works might be considered the most famous in this genre, the presentation of texts on opposite pages hinders the immediate link between words and their semantic equivalence in our native tongue (or one we have a strong mastery of).

---

1 Some further ways of using the present work include:

1. As you progress through the stories, focus less on the lower line (the English translation). Instead, try to read through the upper line, staying in the foreign language as long as possible.
2. Even if you find glosses or explanatory footnotes about the mechanics of the language, you should make your own hypotheses on word formation and syntactical functions in a sentence. Feel confident about inferring your own language rules and test them progressively. You can also take notes concerning those idiomatic expressions or special language usage that calls your attention for later study.
3. As soon as you finish each text, check the reading in the original version (with no interlinear or parallel translation). This will fulfil the main goal of this

collection: bridging the gap between readers and original literary works, training them to read directly and independently.

Why interlinear?

Conventionally speaking, tiresome reading in tricky and exhausting circumstances has been the common definition of learning by texts. This collection offers a friendly reading format where the language is not a stumbling block anymore. Contrastively, our collection presents a language as a vehicle through which readers can attain and understand their authors' written ideas.

While learning to read, most people are urged to use the dictionary and distinguish words from multiple entries. We help readers skip this step by providing the proper translation based on the surrounding context. In so doing, readers have the chance to invest energy and time in understanding the text and learning vocabulary; they read quickly and easily like a skilled horseman cantering through a book.

Thereby we stress the fact that our proposal is not new at all. Others have tried the same before, coming up with evident and substantial outcomes. Certainly, we are not pioneers in designing interlinear texts. Nonetheless, we are nowadays the only, and doubtless, the best, in providing you with interlinear foreign language texts.

Handling instructions

Using this book is very easy. Each text should be read at least three times in order to explore the whole potential of the method. The first phase is devoted to comparing words in the foreign language to those in the mother tongue. This is to say, the upper line is contrasted to the lower line as the following example shows:

Das	wußte	der	alte	dicke	Crofts	nicht	mehr.
That	knew	the	old	fat	Crofts	not	(any)more

The second phase of reading focuses on capturing the meaning and sense of the original text. As readers gain practice with the method, they should be able to focus on the target language without getting distracted by the translation. New users of the method, however, may find it helpful to cover the translated lines with a piece of paper as illustrated in the image below. Subsequently, they try to understand the meaning of every word, phrase, and entire sentences in the target language itself, drawing on the translation only when necessary. In this phase, the reader should resist the temptation to look at the translation for every word. In doing so, they will find that they are able to understand a good portion of the text by reading directly in the target language, without the crutch of the translation. This is the skill we are looking to train: the ability to read and understand native materials and enjoy them as native speakers do, that being, directly in the original language.

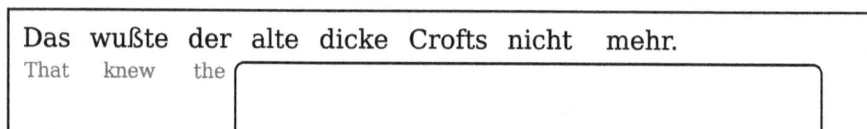

Das wußte der alte dicke Crofts nicht mehr.
That knew the

In the final phase, readers will be able to understand the meaning of the text when reading it without additional help. There may be some less common words and phrases which have not cemented themselves yet in the reader's brain, but the majority of the story should not pose any problems. If desired, the reader can use an SRS or some other memorization method to learning these straggling words.

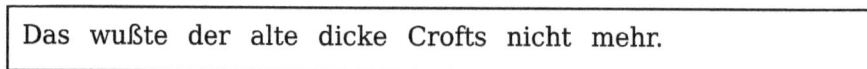

Das wußte der alte dicke Crofts nicht mehr.

Above all, readers will not have to look every word up in a dictionary to read a text in the foreign language. This otherwise wasted time will be spent concentrating on their principal interest. These new readers will tackle authentic texts while learning their vocabulary and expressions to use in further communicative (written or oral) situations. This book is just one work from an overall series with the same purpose. It really helps those who are afraid of having "poor vocabulary" to feel confident about reading directly in the language. To all of them and to all of you, welcome to the amazing experience of living a foreign language!

Additional tools

Check out shop.hyplern.com or contact us at info@hyplern.com for free mp3s (if available) and free empty (untranslated) versions of the eBooks that we have on offer.

For some of the older eBooks and paperbacks we have Windows, iOS and Android apps available that, next to the interlinear format, allow for a pop-up format, where hovering over a word or clicking on it gives you its meaning. The apps also have any mp3s, if available, and integrated vocabulary practice.

Visit the site hyplern.com for the same functionality online. This is where we will be working non-stop to make all our material available in multiple formats, including audio where available, and vocabulary practice.

Table of Contents

Kapitel I

Ein mysteriöser Vorfall, der der näheren Aufklärung
A mysterious incident which the closer explanation
more in detail

noch bedarf, wird gegenwärtig viel diskutiert an der
still needs becomes currently much discussed on the

französischen Riviera.
French Riviera

Am Karnevalsdienstag erklärte nach größeren
At the carnival Tuesday declared after great

Spielverlusten im Kasino von Monte Carlo der Kapitän
game losses in the Casino of Monte Carlo the Captain

eines im Hafen liegenden auswärtigen Kreuzers, daß er
of one in the harbor laying outward cruiser that he
foreign warship

soeben die Schiffskasse verspielt habe und sie von
just now the ships cash (box) gambled away had and her from
it

der Bank zurückerbitten müsse, widrigenfalls er am
the (Casino) bank ask back must otherwise he at the

nächsten Morgen das Kasino beschießen werde.
next morning the Casino shoot at would

Unter den Gästen entstand zunächst eine Panik. Am
Under the guests arose first a panic At the

nächsten Morgen war der Kreuzer aus dem Hafen
next morning was/had the cruiser/warship from the harbor

verschwunden. Die Bank gab beruhigende Erklärungen ab.
disappeared The bank gave soothing/reassuring explanations -off-

Die Regelung des noch recht unaufgeklärten Vorfalles
The arrangement of the still right/indeed unexplained incident

wird mit dem Eingreifen der gegenwärtig zur Kur
will with the intervention of the currently to the/for a cure/treatment

in Monte Carlo anwesenden Fürstin eines kleineren
in Monte Carlo present queen of a smaller

Balkanstaates in Verbindung gebracht.
Balkan state in connection brought

Zeitungsmeldung des ›Meridional‹
Newspaper Announcement of the Meridional

vom 8. März 1922.
From the 8th March 1922

Dies ist, wie ich meine, eine fröhliche, eine beschwingte
This is as I mean/believe a happy an exhilarated

Geschichte – ich glaube, daß sie in dem nun etwas
story – I believe that she in the now somewhat

mürrisch und rauchgrau gewordenen Europa eine der
grumpy and smoky gray become Europe one of the

letzten fröhlichen und übermütigen Geschichten ist.
last joyful and high-spirited stories is

Weswegen sie damals vor sieben Jahren, als sie sich
For what she at that time before seven years as she herself
seven years ago

zutrug, gerade in Deutschland nicht bekanntgeworden ist,
happened just in Germany not known is

habe ich mir nie recht erklären können, da sie
have I myself never right explain been able there she
really

ja doch um den ganzen Erdball herum ihren
indeed however around the whole earth-ball -around- her
globe

Weg gemacht hat: von Port Said (wo die Welt notorisch
way made has from port said where the world notoriously

am unanständigsten ist) ist sie durch alle die unzähligen
at the most indecent is is she through all the countless

Überseeklubs in Aden und Singapore gewandert ... in der
oversea clubs in Aden and Singapore wandered in the

Tent-Bar in Yokohama ist über sie gelacht worden, und in
tent bar in Yokohama is over her laughed become and in

Sydney und in Kapstadt, als wir frostklappernd im
Sydney and in Cape town as we rattling frost in the

Südwinter vor den Kaminfeuern des »India-Hotels«
South winter before the chimney fires of the India hotel

saßen, und sich puritanische und bibelfeste alte
sat and themselves puritanical and bible-proof old

Holländer ärgerten über unseren Alkoholkonsum: immer
dutch irritated about our alcohol consumption always

war es diese lustige Geschichte von dem Kapitän Cradock,
was it this merry story from the Captain Cradock

der zum Entsetzen der ganzen Welt eines Tages seine
who to the fright of the whole world one day his

Kanonen auf das Kasino von Monte Carlo richtete. Bis
cannons on the Casino of Monte Carlo aimed Until

dann eine Frauenhand dazwischenfuhr und diesen
then a woman's hand intervened and this

grimmigen Abenteurer zu einem wohlgesitteten und
grim adventurer to a well-mannered and

ordentlichen Mitglied der menschlichen Gesellschaft
ordinary member of the human company

machte. –
made

Was nun diesen Kapitän Cradock anbelangt, so muß ich
What now this Captain Cradock concerned so must I

ja wohl, ehe ich seine Geschichte erzähle, eine
indeed well before I his story relate a

persönliche Feststellung machen. Ich für mein Teil glaube
personal conclusion make I for my part believe

zwar, daß diese ganz großen Abenteurer sozusagen
indeed that these very great adventurers so to speak

5

Weltwunder sind, daß sie unabhängig von
wonders of the world *are* *that* *they* *independent* *of*

Nationalitäten und politischen Sentiments durch den
nationalities *and* *political* *sentiments* *through* *the*

Weltenraum schwirren wie Kometenschwänze und
world space *buzz* *as* *comet tails* *and*

Planetentrümmer. Immerhin möchte ich in aller Form
planetary debris *After all* *may* *I* *in* *all* *form*

feststellen, daß dieser Cradock, obwohl er vor dem
determine *that* *this* *Cradock* *although* *he* *before* *the*

Kriege ganz kurze Zeit die Uniform eines britischen
War *(a) very* *short* *time* *the* *uniform* *of a* *british*

Marineoffiziers getragen hatte, durchaus kein Engländer
naval officer *carried* *had* *throughout at all* *no* *Englishman*

von Blut war, sondern aus einem durchaus
from *blood* *was* *but* *from* *a* *throughout at all*

internationalen Raufbold- und Seeräuberadel stammte.
international *brawler* *and* *pirate nobility* *stemmed came from*

Zuzugeben ist, daß einer seiner Vorfahren vor
Admitted *is* *that* *one* *of his* *ancestors* *before*

fünfhundert Jahren um die Zeit der britisch-französischen
fivehundred *years* *for* *the* *time* *the* *British-French*

Kriege englischer Oberst gewesen war und als solcher der
war *(an) English* *Colonel* *been* *was had* *and* *as* *such* *the*

Familie	Cradock	ein	ganz	merkwürdiges	Privileg
family	Cradock	a	completely	strange	privilege

erstritten	hatte.	Das	von	jenem	mittelalterlichen	Cradock
disputed conquered	had	The	from	that	medieval	Cradock

befehligte	Regiment	nämlich	hatte	an	der	Ruhr	gelitten,
commanded	regiment	namely	had	on	the	Ruhr	suffered

hatte	infolgedessen	öfter	als	andere	Regimenter
had	consequently	more often	than	other	regiments

Ursache	gehabt,	sich	seiner	Hosen
root cause reason	had	itself	their	pants

zeitweilig	zu	entledigen,	und	war	in	einem	solchen
at times ?because of German beer?	to	get rid of	and	was	in	a	such

Zustande	der	Hosenlosigkeit	von	den	Franzosen	–
to-stand condition	of the of	pantlessness	from by	the	Frenchmen	–

unschicklicherweise	vermutlich	unter	der	persönlichen
inappropriately	probably	under	the	personal

Führung	der	Jungfrau	von	Orleans	–	angegriffen	worden.
guidance	of the	maiden	of	Orleans	–	attacked	become

Nun	also,	der	damalige	Cradock	hatte	mit	seinem
Now	thus	the	then	Cradock	had	with	his

hosenlosen	Regiment	den	Feind	in	die	Flucht	geschlagen
pantless	regiment	the	enemy	in	the	flight	struck

und	dadurch	für	alle	Zeiten	für	sich	und	seine
and	there-through through that	for	all	times	for	himself	and	his

Nachkommen von den britischen Königen ein ganz
progeny from the British kings a completely

seltsames, in Europa viel belachtes Privileg erstritten: das
strange in Europe much laughed at privilege conquered the

glücklicherweise nie ausgeübte Privileg, jederzeit und
fortunately never practiced privilege at any time and

unangemeldet bei sämtlichen Mitgliedern des Hofes –
unannounced at all members of the court –

ohne Hosen zu erscheinen ...
without pants to appear

So also verhielt es sich mit dem Stammvater aller
So thus related it itself with the progenitor of all

Cradocks, und seine Nachkommen hatten so ziemlich in
Cradocks and his progeny had so rather in

allen Armeen Europas und auf allen Schlachtfeldern des
all armies (of) Europe and on all battlefields of the

Erdballes gerauft und sich die Schädel blutig schlagen
globe robbed and himself the skull bloody strike

lassen. Für den Schwedenkönig und die reine Lehre
let For the king of Sweden and the pure teaching

hatten sie gefochten. Für die Ostindische Kompanie und
had they fought For the East Indian Company and

den Großen Friedrich. Und sogar für die Sterne und
the great Friedrich And even for the stars and

Streifen des jungen Amerika. Es gibt eben solche über
stripes of the young America It gives just such over
There are

alle Staaten verteilte Raufbolde, die ebensogut in Hu- wie
all States divided scoundrels who just as well in Hu as

in Büsum oder selbst auf dem Monde zu Hause
in bussum or even on the Moon to house
at home

sein können. Leute, die heute Soldaten für Amanullah und
be can People who today soldiers for Amanullah and
can be

morgen für die chinesischen Marschälle ausbilden, und
tomorrow for the Chinese Marshals form and
generals

deren ewiges Schicksal es ist, wie Kometen ruhelos durch
whose eternal fate it is like comets restless through

das Weltall zu sausen. Wenn es ihnen eben nicht passiert,
the space to zoom When it them just not happened

was im Jahre neunzehnhundertundzweiundzwanzig diesem
what in the year nineteen twenty-two this

langen Kapitän Cradock passierte: daß sie von
tall Captain Cradock happened that they from
by

Frauenhänden gezähmt und schließlich doch noch zu
female hands tamed and finally indeed still to

leidlich gesitteten Europäern gemacht werden. Ja. –
tolerable mannered Europeans made become Yes

Und nun: es tut mir innig leid, daß diese an sich
And now it does me intimate suffering that this on itself
I'm very sorry

so unromantische und beschwingte Geschichte eine ganz
so unromantic and exhilarated story a very

kleine Vorgeschichte hat – eine Vorgeschichte, in der
small prehistory has – a prehistory in which

sogar eine so romantische und rar gewordene
even a so romantic and rare become

Angelegenheit wie eine Prinzessinnenhochzeit eine Rolle
matter as a princess wedding a role

spielt. In den allerletzten Jahren vor dem Kriege nämlich
plays In the very last years before the War namely

hatte dieser »lange Cradock« (wie er wegen seiner ganz
had this tall Cradock as he because of his very

unwahrscheinlichen Körpermaße genannt wurde!) in
improbable body measurements called was in

London als eben beförderter Flottenleutnant einen Flirt
London as just promoted fleet lieutenant a flirt

gehabt. Einen Flirt mit einer Prinzessin aus einer
had A flirt with a princess from a

Nebenlinie des königlichen Hauses von Großbritannien
branch line of the royal house from Great Britain

und Irland. Einen Flirt, von dem nur bekannt ist, daß die
and Ireland A flirt from which only known is that the

gemeinsamen Ausritte der beiden Beteiligten etwas
shared rides of the both involved somewhat

länger dauerten, als nach den Grundsätzen der höfischen
longer lasted as to the principles of the courtly

Schicklichkeit solche Ritte zu dauern haben. Ferner, daß
decency such rides to last have Further that
should last

dieser Flirt einige Zeit Gegenstand des Hofklatsches von
this flirt some time object of the court gossip of

alten silberbestickten Palastdamen war. Drittens, daß der
old silver embroidered palace ladies was Thirdly that the

Flirt zwischen dem neubeförderten Flottenleutnant Cradock
flirt between the newly promoted fleet lieutenant Cradock

und der Prinzessin Maria so endete, wie alle solche Flirts
and the princess Maria so ended as all such flirts

zu enden pflegen. Damit nämlich, daß der Hof die
to end use to do There-with namely that the court the

Prinzessin Maria standesgemäß verlobte.
princess Maria according to her rank engaged

Mit dem Potentaten eines kleinen armen Balkanstaates,
With the potentate of a small poor Balkan state

der hier, damit durch diese fröhliche Geschichte um
which here there-with through this happy story for
so because of

Gottes willen keine internationalen Spannungen verursacht
God's will no international tensions caused

werden, mit dem Phantasienamen »Labrador« bezeichnet
become with the fantasy name Labrador designated

sein mag. Mit diesem, um mindestens dreißig Jahre
be may With this about at least thirty years

älteren Sixtus von Labrador, der diese fröhliche und
older Sixtus of Labrador who this happy and

beschwingte Geschichte mit dem Gewichte seiner
exhilarated story with the weights of his

Persönlichkeit und seines Namens nicht im allermindesten
personality and of his name not in the most least

beschweren wird. Da er nämlich schon bei seiner
weigh down will Since he namely already at his

Heirat ein verlebtes altes Scheusal, ein altes Austerngrab
marriage a passed out old monster an old oyster grave

mit pontacroter Burgundernase gewesen war. Und im
with big red Burgundy nose been was And in the

achten Jahre dieser im November
eight year of this in -the- november

neunzehnhundertundzwölf zu London geschlossenen Ehe
nineteen hundred and twelve at / in london closed / concluded marriage

vom Darmkrebs geholt wurde und die Mary als
from the colon cancer fetched killed became and the Mary as

Fürstin-Witwe von Labrador zurückließ. Und begraben
princess-widow of Labrador left behind And buried

wurde mit allen Zeremonien seines Landes und damit
became with all ceremonies of his country and there-with

gottlob ein für allemal ausscheidet aus dieser
praise God once for all is eliminated from this

Geschichte, die mit Hoheiten gar nichts ... aber auch
story that with sovereignty at all nothing but also

gar nichts zu tun hat. Sondern eben nur mit diesem
at all nothing to do has However just only with this

wilden Abenteurer Cradock, der partout das Kasino von
wild adventurer Cradock who right away the Casino of

Monte Carlo in Brand schießen wollte und dann doch auf
Monte Carlo in fire shoot wanted and then indeed on

unerwartete Weise von einer Frauenhand zu einem
unexpected manner from a woman's hand to a

zivilisierten Manne gemacht wurde. Ja.
civilized man made became Yes

***
***

Diese Verlobung und diese Hochzeit der Mary aber,
This engagement and this wedding of the mary however

sie bildet den einzigen mit höfischem Ballast beschwerten
she forms the only with courtly ballast weighed (down)

Bestandteil meiner Geschichte. Daß man sie an diesen
component of my story That one her to this

greulichen alten Mann verlobt habe, das hatte sie dem
horrible old man engaged have had that had she the

13

langen Cradock unter Tränen erzählt am Tage, ehe der
long Cradock under in tears told at the day before the

Hofbericht die Verlobung bekanntgab, bei einer Fuchsjagd
court notice the engagement announced at a fox hunt

in Hampton, bei der sie (absichtlich oder zufällig)
in Hampton at which she intentionally or coincidentally

sich verirrt hatten und für eine halbe Stunde allein
herself lost had and for a half hour alone

geblieben waren. Und als sie es ihm gesagt hatte, da
remained were And as she it him said had there

war der lange Cradock kurzerhand zum Angriff
was the tall Cradock without further ado to the attack

übergegangen und hatte diese Prinzessin furchtbar geküßt.
passed over and had this princess terribly kissed

Ganz furchtbar und mit Küssen, auf die
Completely terribly and with kisses, on (which) the

Prinzessinnen eigentlich nicht eingerichtet sind. Dann war
princesses actually not furnished are Then was had

er aufgesessen und hatte sie zum Jagdfelde
he up-sat stood up and had her to the hunt field

zurückbegleitet. Und hatte sich sehr formell verabschiedet
accompanied back And had himself very formally taken leave

und hatte sie in den acht bis zur Hochzeit
and had her in the eight until to the wedding

verstrichenen Wochen nie wieder gesehen, und nur das
elapsed weeks never again seen and only that

war bekanntgeworden, daß er in diesen Wochen wilder
was known that he in these weeks more wild

trank und noch wilder ritt als gewöhnlich. Bis dann
drank and even more wild rode as usual Until then

eben die Hochzeit gekommen war, und sie sich bei
just the wedding come was and they each other at

dieser Hochzeit für lange Jahre ein letztes Mal gesehen
this wedding for long years a last time seen

hatten ...
had

Diese Hochzeit aber fand in London an
This wedding however found in London on
(fand statt; occurred)

einem kalten windigen Novembertage statt. In der
a cold windy November day place In the

Westminsterabtei, in der bekanntlich alle englischen
Westminster abbey in which as known all English

Könige begraben liegen – der blutige Richard und der
kings buried lie – the bloody Richard and the

fröhliche Prinz Heinz und dann der achte Heinrich, der
happy Prince Heinz and then the eighth Heinrich who

bekanntlich neben dem Rekord von acht Frauen den
as known besides the record of eight women the

anderen Rekord von dreihundertundfünfundsechzig Bastarden
other record of three hundred sixty-five bastards

aufgestellt hat, und wenn es gerade ein Schaltjahr gewesen
set up / set had and when it just a leap year been

wäre, so wären es todsicher
would be so were it surefire

dreihundertundsechsundsechzig gewesen ... An diesem mit
three hundred sixty six been At this with

Geschichte und Romantik schwer belasteten Orte also
stories and romance heavy burdened place thus

vollzog sich die Trauung des Paares so, wie nach alter
fulfilled itself the wedding of the couple so as after old

Sitte sich Trauungen von englischen Prinzessinnen
habits itself wedding ceremonies from English princesses

immer vollziehen. Daß nämlich Braut und Bräutigam bei
always fulfill That namely bride and bridegroom at

ihrem Gange zum Kirchenportal durch ein Spalier von
their progress to the church portal through a latticework of

Flottenoffizieren schritten, und daß diese Offiziere über das
fleet officers stride and that these officers over the

Paar dachsparrenartig und schützend ihre entblößten Degen
pair rafters like and protective their bared swords

hielten. So, wie das heute noch geschieht, wenn ein
held So as the today still happens when a

Mitglied des königlichen Hauses heiratet. Höchst
member of the royal house marries Most high
Most

romantisch und unzeitgemäß eigentlich. Ich kann's nicht
romantic and out of date actually I can it not

ändern. –
change

So also war das auch dieses Mal. Und zuerst standen da
So thus was it also this time And first stood there

alte eisgraue Admirale mit beträchtlichem Leibesumfang
old ice gray admirals with considerable body size

und Leberverhärtung und goldbetreßten Schiffshüten und
and liver hardening and gold-pressed ship's hats and

blitzenden Victoriakreuzen auf Milz und Blinddarm. Dann
flashing Victoria crosses on spleen and appendix Then

– näher schon dem Portal – waren es magere
– closer already to the portal – were it skinny

Linienschiffskapitäne in mittleren Jahren mit harten
Battle ship captains in middle (aged) years with hard

Gesichtern, und auf diesen Gesichtern war zu lesen, daß
faces and on these faces was to read that

man hier sei, um mit Anstand eine etwas romantische
one here were for with decency a somewhat romantic

Zeremonie zu erledigen, und daß man im übrigen diese
ceremony to take care of and that one in the rest this

süße Mary bedauere, weil sie nun ein solch altes
sweet Mary regret because she now a such old

verlebtes Laster heiraten müsse. Ganz dicht am Portal
worn out wagon marry must Very close to the portal

aber, da stand unter sechs blutjungen, eben
however there stood under six very young just

beförderten Flottenleutnants einer, der mit seiner
promoted fleet lieutenants one which with his

verwegenen Nase und den kühlen und vielleicht ein wenig
daring nose and the cool and perhaps a little

frechen Augen eigentlich wie ein vorzeitig in die Uniform
cheeky eyes actually like a prematurely in the uniform

gepreßter Schuljunge aussah. Das also war der Leutnant
pressed school boy looked That thus was the lieutenant

Frederic William Cradock. –
Frederic William Cradock

Ja, so war das, und alles vollzog sich, wie die
Yes so was it and everything took place itself as the

Etikette es vorschrieb und heute noch vorschreibt. Und
etiquette it prescribed and today still prescribes And

Zeremonienmeister, leuchtend in ihren zinnoberroten
masters of ceremonies bright shining in their vermilion

Hoffräcken wie riesige seltene Vögel, waren eingeschwenkt
court jackets as giant rare birds were swung in

und hatten Front gemacht und ihre Stäbe aufstampfen
and had front made and their staffs pound

lassen ... die Kameras der Presseleute hatten geschnappt,
let the cameras of the press people had snapped

und unter dem Dach von entblößten Säbelklingen schritt
and under the roof of bared saber blades stepped

auf das Portal zu mit ihrem abgelebten alten
on the portal towards with her worn out old

Bräutigam diese in der Gloriole ihrer zwanzig Jahre
bridegroom this in the prime of her twenty years

strahlende Braut. Und erst da, als dieses ungleiche Paar
radiant bride And first there as this unequal pair
only

schon auf der obersten Stufe der Treppe stand, und als
already on the highest step of the stairs stood and as

aus dem Dunkel von Westminsterabtei schon die bunten
from the dark of Westminster abbey already the colorful

Meßgewänder der amtierenden Geistlichkeit leuchteten,
Mass vestments of the incumbent clergy shone

da hatte sich etwas ereignet, was als eine, wenn
there had itself something occurred what as a when

auch nur flüchtige Störung dieser feierlichen Zeremonie
also only fleeting disturbance of this solemn ceremony

bezeichnet werden muß, und was dann auch für den
designated become must and what then also for the

weiteren Verlauf dieser Geschichte allerlei Folgen
further process of this story all kinds of consequences

hatte.
had

Die Sache war eben die, daß es ein kalter, unfreundlicher
The thing was just this that it a cold unfriendly

Novembertag war mit eisigem Nordost, und daß
November day was with icy northeast(er wind) and that

gerade, als das Brautpaar das Portal durchschreiten wollte,
just as the wedding pair the portal step through wanted

ein solch grober Bursche von Windstoß über den Platz
a such rough lad of gust of wind over the square
                    gust of wind

gefahren kam. Zuerst war es nur so, daß weißhaarige
driven came First was it only so that white-haired
was blown

Hofdamen zusammenschauerten und alte Kammerherren die
court ladies huddled together and old chamberlains the

Gicht in ihren Knochen fühlten und wohl auch daran
gout in their bones felt and well also to it

dachten, daß jetzt ein männlicher Whisky guttun könnte.
thought that now a more masculine whiskey do well could

Das Gros dieses unheiligen Windes aber, das mit
The large(st part) of this unholy wind however that with

voller Wucht und mit tanzenden Wirbeln von Staub und
full force and with dancing swirls of dust and

Papierfetzen und Strohhalmen daherkam, das
scraps of paper and straws came along that

richtete schlimme Verheerungen an. Zuerst flogen
arranged bad devastation on First flew
(richtete an; caused)

von den kammerherrlichen Häuptern etliche Schiffshüte
from the chamber-masters' heads several ship hats

davon, ließen schön polierte Glatzen sehen und
there-from let beautiful polished bald see and
away

erregten einiges Lachen ringsum. Dann stürzte der
excited some laughing all around Then crashed the

Kurbelapparat eines Kinomannes um, dann
crank set of a cinema man for then

machten, scheu geworden durch die allgemeine
made shy become through the general
(machten Miene: started)

Wirrnis, vor einer der Galakutschen die à la Daumont
tangle before one of the gala carriages which à la Daumont

gespannten Schimmel und Rappen Miene,
harnessed gray and white horse signs
(machten Miene: started)

durchzugehen. Zum Schluß aber fuhr dieser Lümmel
to go through At the end however drove this lout

von einem Wind mitten hinein in das Kirchenportal, nahm
of a wind middle inside in the church portal took
right

den Schleier der Braut und bauschte ihn wie eine Fahne
the veil of the bride and bagged him as a flag
it

auf, bis er sich da oben an irgend etwas verfing.
up until he itself there above on any something caught
it

Dieses »Irgendetwas« aber, das war die Degenspitze
This anything however that was the rapier tip

des Leutnants Frederic William Cradock.
of the lieutenant Frederic william cradock

Das war ja nun wirklich ein störendes, um nicht zu
That was yes now really an annoying for not to
indeed

sagen peinliches Ereignis. Die Braut hatte es zunächst
say embarrassing event The bride had it first

nicht bemerkt und war einfach weitergegangen; da hatte
not noticed and was simply walked on there had

sie alles nur noch schlimmer gemacht und den
she everything only still worse made and the

Schleier über die ganze Länge der Klinge gezerrt bis
veil over the whole length of the blade tugged until

zum Degengefäß. Und als der Leutnant Cradock den
to the rapier handle And as the lieutenant Cradock the

Degen gesenkt und versucht hatte, den inzwischen
rapier lowered and tried had the In the meantime

schon stark beschädigten Brautschmuck von der Klinge
already strong damaged bridal decoration from the blade

zu ziehen, da war ein zweiter Windstoß gekommen und
to pull there was a second gust of wind come and

hatte ihm den Schleier um die Schulter geweht. Und als
had him the veil around the shoulder blown And as

sie dann beide durch allerlei Manipulationen versucht
they then both through all kinds of manipulations tried

hatten, sich von diesem Erzeugnis der englischen
had themselves from this product of the english

Textilindustrie und seinen mannigfachen Umschlingungen zu
textile industry and its manifold entwines to

befreien, da war es ganz schlimm geworden. Da
free there was it completely bad become There

standen sie nämlich und waren untrennbar verbunden
stood they namely and were inseparable connected

durch eine Boa constrictor aus Tüll. Notgedrungen
through a boa constrictor of tulle Inevitably

blieb natürlich der ganze Brautzug stehen, und
remained of course the whole bridal train stand and
(blieb stehen: stopped)

natürlich fingen alte Hofdamen an, mokante Blicke zu
of course caught old court ladies on mocking looks to

tauschen. Da nahm denn die resolute Braut ihren
exchange There took then the resolute bride her

Brautschleier und riß ihn … ritsch – ratsch … mitten
bridal veil and ripped it rip rap middle

durch. Dann blieb sie noch eine kleine Weile stehen
through Then remained she still a little while stand

neben dem langen Cradock, und beide sahen sich ins
beside the tall Cradock and both saw himself in the

Gesicht und mußten zuerst lachen und waren hinterher
face and must first laugh and were after
                                           had

doch beide ein wenig rot geworden ...
indeed both a little red become

Grober Unfug wäre es natürlich, in diesem Falle von
Rude nonsense would be it of course in this case of

»Liebe auf den ersten oder auch nur auf den zweiten
Love on -the- first or also only on -the- second

Blick« zu reden – beide waren sie für derlei
sight to speak – both were they for such

Sentimentalitäten viel zu lebenstüchtige Menschenkinder.
sentimentalities much too vivacious human children

Es war einfach so, wie es eben manchmal ist zwischen
It was simply so as it just sometimes is between

jungen Leuten, die sich einmal gut gewesen sind
young people who each other once good been are

und sich unvorhergesehenerweise noch einmal
and each other unforeseen still once

begegnen, ehe sie sich auf immer trennen müssen.
meet before they themselves on always separate must
                                      for

Und sich das, was sie sich zu sagen haben, in
And each other that what they each other to say have in

aller Verschwiegenheit mit den Augen sagen ...
all secrecy with the eyes say

»Dank dir«, sagten die Augen der kleinen Mary, »daß du
Thank you said the eyes of the small Mary that you

mir nun ein so schöner Brautkavalier bist.«
to me now a such beautiful bridal cavalier are

»Laß dir's nicht zu schwer werden«, sagten die Augen
Let to you it not too heavy become said the eyes

des langen Cradock und streiften dabei den alten,
of the long Cradock and grazed there-by the old

klapprigen Bräutigam, »laß dir's nicht allzu schwer
rickety bridegroom let you it not all too heavy

werden, wenn du nun dieses alte Laster heiraten mußt!«
become when you now this old wagon marry must

Das war alles, und damit setzte sich der Brautzug
That was everything and there-with set itself the bridal train

auch schon wieder in Bewegung. Und nur noch einmal,
also already again in movement And only still once

dicht an der Tür, drehte sie sich um nach dem langen
close on the door turned she herself for to the long

Cradock. »Zum Andenken an Mary«, sagte ganz leise
Cradock To the memories on mary « said completely softly

die Braut und reichte dem langen Cradock einen Fetzen
the bride and reached the long Cradock a shred
handed

ihres zerrissenen Schleiers hin. Das aber war auch
of her torn veil -to- That however was also

wirklich alles. Und alles Weitere vollzog sich so,
really everything And everything further took place itself so

wie es nach altem Brauch sich zu vollziehen hatte. Und
as it to old usage itself to fulfill had And

höchstens dieses eine nur noch wurde von älteren
at most this one (thing) only still became from older
was by

Hofdamen flüsternd vermerkt, daß am Abend die
court ladies whispering noted that at the evening the

Prinzessin-Braut den langen Cradock ungebührlich oft
princess bride the long Cradock undue often

zum Tanz auffordern ließ. Das war alles, und das ist
to the dance up-demand let That was everything and that is
prompt

eigentlich die ganze Vorgeschichte zu dem, was sich dann
actually the whole prehistory to that what itself then

zehn Jahre später in Monte Carlo ereignete. –
ten years later in Monte Carlo occurred

Was die Mary anbelangt, so habe ich schon angedeutet,
What the mary concerned so have I already indicated

daß ihr Gatte nach siebenjähriger Ehe schon vom
that her spouse after seven year marriage already from the

Darmkrebs geholt wurde und sie als Fürstin-Witwe jenes
colon cancer fetched became and her as princess-widow of that
killed

kleinen Balkanstaates zurückließ, den wir, »den Gesetzen
small balkan state left behind which we the laws

internationaler Courtoisie folgend«, unter dem Namen
of international courtesy following under the name

»Labrador« verbergen wollen.
Labrador hide will

Da war sie denn also Herrin über fünf Millionen
There was she then thus Mistress over five million

halbwilder Menschen, die von Schweinemast en gros,
semi-wild people who from pig fattening in wholesale
pig raising (French)

von ein paar schlechten Petroleumquellen, vom
from a few bad oil wells from the

Grenzschmuggel nach der Türkei hinüber und vom
border smuggling to -the- Turkey over and from the

Hammeldiebstahl lebten ..., Herrin über eine Liliputarmee
pickpocketing lived Mistress over a liliput army

und eine aus drei asthmatischen alten Kreuzern
and one out (of) three asthmatic old cruisers
warships

bestehende »Flotte«, für die sie die Offiziere aus allen
existing fleet for which she the officers from all

Marinen der europäischen Staaten ... mit Vorliebe wohl
marines from the European states with preference well

auch aus der ihres Heimatlandes bezog. Im ganzen eine
also from that of her home country drew In the whole a
recruited

kleine   korrekte   konstitutionelle   Balkanfürstin   von
little   correct   constitutional   Balkan princess   from

weltberühmter   Schönheit.   Und   nur   das   eine   noch
world famous   beauty   And   only   that   one (thing)   still

wäre   zu   erwähnen,   daß   sie   ein   wenig   zart   und
would be   to   mention   that   she   a   little   tender   and

anfällig   geworden   war.   Daß   ihre   Lungen   das   skythische
susceptible   become   was   That   her   lungs   the   scythian

Klima   ihres   Landes   nicht   recht   vertrugen,   und   daß   sie
climate   of her   country   not   right   tolerated   and   that   she

eigentlich   jeden   Winter   in   Ägypten   zubringen   mußte ...
actually   every   witer   in   Egypt   bring through spend   had to

Was   aber   den   langen   Cradock   betrifft,   so   hatte   es
What   however   the   tall   Cradock   concerns   so   had   it

gleich   nach   der   eben   beschriebenen   Hochzeit   ein
immediately   to   the   just   described   wedding   a

etwas   voreiliges   Ende   genommen   mit   seiner   Laufbahn   in
somewhat   hasty   end   taken   with   his   career   in

der   großen   Flotte.   Daß   er   mit   allen   seinen   verwegenen
the   large   fleet   That   he   with   all   his   daring

Wetten   und   Poloponys   und   seiner   heillosen   Passion   für
bets   and   polo-ponies   and   his   hopeless   passion   for

Roulette   und   Baccarat   sein   ziemlich   beträchtliches
roulette   and   baccarat   his   rather   considerable

Vermögen in anderthalb Jahren vertan und vermöbelt
capital in one and a half years wasted and thrashed

hatte und bis zum Hals in Schulden stak, das war nur
had and until to the neck in debts stuck that was only
was

der eine Grund gewesen. Daß er aber dann (kurz vor
the one reason been That he however then short before
only

dem Weltkriege!) als Dritter Offizier des kleinen Kreuzers
the world wars as third officer of the small cruiser

»Thunderer« im Hafen von Bangkok in Siam in stark
Thunderer in the harbor of Bangkok in Siam in strong
(Thailand)

angeheitertem Zustande die im Po-Wat-Tempel gehaltenen
tipsy to-stand the in the Po-Wat temple held
condition

heiligen Tempelkatzen mit Hilfe von Baldriantropfen auf die
holy temple cats with help of valerian drops on the

Straße gelockt und zu einem in der buddhistischen
street lured and to a in the buddhist

Religion durchaus nicht vorgesehenen Konzert veranlaßt
religion throughout not seen before concert impelled
at all

hatte: das war der Streiche zuviel gewesen. Ernsthafte
had that was the prank too much been Serious
had a

diplomatische Verwicklungen hatte es damals wegen
diplomatic entanglements had it at that time because of
complications

dieses Frevels gegeben zwischen den Regierungen von
this outrage given between the governments from
caused

England und Siam. Und dann hatte auch die Herzogin
England and Siam And then had also the duchess
(Thailand)

von Fife ihrem als Dritten Seelord im Flottenamt
from Fife her as third seelord in the fleet office

sitzenden Vetter einen Besuch gemacht in ihrer Eigenschaft
sitting cousin a visit made in her property
appointed

als Protektrice der internationalen Liga für Katzenzucht
as protector of the international league for cat breeding

und Katzenschutz: da war denn der lange Cradock (der
and cat protection there was then the tall Cradock who

ja sowieso eigentlich kein Brite von Geblüt war!) in
yes anyway actually no Brit from blood was in
indeed birth

weitem Bogen und für alle Zeiten hinausgeflogen aus dem
(a) wide arc and for all times flown out from the

Dienste in der königlichen Flotte.
service in the royal fleet

Zu berichten ist, daß er, der internationale Abenteurer,
To report is that he the international adventurer

während des Krieges durch die üblen Gebiete am
during -of- the war through the foul areas at the
in the

mittleren Kongo sich mühselig mit einer Expedition
middle of Congo himself laborious with an expedition

durchschlug, von der außer ihm nur zwei zum Skelett
through-struck from which except him only two to the skeleton
penetrated

abgemagerte Träger und sein Terrier »Quidam«
emaciated carriers and his terrier Quidam

zurückkehrten. Zu berichten ist ferner, daß er sich im
returned To report is further that he himself in the

Jahre 1918 in Betschuana-Land mit den allerletzten
year 1918 in Betschuana country with the very last

Vermögenstrümmern eine Farm kaufte und Schafe züchtete.
assets a farm bought and sheep bred

Daß er für zwei weitere Jahre verschollen blieb für die
That he for two further years hidden remained for the

große Welt. Bis ihn im Jahre
great world. Until him in the year

neunzehnhundertundzwanzig eine fabelhafte Schafpest
nineteen hundred and twenty a fabulous sheep plague

vollends ruinierte und er zum namenlosen Erstaunen
completely ruined and he to the nameless astonishment

aller alten Klub- und Flottenkameraden in San Sebastian
of all old club and fleet comrades in San Sebastian

aufgetaucht war, wo er mit einem geradezu lächerlichen
duck-up was where he with an almost ridiculous
surfaced

Betriebskapital in drei Nächten fast die Bank
working capital in three nights almost the (casino) bank

gesprengt hatte, um dann binnen eines besonders tollen
blown up had for then within of a particularly great

Jahres auch dieses recht beträchtliche Sümmchen an den
year also this right considerable little sum on the

Mann zu bringen: mit dem berühmten Steeplerhengst
man to bring with the famous Steepler stallion

»Nevermind«, der sich dann beim Derby
Nevermind which itself then at the derby

neunzehnhundertundzwanzig auf dem letzten Sprung das
(of) nineteen hundred and twenty on the last jump the

Erbsbein gebrochen hatte. Und mit der fabelhaften
pea leg broken had And with the fabulous

Segeljacht »Rhadames«, die er vor Spezia auf die
sailing yacht Rhadames which he before Specia on the

Felsen gejagt hatte. Und endlich mit der alten Passion für
rocks chased had And finally with the old passion for
crashed

Baccarat und sonstiges Spiel und mit großartigen
baccarat and other play and with great

Dotationen für hundert in Not geratene Freunde und
endowments for hundred in need become friends and

Feinde von ehedem und mit seiner notorisch offenen
enemies from before and with his notoriously open

Hand für alle die sonstigen zahllosen Parasiten, die für
hand for all the other countless parasites who for

solche plötzlich vom Monde gefallenen Gelder ja eine
such suddenly from the moons fallen funds yes a
indeed

notorisch gute Witterung haben.
notoriously good scent have

Item – in einem weiteren Jahre war auch dieses der Bank
Also – in a further year was also this the bank
(latin) had

von San Sebastian abgenommene Geld zu Ende gewesen,
of San Sebastian taken off money to end been
come

und der lange Cradock hatte sich schließlich und endlich
and the tall Cradock had himself closely and finally
lastly

darauf besinnen müssen, daß er von Hause aus
thereupon reflection must that he from house out

Seemann war: am Ende des Jahres hatte die (wie
sailor was at the end of the year had the as

gesagt, aus drei asthmatischen Kreuzern bestehende)
said out (of) three asthmatic cruisers existing
war ships

Marine von Labrador gerade Offiziere gesucht, und da
marine from Labrador just officers sought and there

hatte er sich eben um eine Stelle beworben. Hatte
had he himself just for a spot applied Had

wieder einmal Glück gehabt, hatte das Kommando des
again once luck had had the command of the

Kanonenbootes »Persimon« erhalten und war somit
gunboat Persimon become and was consequently

Offizier und sozusagen auch Untertan seiner ehemaligen
officer and so to speak also subject of his former

Reitgenossin und Tänzerin geworden. Wobei
riding companion and dancer become Where-by
dance-partner

übrigens zu bemerken ist, daß er sie nie wiedergesehen
by the way to notice is that he her never seen again

hatte seit dem Tage ihrer Hochzeit, und daß er, der alte
had since the days of her wedding and that he the old

abergläubische Spieler, nur den geschenkten Schleierfetzen
superstitious player only the gifted scrap of veil

als Talisman in allen kitzligen Situationen seines etwas
as talisman in all ticklish situations of his somewhat

bewegten Lebens bei sich getragen hatte. In Afrika,
moved life with himself carried had In africa

wo er in seiner entlegenen Farm mit drei weißen
where he in his remote farm with three white

Arbeitern zusammen einmal von neunzig bolschewistisch
workers together once from ninety (by) Bolshevism
by

infizierten Kaffern belagert worden war. In Suez, wo er
infected kaffirs besieged become was In Suez where he

aus dem von Haien wimmelnden Hafen einen aus
from the of sharks teeming harbor a out (of)
with

Liebeskummer über Bord gegangenen deutschen Kellner
lovesickness over- board gone German waiter

nach viertelstündiger Katzbalgerei mit dem Tode doch
after quarter of an hour catfighting with -the- death indeed

noch herausgeholt hatte. In San Sebastian endlich, wo
still brought out had In San Sebastian finally where

ihm, wie gesagt, der größte Baccarat-Coup seines
him as said the greatest baccarat coup of his

baccaratreichen Lebens gelungen war. So war das. Im
rich in baccarat life succeeded was So was that In the
had For the

übrigen war es gar nicht so einfach, nach einer so
rest was it at all not so simple after a such

glanzvollen Jugend und mit einem so unruhigen
glamorous youth and with -a- such restless

Abenteurerblut ums liebe Brot zu dienen in der
adventurer blood for the dear bread to serve in the

armseligen Marine eines armen, halbexotischen Staates,
poor marine of a poor semi-exotic state

der die Gehälter notorisch unpünktlich anwies und
of which the wages notoriously unpunctual instructed and
were paid out

oft nicht einmal die Kohlen seiner Flotte bezahlen
often not once the coals of its fleet pay
even

konnte.
could

Ja, so stand es mit dem langen Cradock. Am
Yes so stood it with the tall Cradock at the

sechsundzwanzigsten Februar
twenty sixth of February

neunzehnhundertzweiundzwanzig aber – an solch einem
nineteen hundred and twenty two however – on such a

Tag, an dem der Frühling zum erstenmal erfolgreich sich
day on that the spring to the first time successful itself

mit dem Winternebel herumbalgte –, an diesem Tage also
with the winter fog wrangled around on this day thus

brachte im Hafen von Genua der diensttuende
brought in the harbor from Genoa the on duty

Funker dem Kapitän Cradock ein Telegramm. Der
radio operator the Captain Cradock a telegram The

Kapitän Cradock saß gerade bei Tisch mit seinem
Captain Cradock sat just at (the) table with his

aus alten Sündern und Abenteurern aller europäischen
out (of) old sinners and adventurers of all European

Staaten zusammengewehten Offizierskorps: der alte
States blown together officer corps the old

Schiffsarzt Crofts war da (ein dicker Schotte,
ship doctor Crofts was there a fat Scotsman

mit dem Cradock sich duzte) ... der Navigationsoffizier
with whom Cradock himself you-d the navigation officer
who Cradock used informal you with

Bromley aus Gravesend (wo bekanntlich die größten
Bromley from Gravesend where as known the great

Spitzbuben der Welt zu Hause sind) ... und der kleine
rascals of the world to house are and the little
home

stiernackige Ostpreuße Kries, der so stark war, daß er
bull-nosed East Prussian Kries who so strong was that he

Tischkanten abbeißen und Fünfschillingstücke zerbrechen
table edges bite off and five shilling pieces break

konnte. Dann noch der alte Chefingenieur Pavlicek, der
could Then still the old chief engineer Pavlicek who

noch in der verwehten Seemacht der Habsburger
still in the blown away sea power of the Habsburg

Doppelmonarchie gedient hatte, und endlich noch der
double monarchy served had and finally still the

blutjunge Williams aus Cornwall, der eigentlich nur »Ja«
very young Williams from Cornwall who actually only yes

und »Nein« sagen konnte und seinen Liebeskummer um
and no say could and his lovesickness for

irgendein kleines Berberiner-Mädchen aus Alexandria in
some little Berber girl from Alexandria in

ungeheuren Whiskymengen zu ersäufen pflegte. Es
tremendous amounts of whiskey to drown used It
There

wurde, wie gewöhnlich, scharf getrunken und dann, beim
became as usual sharp drunk and then at the
much

Kaffee, ziemlich hoch gespielt: das Telegramm, das ihm
coffee rather high played the telegram that him

eben überbracht worden war, hatte der lange Cradock
just brought become was had the tall Cradock

zunächst uneröffnet in den Ärmel geschoben.
first   unopened in the sleeves pushed

Erst nach Tisch, als er allein auf der Brücke noch eine
First after table as he alone on the bridge still a
Only   dinner

Zigarette rauchte, öffnete er es. Es war ein kurzes
cigarette smoked opened he it It was a short

Telegramm seiner Regierung, die ihm auftrug, sofort
telegram of his government which him ordered immediately

nach Monte Carlo zu dampfen und weitere Befehle dort
to Monte Carlo to steam and further orders there

zu erwarten. Was er dort eigentlich sollte, und wie
to expect What he there actually should (do) and how

lange er dort zu liegen haben würde, war nicht gesagt. Er
long he there to lie have would was not said He

ließ das Monokel fallen und steckte kopfschüttelnd das
let the monocle fall and stuck head shaking the

Papier fort. Als er es in seiner Brieftasche barg, fiel ihm
paper away As he it in his letter-bag hid fell him
                                  wallet

der bewußte Schleierfetzen in die Hand.
the mentioned scrap of veil in the hand

Es war ein Fetzen Seidentüll mit Silberfäden, die nun
It was a shred of silk tulle with silver threads which now

schon rot angelaufen waren - er selbst war ein alter,
already red on-run were - he himself was an old
         were becoming red

hartgesottener Sünder, dessen Herz nicht eben sentimental
hard boiled sinner of that heart not just sentimental

genannt werden konnte. Aber da, als der lange Cradock
called become could But there as the tall Cradock

seinen Talisman in der Hand hielt, mußte er doch an
his talisman in the hand held must he indeed on
of

jenes rotblonde Haar denken, auf dem dieser Schleier
that red blonde hair think on which this veil

einmal befestigt gewesen war; und an die Besitzerin dieses
once attached been was and on the owner this
of

rotblonden Heiligenscheines, die man seit zehn Jahren
red blonde saints-shine which one since ten years
halo

nicht gesehen hatte, und die nun »oberste Kriegsherrin«
not seen had and which now top warlord

und »grundgütige Landesmutter« war. Und in diesem
and ground-goody country mother was And in this
principal kind mother of the nation

Augenblick, wo der lange Cradock zum ersten Male
moment where the tall Cradock for the first time

wieder an seine kleine Tänzerin von einst dachte, da
again on his little dancer of once thought there
of dancepartner

geschah ringsum in der spätwinterlichen Hafenbucht
happened all around in the late winter harbor bay

etwas Seltsames und beinahe Aufregendes ...
something strange and almost exciting

Es war eine scharfe Bö, die vom offenen Meer
It was a sharp gust that from the open sea
There nasty

hineinfuhr in den griesgrämigen Tag und die Nebel über
carried in in the grouchy day and the fog over
grayish

den Höhen lockerte und zum erstenmal so etwas wie
the heights loosened and for the first time so something like

Sonne hineinließ in den traurigen Nachmittag. Es war
(a) sun let in in the sad afternoon It was

nichts weiter als der erste entscheidende
nothing further as the first decisive
more than

Frühlings-Schirokko, der sich am Südhimmel meldete.
spring sirocco which itself at the southern sky reported
spring wind from Africa

Aber er war geladen mit Sonnenfeuer und Meereshauch
But it was loaded with sunfire and breath of sea

und wußte von dem glühenden Granit des fernen
and knew from the glowing granite of the distant

Atlas und von den Fanfaren nordwärts
Atlas (mountains) and from the Fanfare (of) northward

ziehender Kraniche und den Brunstschreien numidischer
pulling cranes and the mating calls of Numidian
traveling

Stuten und den Brautliedern der westlichen Berberstämme
mares and the bridal songs of the western Berber tribes

an der roten Afrikaküste.
on the red Africa coast

Solch ein verbuhlter Wind war das, und er machte, daß
Such a fated wind was that and he made that
it

Mensch und Tier und das ganze noch winterliche Genua
human and animal and the whole still wintry Genoa

sofort seine Sprache verstanden. Daß drüben auf
immediately his language understood That over there on
its

dem Kai die mit dem Ausklarieren ihrer Schiffe
the quay the with the clearing out of their ships

beschäftigten italienischen Clerks Verdi-Koloraturen in die
employed Italian clerks verdi colors in the

Lüfte schmetterten und bei den Zollspeichern verliebte
air threw and at the customs store in love being

Katzen schrien und selbst hier auf der Brücke der mit
cats screamed and even here on the bridge the with

dem Putzen des Maschinentelegraphen beschäftigte
the scrubbing of the machine telegraph employed

Quartermeister Jackson ohne Rücksicht auf die
quartermaster Jackson without consideration on the

Anwesenheit des Kapitäns in hohem Tenor leise zu
presence of the captain in high tenor softly to

singen begann.
sing began

Der lange Cradock aber, der zum erstenmal wieder
The tall Cradock however who for the first time again

ganz — completely
bewußt — conscious
an — on / of
einen — a
Heiligenschein — saints-shine / halo
aus — out (of)

rotblondem — red blonde
Haar — hair
und — and
an — on / of
eine — a
kleine — little
übermütige — cocky

Jagdreiterin — hunting rider
gedacht — thought
hatte, — had
steckte — stuck
seinen — his
Talisman — talisman
fort — away

und — and
ging — went
mit — with
gerunzelter — wrinkled
Stirn — forehead
in — in
seine — his
Kabine. — cabin
Noch — Still

immer — always
war — was
er — he
schlank — slim
und — and
drahtig — wiry
wie — as
früher — before
und — and
konnte — could

noch — still
immer — always
für — for
einen — a
schönen — handsome
Burschen — lad
gelten. — be valid / go through
Das — The

Leben — life
aber — however
war — was
das — that
eines — of a
einsamen — lonely
und — and
nicht — not
mehr — (any)more

so — so
übermäßig — excessive
jungen — young
Abenteurers — adventurer
geworden. — become
Das — The
Leben — life
war — was

eine — a
Kette — chain
von — of
Erinnerungen — memories
an — on
gute — good
und — and
schlechte — bad

Baccarat-Tage, — baccarat days
an — on
schwarze, — black
weiße, — white
braune, — brown
gelbe — yellow
und — and

selbst — even
grüne — green
Weiber — women
aus — from
allen — all
Strichen — areas
des — of the
Globus ..., — globe
an — on

Spelunken — late nights
in — in
Yokohama — Yokohama
und — and
in — in
Kapstadt, — Cape town
an — on
zahllose — countless

Blenton- und Ginfizz- und Chocolate-Cocktails. Das Leben
Blenton and Ginfizz and chocolate cocktails The life

war ein wenig ärmlich geblieben, und manchmal begann
was a little poor remained and sometimes began
had

schon ein etwas kalter und scharfer Wind von seiner
already a something colder and sharper wind from its

Bühne zu wehen. Der Steward Blix erzählte an diesem
stage to blow The steward Blix told at this

Abend seinen Kameraden, daß der Kapitän heute lange
evening his comrades that the Captain today long

vor seinem Spiegel gestanden und schließlich ihn (Blix)
before his mirror stood and finally him Blix

gefragt habe, ob man hinten bei ihm graue Haare
asked have whether one in the back at him gray hair
had

entdecken könne ...
discover can
could

An diesem Abend gab es übrigens noch einigen Krach
At this evening gave it by the way still some noise
was there

zwischen dem Kapitän Cradock und der Genueser
between the Captain Cradock and the Genoese

Kohlenfirma Zanelli & Peto, die der fürstlichen Marine
coal company Zanelli Peto which the princely marine

von Labrador ohne Barzahlung (denn die Bordkasse
from Labrador without cash payment then the board account
ship's cashbox

war ziemlich leer) Brennstoff partout nicht liefern wollte.
was rather empty fuel at all not deliver wanted

Und in der Nacht lief mit ihren letzten, aus den
And in the night ran with her last out (from) the

Bunkern zusammengekratzten Kohlen unter den Kesseln die
bunker scraped together coals under the kettles the
coal hold

»Persimon« nach Monte Carlo aus. Und erst hier in Monte
Persimon to Monte Carlo out And first here in Monte
only

Carlo konnte dann der Kapitän Cradock tausend für die
Carlo could then the Captain Cradock (a) thousand for the

Schiffskasse telegraphisch angeforderte Pfunde erheben.
ship's account telegraphically requested pounds raise
ship's cashbox

Was er sonst noch in diesem mit seinem Karneval auf
What he otherwise still in this with his carnival on

das intensivste beschäftigten Monte Carlo sollte, konnte er
the most intense employed Monte Carlo should could he

nirgends erfahren.
nowhere experience

Auch nicht auf dem fürstlichen Konsulat von Labrador mit
Also not on the princely consulate from Labrador with

seiner mehr als dürftigen Office und dem verblaßten
its more as poor office and the faded
than

Wappenschild und dem Porträt der süßen kleinen Mary,
heraldic shield and the portrait of the sweet small Mary

die	nun	als	Fürstin-Witwe	und	grundgütige
who	now	as	princess-widow	and	ground-goody principal kind

Landesmutter	über	dem	Schreibtisch	ihres	Konsuls	hing.
country-mother mother of the nation	over	the	desk	of her	consul	hung

***
***

Bis	Weihnachten	hatte	sie,	die	Fürstin-Witwe,	den	Winter
Until	Christmas night	had	she	the	princess-widow	the	winter

ihres	in	Europas	Wetterwinkel	auf	des	Teufels	Rinne
of her	in	Europe's	weather corner	on	of the	devil's	gutter

gelegenen	Landes	leidlich	vertragen.	Im	Januar	war	auf
situated	land	suffering	born	In -the-	January	was	on

Wintergewittern	von	unwahrscheinlicher	Heftigkeit	und
winter-thunderstorms	from	unlikely	violence	and

auf	groben	Schneestürmen	eine	schwere	Grippe
on	rough	snow storms	a	heavy	flu

dahergefahren	gekommen,	hatte	sie,	die	ehedem	so
there-to-driven added (to her misery)	come	had	she	who	before	so

gesunde	Mary,	für	Wochen	aufs	Krankenlager	geworfen:
healthy	Mary	for	weeks	on the in the	hospital	thrown

da	hatten	die	Ärzte	zuerst	Madeira	und	dann,
there	had	the	doctors	first	Madeira	and	then

im	Hinblick	auf	die	ernstlich	affizierten	Lungen,	sogar
in the	look seeing	on	the	seriously	affected	lungs	even

eine längere Überseereise verordnet. Da aber der
a longer overseas trip prescribed There however the

Verwalter der etwas mageren fürstlichen Schatulle
administrator of the something skinny princely treasure chest

(irgend so ein fetter armenischer Anwalt) ein Veto eingelegt
any so a fat Armenian lawyer a veto inserted

hatte, so hatte die resolute Patientin sich wieder mit
had so had the resolute patient herself again with

Ägypten begnügt und hatte ausgerechnet, daß erhebliche
Egypt satisfied and had of all places that substantial

Kosten sich ersparen ließen, wenn man zur Überfahrt
costs herself spare let when one to the crossing

einen der gerade im Mittelmeer liegenden alten
one of the just in the Mediterranean sea laying old

Kasten von der fürstlich-labradorischen Kriegsmarine
cupboards of the princely Labradorian navy

beordere. Die alte Gräfin Hensbarrow (noch aus London
order The old countess Hensbarrow still from london

importiert und einzige »Palastdame« Ihrer Hoheit und
imported and only palace lady of her highness and

über die alten Flirtgeschichten mit Cradock noch gut
over the old flirting stories with Cradock still good

unterrichtet) hatte zwar protestiert, hatte, als der gerade
informed had indeed protested had as the just

46

in Genua liegende alte Kreuzer »Persimon« in Betracht
in Genoa lying old cruiser/warship Persimon in consideration

gezogen war, unverblümt Ihre Hoheit auf das wenig
pulled/taken was bluntly her highness on the little

Schickliche dieses Projektes aufmerksam gemacht... hatte
chicness of this project attentive made had

sogar zu verstehen gegeben, daß sie in dem
even to understand given that she in the

diesbezüglichen Plan nur einen Vorwand Ihrer Hoheit
in this regard plan only a pretext of her highness

sähe, diesem Cradock (der doch nicht einmal Brite von
see this Cradock who indeed not one-time even Brit from

Geburt war!) wieder zu begegnen.
birth was again to meet

Geholfen hatte dieser Protest nicht im mindesten. Gegen
Helped had this protest not in the least Against

die Energie der kleinen Hoheit hatte man eben wieder
the energy of the small highness had one just again

einmal nicht ankommen können, und so war dem in Genua
once not arrive can/been able and so was the in Genoa

ankernden Kreuzer »Persimon« (Kapitän Cradock) der Befehl
anchoring cruiser/warship Persimon Captain Cradock the order

gegeben, am siebenundzwanzigsten Februar
given at the twenty-seventh of February

neunzehnhundertundzweiundzwanzig Monte Carlo anzulaufen
nineteen hundred twenty-two   Monte Carlo   on-to-run
                                             to sail towards

und dort weitere Befehle zu erwarten. Zweck und Ziel
and there further orders to expect Purpose and target

dieser Fahrt waren in dieser Order mit keinem Worte
of this trip were in this order with no words

angegeben: Ihre Hoheit hatte streng befohlen, die
specified Her highness had strictly ordered the

Ägyptenreise und ihre beabsichtigte Anwesenheit an Bord
Egypt trip and her intended presence on board

geheimzuhalten, und hatte sich auch jede besondere
to keep secret and had herself also each special

Vorbereitung des Schiffes verbeten.
preparation of the ship forbid

Am fünfundzwanzigsten Februar schon waren als
At the twenty-fifth of February already were as
                                                      had

Avantgarde in Monte Carlo im Hotel de Paris fünf große
avant-garde in Monte Carlo in the Hotel de Paris five great

Koffer angekommen ... Ledergebirge von einer
suitcases arrived leather mountains from an

altmodischen uneuropäischen und beinahe schon
old fashioned non-European and almost already

barbarischen Solidität, und der Portier Chazel hatte auf
barbaric solidity and the porter Chazel had on

»russische Aristokratie mit mäßigem, in die Schweiz
Russian aristocracy with moderate in -the- Switzerland

gerettetem Vermögen« geraten. Dann war am Morgen
saved capital guessed Then was at the morning

des sechsundzwanzigsten die Zofe Susan gekommen, hatte
of the twenty sixth the maid Susan come had

für zwei Damen Quartier gemacht, hatte die zwei Zimmer
for two ladies camp made had the two rooms

der einen Dame in der dritten Etage und die der
of the one lady in the third floor and that of the
on

jüngeren seltsamerweise in der ersten gewählt; hatte die
younger strangely enough in the first chosen had the

Preise des Hotel de Paris als ungebührlich hoch
prices of the Hotel de Paris as undue high

bezeichnet und den Portier Chazel in der Annahme
designated and the porter Chazel in the assumption

»emigrierte russische Aristokratie mit mäßigem, in die
emigrated Russian aristocracy with moderate in -the-

Schweiz gerettetem Vermögen« nur bestärkt. Zum
Switzerland saved capital only encouraged At the

Schluß freilich, als mit dem Mittagszuge von Mailand die
end indeed as with the lunchtime train from Milan the

beiden Damen eingetroffen waren, hatte der alte Chazel
both ladies arrived were had the old Chazel

diese seine Diagnose wieder verworfen. Engländerinnen
this his diagnosis again discarded English women

waren die beiden, da die jüngere die Zimmerpreise
were -the- both there the younger the room prices

sofort um zwanzig Prozent heruntergehandelt hatte,
immediately for twenty percent traded down had

sicherlich. Die etwas phantastisch klingenden gräflichen
surely The somewhat fantastic sounding countess

Titel waren sicherlich Decknamen, und nur das eine war
titles were surely aliases and only the one was
one thing

dem alten Routinier unklar, in welcher illustrierten
the old routinier not clear in which illustrated

Zeitschrift er schon das Gesicht der jüngeren, der
magazine he already the face of the younger the

kleineren mit dem Helm aus kupferrotem Haar und dem
smaller one with the helmet from copper red hair and the

etwas knabenhaften Gesicht gesehen haben mochte: der
somewhat boyish face seen have might the

alte Chazel beschloß, sich bei dem Barmixer zu
old Chazel decided himself at the bartender to

erkundigen, der als ehemaliger österreichischer
inquire who as former Austrian

Dragoneroffizier als Autorität für berühmte Schönheiten
dragon officer as authority for famous beauties

der internationalen Aristokratie gelten konnte.
of the international aristocracy be valid could
go through

So war also der Einzug gewesen im Hotel de Paris.
So was thus the entry been in the Hotel de Paris
had

Vor dem etwas verspätet servierten Luncheon lag man
Before the somewhat delayed served luncheon lay one

wohlverpackt in den Liegestühlen des Balkons, sah ein
well packed in the deckchairs of the balconies saw a

wenig sehnsüchtig hinunter in den tobenden Mittagskorso
little longingly down in the raging afternoon parade

dieses nun doch etwas heruntergekommenen Monte
of this now indeed somewhat run down Monte

Carlo. Unter dem Balkon klapperten eifrig gelbrote
Carlo Under the balcony rattled zealously yellow-red

Sonnendächer im Seewind, und unnatürlich nahe stand in
canopies in the sea wind and unnatural close stood in

den dunklen Katarakten von Lorbeer und Feigen und
the dark cataracts from laurel and figs and

Myrten der braune Granit des Gebirgsstockes. Und
myrtle the brown granite of the mountain range And

ziegelrote und kobaltblaue und gurkhafarbene Limousinen
brick red and cobalt blue and cucumber-colored limousines

zogen vorüber auf der großen Autostraße nach Cannes und
drew past on the large highway to Cannes and
drove

Antibes mit ihrer Last von Chicagoer Schweinemetzgern
Antibes with their load from (from) Chicago pig-butchers

und Berliner Großverdienern und mimosenhaft zarten
and (from) Berlin big earners and mimosaic gentle

und müden Luxusweibern, und in das vielstimmige Geschrei
and tired luxury wives and in the polyphonic shouting

ihrer Sirenen mischten sich wieder die langgezogenen
of their sirens mixed itself again the elongated

Rufe der kleinen Liftboys bei dem Elevator unten an der
call of the small liftboys at the elevator under on the

See. Monegasser Fischer, braun und statuenhaft wie antike
lake Monegasser fisherman brown and statuesque as ancient

Hirten, ließen sich begaffen von lodengepanzerten
shepherds let themselves gawk from loden armored

sächsischen Provinzialen, und aus den großen Hotels die
saxon provincials and from the large hotels the

kleinen dienstfreien Zimmermädel zwitscherten und
small off duty chambermaids chirped and

kicherten unter primitiven Masken und wiegten sich
giggled under primitive masks and swayed themselves

in schwarzbespannten Hüften, Arm in Arm mit den
in black-covered hips arm in arm with the

Urlaubsmatrosen der Flottenstation von Cap
vacation sailors of the fleet station from Cap

d'Antibes. Seehauch kam, beladen mit dem Parfüm der
d'Antibes Lake-breath came loaded with the perfume of the
Sea breeze

nahen Exotik. Sehnsucht kam ihr, der doch noch so
sew exotic Desire came her the indeed still so

jungen kleinen Hoheit, etwas noch zu erhaschen von
young small highness somewhat still to catch from

der allzu früh und allzu jäh beendeten Jugend ...
the all too early and all too abruptly ended youth

Sehnsucht, mitzutun mit den jungen, fröhlichen
Desire to participate with the young happy

Menschenkindern, als unerkannte Maske mitzuschwimmen in
human children as undetected mask to swim along in

dem Strom, von dem man ja nicht unbedingt zu
the flow from which one yes not absolutely to
indeed

wissen brauchte, wohin er trieb. So beschaffen also
know needed where-to he drove So made up also
it

waren zur Stunde die Wünsche der kleinen Mary – ich
were at the hour the desires of the small Mary – I

glaube, daß in dieser Stunde schon der Plan entworfen
believe that in this hour already the plan designed

wurde zu dem, was dann im Laufe des nächsten
became to that what then in the course of the next

Tages einiges Leben brachte in dieses etwas schläfrig,
day some life brought in this somewhat sleepy

etwas verstaubt, etwas provinzial gewordene Monte
somewhat dusty somewhat provincial become Monte

Carlo.
Carlo

Sie, die alte Violet, tat das, was sie eigentlich immer tat:
Shee the old Violet did that what she actually always did

sie jammerte ...
she wailed

Sie jammerte über die Uneleganz von Monte Carlo. Sie
She wailed over the inelegance of Monte Carlo she

jammerte, daß man nicht in Cannes oder wenigstens in
wailed that one not in Cannes or at least in

Nizza abgestiegen war, und sie jammerte vor allem, daß
Nice descended were and she wailed before all that

man nun auf ein primitives Kriegsschiff müsse, und daß
one now on a primitive warship must (go) and that

das Ganze ja doch nur ein Vorwand Ihrer Hoheit sei,
the whole yes indeed only a pretext of her highness be

die ihren alten Flirt Cradock wiedersehen wolle ...
who her old flirt Cradock see again wanted

Sie, die Mary, hörte nicht weiter darauf und beäugte
She the Mary heard not further thereupon and eyed

mit dem Glase lieber die kleine Rauchwolke, die im
with the glass rather the little smoke cloud that in the

Südosten zu sehen war. Serviert wurde schon, als aus der
southeast to see was Served became already as from the
Lunch was already served

Rauchwolke zuerst ein kleines silbergraues Schiffchen und
smoke cloud first a little silver gray boat and

dann ein wirklicher Kreuzer geworden war mit zierlichen
then a more real cruiser become was with dainty
warship

Miniaturkanonen und zwei pathetisch qualmenden
miniature cannons and two pathetic smoking

Schornsteinen und der fürstlich-labradorischen Flagge am
chimneys and the princely Labrador flag at the

Stock. Der Nachtisch wurde schon aufgetragen, als dieses
mast The after-platter became already carried up as this

kleine Spielzeug unten zu Anker ging. Da hatte die
little play-toy under (them) for anchor went There had the

Mary sehr resolut erklärt, daß »Eio-Mammy« (so nannte
Mary very resolutely explained that Eio Mommy so called

sie, seit Babytagen schon, ihre alte einstige Erzieherin) ...
she since baby days already her old former educator

daß »Eio-Mammy« jetzt müde sei von der Nachtfahrt
that Eio Mommy now tired be (must) from the night drive

und unbedingt schlafen müsse. Und als die alte Violet
and absolutely sleep must And as the old Violet

dann wirklich und übrigens nicht ohne boshafte
then really and by the way not without mischievous

diese übertriebene Sorge um ihren Mittagsschlaf das Feld
this exaggerated worry for her afternoon nap the field

endlich geräumt hatte, da war die Mary aufgesprungen
finally cleared had there was the Mary jumped up
had

und war hinuntergelaufen zu dem großen Fernrohr auf der
and was walked down to the large telescope on the
had

Frühstücksterrasse. Die dunklen Massen auf den
breakfast terrace The dark mass on the

Ankerwinden bei der Back, das waren
windlass at the back that were

fürstlich-labradorische Matrosen und mithin (was sie mit
princely-Labrador sailors and therefore what she with

einem etwas ironischen Lächeln vermerkte) ihre
a somewhat ironic smile noticed her

Landeskinder. Dann hatte unten das Schiffchen
country children Then had under the boat
the children of her country below

diese dunklen Massen wieder eingesogen in seinen
this dark mass again sucked in in its

Silberleib, und dann hatte es ein Boot heruntergelassen,
silver body and then had it a boat lowered

das vorläufig wie ein kleines gelbes Entenjunges neben
that for now as a little yellow duck cub beside
duckling

dem Leibe der Mutter schwamm. Endlich aber, nach
the body of the mother swam Finally however after

langem und hastigem Suchen, war da ganz oben auf
long and hasty search was there completely above on

dem Kompaßdeck in schneeweißer Sommeruniform ein
the compass deck in snow white summer uniform a

schlankes, elegantes Figürchen zu entdecken gewesen. Das
slim elegant little figure to discover been The

Figürchen aber lehnte mit untergeschlagenen Armen in
little figure however leaned with down-struck arms in
crossed

einer lässigen, der Mary gut bekannten Haltung an der
a casual the Mary well known posture on the

Reling, verschwand und tauchte wieder auf und verschwand
railing disappeared and duck again up and disappeared
appeared again

dann definitiv in dem Menschengetümmel der Decks. Als
then definitely in the crowds of people of the deck As

dann nach zehn Minuten das Boot sich trennte von dem
then after ten minutes the boat itself separated from the

Leibe der Mutter und über die Bucht auf die
body of the mother and over the bay on the
across

Landungsbrücke zugeschwommen kam: da war die Mary
jetty swam to came there was the Mary
had

atemlos in ihr Zimmer gestürmt und hatte die Zofe Susan
breathless in her room stormed and had the maid Susan

in die obere Etage geschickt und erkunden lassen,
in the upper floor sent and explore let

ob   die alte Dame schon schlafe. Dann, als es sich
whether   the old lady already sleep Then as it itself

ergeben hatte, daß »Ihre Exzellenz« wie ein Sägewerk
given up had that your excellence as a sawmill
reported

schnarche, da hatte man sich für zehn Minuten
snore there had one oneself for ten minutes

eingeschlossen mit der Zofe. Und wieder zehn Minuten
locked in with the maid And again ten minutes

später hatte der Portier Chazel, der sich als
later had the porter Chazel who himself as

welterfahrener Mann über nichts mehr wunderte,
world-experienced man over nothing (any)more surprised

einen schwarzmaskierten Domino blitzschnell die Halle
a black masked domino lightning fast the hall

passieren und in dem Menschengewühl beim Café
pass and in the crowds of people at the coffee shop

drüben verschwinden sehen.
over there disappear see

Dominos gab es heute am Faschingdienstag an sich in
Domino's gave it today at the mardi gras on itself in
by

genügender Anzahl in Monte Carlo. Bei diesem hier, den
sufficient number in Monte Carlo At this here who

der alte Chazel in Figur und Bewegung mit der jüngeren
the old Chazel in figure and movement with the younger

der   beiden   gestern   angekommenen   mysteriösen   Damen   in
of the   both   yesterday   arrived   mysterious   ladies   in

Verbindung   bringen   mußte ...   bei   diesem   hier   versprachen
connection   bring   must   could   at   this   here   promised

weitere   Recherchen   immerhin   interessante   Resultate.   Die
further   research   after all   interesting   results   The

beiden   Pagen   nämlich,   die   der   Alte   hinter   dem
both   pages   namely   who   the   old (one)   behind   the

seidenen   Phantom   hergeschickt   hatte,   berichteten
silk   phantom   sent away   had   reported

einstimmig,   daß   sie   den   Domino   hinter   der   Rue   de   la
unanimously   that   she   the   domino   behind   the   road   de   la

Constitution   aus   dem   Auge   verloren   hätten.
Constitution   out (of)   the   eye   lost   had

An   der   Grenze   der   gänzlich   indiskutablen   Altstadt   also,
On   the   limit   of the   completely   indisputable   old town   thus

wo,   nebenbei gesagt,   das   ziemlich   ärmliche   Konsulat   des
where   next by / by the way   said   the   rather   poor   consulate   of the

Fürstentums   Labrador   lag.
principality   Labrador   lay

Kapitel II

Was aber den Kapitän Cradock angeht, so war er, wie
What however the Captain Cradock concerns so was he as

schon berichtet, sofort auf dieses ärmliche Konsulat
already reported immediately on/to this poor consulate

gegangen, hatte dort sein Geld zur Wiederauffüllung
gone had there his money to the refilling

der leeren Kohlenbunker und der leeren Schiffskasse
of the empty coal bunker and the empty ships cash (box)

behoben, hatte in der verräucherten Office das Bild
received had in the smoked office the picture

seiner Herrin gesehen, hatte nichts ... aber auch gar
of his Mistress seen had nothing but also at all
indeed

nichts über den mysteriösen Grund dieser mysteriösen
nothing over the mysterious reason of this mysterious

Order erfahren und war wieder gegangen.
order experienced and was again gone
heard

Im Kasino, wohin er ganz automatisch sich
In the Casino where-to he completely automatically himself

begeben hatte, war es offensichtlich noch zu früh: müßige
issued had was it obviously still too early idle

Saaldiener rekelten sich herum in ihren olivgrünen
room attendants reclined themselves around in their olive green

Uniformen ... ein schlanker älterer Herr in etwas
uniforms a slender older gentleman in something

abgeschabtem Dreß überzählte in einem Winkel mit
scraped dress recounted in a corner with
ragged

sorgenvollem Gesicht seine Barschaft ... in einem der Säle
worrying face his cash in one of the halls

handhabten gähnende Croupiers vor dicken Pfahlbürgern
handled yawning croupiers before thick stake citizens

aus dem Limousin zum Einsatz von drei Gulden die
from the limousine to the commitment of three guilders the
(money)

Roulette. Das Ganze machte den gespenstischen und
roulette The whole (thing) made the ghostly and

übernächtigen Eindruck eines Nachtcafés, das man zu früh
stay overnight impression of a night cafe that one too early

betritt – der Kapitän Cradock ging wieder.
enters – the Captain Cradock went again
left

Er ging die Rue de la Paix entlang. Nun, nach dem
He went the road of the peace along Now after the
(French)

Verebben des offiziellen Faschingszuges und in der
ebbing away of the official carnival procession and in the

hereinbrechenden Dämmerung war es ganz und gar
breaking in dusk was it completely and at all
rising had

der Karneval der kleinen Leute geworden: Arbeiter aus
the carnival of the small people become Workers from
common

den Marmorbrüchen und den Ölpressen waren erschienen ...
the marble breaks and the oil presses were appeared
marble digs had

Fischer und ältliche Kokotten, Marseiller Spießer und
fisherman and elderly cocots from Marseille philistines and
rabble

italienische Schiffsjungen mit wiegenden Hüften und
Italian ship boys with swaying hips and

unheiligen Lastern in den übergroßen Samtaugen ...
unholy blasphemes in the oversized velvet eyes

wieder angetrunkene Matrosen, und vor allem in ihren
again drunk sailors and before all in their

zerlumpten Uniformen die entlassenen Negersoldaten des
ragged uniforms the laid off black soldiers of the

französischen Heeres: hellhäutige Marokkaner und
French army fair-skinned Moroccans and

Madagassen und massige Senegalesen mit blinkendem
Malagasy and bulky Senegalese with flashing

Gebiß. Dieser johlende, kichernde, singende Zug also
teeth This hooting giggling singing train thus
procession

trieb durch die Rue de la Paix, wo rechts und
drove through the road of the peace where to the right and
(French)

links in blinkenden Vitrinen Kleider von Poiret und
left in flashing showcases dresses from Poiret and
(brand)

Handschuhe von Roguin & ses fils und Geschmeide und
hand-shoes from Roguin and his sons and jewelry and
(gloves) brand

Seidenfetzen und Schminkbüchsen und verliebte
scraps of silk and makeup boxes and in love being

Niedlichkeiten für den Gebrauch von New-Yorker
cuteness for the use of the New Yorker

Shopkeeper-Töchtern ausgestellt waren. Dort aber, wo
shopkeeper daughters exhibited were There however where

die Firma Lebas die schwarze Samtfläche ihrer Auslagen
the company Lebas the black velvet area of their exhibits

mit nichts als einem einzigen, ganz erlesenen
with nothing as a single completely exquisite
but

Perlenkollier bedacht hatte: dort begann dann das, was
pearl necklace considered had there began then that what
decorated

in den nächsten vierundzwanzig Stunden die Menschen
in the next twenty four hours the people

dieser Geschichte in einem ziemlich tollen Wirbel
of this story in a rather great whirl

durcheinanderhetzen sollte ...
through each other rush should

Was dort lag, war wirklich nichts anderes als ein einziger
What there lay was really nothing other as a single
than

Schmuck. Müde Farben spielten über das livide Weiß der
jewel Tired colors played over the livid white of the

Perlen, küßten und umwarben einander, bis es,
pearl kissed and wooed each other until it

schmächtiger werdend, wie Frauentränen sich verlor in den
slimmer becoming like woman's tears itself lost in the

schwarzen Samtfalten. Ein Preis war wohlweislich nicht
black velvet folds A price was well-wisely not
wisely

angegeben, ein Zettel verkündete, daß das Kollier aus
specified a note announced that the necklace from

dem Besitz der kaiserlich russischen Familie stamme,
the possession of the imperial Russian family stem

daß es von den Bolschewiken ausgeboten und in Paris
that it from the Bolsheviks offered and in Paris

von Lebas ersteigert sei: der Kapitän Cradock aber
from Lebas bought at auction be the Captain Cradock however
by

wurde, als er diesen Zettel las, aufgeschreckt von einem
became as he this note read startled from a
by

heftigen trockenen Frauenhusten. Als er dann aufsah,
violent dry women's cough As he then looked up

stand neben ihm in schwarzem Domino und schwarzer
stood beside him in black domino and black

Maske ein weibliches Wesen, das, ohne weitere Notiz
mask a feminine being that without further notice
who

von ihm zu nehmen, gleich ihm den Schmuck besah.
from him to take like him the decoration looked at

Bei jedem Manne aber gibt es Erinnerungen an
At each man however gives it memories on
                              are there   of

allererste Liebesabenteuer, die oft nach Jahrzehnten
(the) very first love adventures which often after decades

erst an unsere Tür pochen und dann meist
first on our door knock and then most

um so gröberen Unfug anrichten in unserem Leben. Als
for so coarser mischief wreak in our life As
       even worse

Midshipman hatte vor siebzehn Jahren der lange Cradock
midshipman had before seventeen years the tall Cradock
                     seventeen years ago

in Port Said sich in ein kleines Arabermädchen namens
in port Said himself in a little Arab girl named

Kaina verliebt. Geschichten, die in Port Said spielen,
Kaina fallen in love Stories which in Port Said play

sind immer mehr oder minder unpassend, und ich will
are always more or less inappropriate and I want

von dieser nicht mehr erzählen, als daß sie begonnen und
from this not more tell as that she begun and
                              than

geendet hatte, wie solch exotische Liebschaften immer
ended had as such exotic loves always

enden. Daß das Schiff eines Tages weitergefahren und daß
end That the ship one day further-sailed and that

eines Tages alles zu Ende gewesen war. Das aber,
one day everything to end been was That however

was nun hier vor dem Schaufenster von Lebas den
what now here before the store window from Lebas the

Kapitän Cradock befiel, das war eben die rein bildmäßige
Captain Cradock attacked that was just the clean pictorial

Erinnerung an jenes Arabermädchen Kaina. Derselbe
memory on that Arab girl Kaina The same
of

überschlanke, fast knabenhafte Wuchs. Dieselben
slender almost boyish growth These self
size The same

Bewegungen und vor allem derselbe adlige,
movements and before all the same noble

blütenstengelzarte und kühne Nacken. Und das, was in
flower stem delicate and bold neck And that what in

diesem Augenblicke jäh hervorbrechender
this moment abruptly more bursting

Jugenderinnerungen ihm durch den Kopf schoß, das war
youth memories him through the head shot that was
flashed

der Gedanke, daß zu diesem adligen Nacken unter allen
the thought that to this noble neck under all

Umständen dieses Kollier gehöre. Im gleichen
circumstances this necklace belong In the (the) same

Augenblick aber, als er es gedacht hatte, da hatte der
moment however as he it thought had there had the

Domino sich abgewandt. Da er aber ein ihm
domino (mask) herself turned away There he however one him

geltendes Lächeln bemerkt zu haben glaubte, so hielt er
applicable smile noticed to have believed so held he

sich für berechtigt, in gemessenem Abstande zu folgen.
himself for entitled in measured distances to follow

Durch das Faschingsgejohle des
Through the carnival hooting of the
carnival festivities

Boulevard du cinquième avril zur
boulevard of the fifth (of) April to the
(French)

Place du commerce, und von dort weiter bis über das
square of the commerce and from there further until over the
(French)

Institut für Meeresforschung hinaus. Bis er sie dann
institute for marine research out Until he her then

überraschenderweise verschwinden sah in jenem Stadtteil,
surprisingly disappear saw in that city-part
district

der von der einheimischen Fischerbevölkerung »Marina«
that from the native fishing population Marina

genannt wird.
called becomes

Es gibt dort hinten so ein Ur-Monte Carlo, das im
It gives there in the back so an old-Monte Carlo that in the
There is

Bädecker nicht besonders verzeichnet ist, und das die
tourist guide not particularly recorded is and that the
(brand)

Bewohner der großen Hotels kaum zu sehen bekommen.
residents of the large hotels hardly to see become

Ein paar Gassen, eng wie Flintenrohre und steil wie
A few alleys close as shotgun barrels and steep as

Hühnerstiegen ... alles aus der Zeit, wo es noch
chicken stairs ... everything from the time where it still
there

keine Hotels und kein Kasino und keine Rouletteeinnahmen
no hotels and no Casino and no roulette earnings

hier gab und das fürstliche Haus von Monaco sich noch
here gave and the princely house of Monaco itself still
were

nicht für Tiefseeforschungen, sondern für den ehedem hier
not for deep sea research but for the before here

blühenden Fisch- und Ölhandel interessierte. Zu bemerken
flowering fish and oil trading interested To notice

ist, daß es in diesen Gassen durchaus nicht nach den
is that it in these alleys throughout not to the
at all of

Parfümen von Houbigant riecht, und daß ihre
perfume of Houbigant smells and that her

Bewohnerinnen sich nicht von Poiret kleiden lassen
residents themselves not of Poiret dress let
with

und ihren Schmuck auch nicht bei Lebas & ses fils
and their decoration also not at Lebas and sons
of

beziehen. Ich glaube nicht einmal, daß es vereinbar mit
draw I believe not once that it compatible with
get

den Geboten der Schicklichkeit wäre, nach dem
the commandments of the decency would be to the

jetzigen Zwecke der hier stehenden, in rosa, bleu, picasso-
current purpose the here standing in rose bleu picasso

und pfefferminzschnapsgrün gemalten Häuser zu fragen. Ich
and peppermint schnapps green painted houses to ask I

glaube auch nicht, daß eine distinguierte Dame guttut,
believe also not that a distinguished lady good does
befits

just diesen Ortsteil für ihre Abendpromenade zu wählen,
just this district for her evening promenade to choose

weiß aber andererseits, daß distinguierte Damen oft
know however on the other hand that distinguished ladies often

recht seltsame Launen haben, und daß diese ganze tolle
right strange whims have and that this whole amazing
quite

Geschichte nun einmal, auf solch seltsame Einfälle gestellt
story now once on such strange ideas set

ist: genug, es war dieser ungehörige Ortsteil, in den der
is enough it was this improper district in which the

Kapitän Cradock jenen Domino verschwinden sah ...
Captain Cradock that domino (mask) disappear saw

Er war nun doch etwas überrascht. Er hatte sie
He was now indeed something surprised He had her

vorhin vor dem Schaufenster wohl beobachtet.
a while ago in front of the store window well observed

Da zwischen Maske und schwarzer Kappe ein rotblonder
There between mask and black cap a red blond

Schopf hervorgelugt hatte, so war sie keine jener
tuft (of hair) peeped out had so was she not that

kleinen Negressen, die jetzt, nach dem Kriege, von
small negress who now to the War from
after

Marseille aus die Mittelmeerstädte überschwemmten. Da
Marseille from the Mediterranean cities over-swam There
flooded Since

sie beim Gang durch das Karnevalsgejohle immerhin
she at the course through the carnival hooting always-through
carnival procession

die Bewegungen und die Haltung der Dame gezeigt hatte,
the movements and the stature of the lady shown had

so war sie erst recht keine Bewohnerin jener rosenfarben
so was she first right no resident of those rose colored

und pfefferminzschnapsgrün gestrichenen Häuser. Und da
and peppermint schnapps green painted houses and there
since

sie nicht in diesen verrufenen Stadtteil gehörte, so hatte
she not in this disreputable city-part belonged to so had
district

sie sich eben verirrt, und da sie sich verirrt hatte,
she herself just lost and there she herself lost had
since

so war es ein simples Gebot der Ritterlichkeit, sie
so was it a simple commandment of the chivalry her

gut im Auge zu behalten: der Kapitän Cradock hatte
good in the eye to keep the Captain Cradock had

somit doppelt ernsthafte Gründe, dem Domino in
consequently double serious reasons the domino (mask) in

den Stadtteil Marina zu folgen.
the city-part Marina to follow
district

Hier, in diesem Fuchsbau, hatte er sie zunächst
Here in this fox building had he her first
burrow

aus den Augen verloren. Die Gasse, eng wie eine
out the eyes lost The alley close as a
lost sight of

Dachsröhre, wand sich in steiler Krümmung bergan – die
roof tube wound itself in steep curvature uphill – the
gutter

Häuser, finster wie Burgen, ließen oben nur ein karges
houses dark as castles let above only a sparse

Streifchen Himmel frei. Es roch, wie es immer riecht in
stripe (of) sky free It smelled as it always smells in

alten Mittelmeersiedlungen – nach Katzen, nach
old Mediterranean settlements – to cats to

Gorgonzola, nach Baldrian, nach gotischem Unrat. Am
Gorgonzola to Valerian to Gothic garbage At the

Eingange dieses Schlauches wurde aus einer Osteria mit
entrance this tube became from a bar with

Fußtritten und frommen Segenswünschen ein Betrunkener
kicks and pious blessings a drunk

auf den Kehricht geworfen, mit monotonem Weinen saß
on the garbage thrown with monotonous crying sat

auf einer Schwelle ein zerlumptes Kind, ein Fuhrmann
on a threshold a ragged child a wagoner

prügelte mit eisenbeschlagenem Stock seinen Maultierkarren
beat with iron-studded stick his mule carts

die steile Gasse hinan. Oben, wo der Lärm einer Kneipe
the steep street upon Above where the noise of a pub

zu hören war und eine alte Öllaterne quer über die
to hear was and an old oil lantern straight over the

Straße hing, sah er sie, wie sie stand und mit aller
street hung saw he her as she stood and with all

Ratlosigkeit den Weg zu suchen schien. Dann war sie
counsel-less-ness the way to search seemed Then was she
helplessness

wieder verschwunden. Als er, ziemlich atemlos, oben
again disappeared As he rather breathless above

angekommen war, stellte er fest, daß die Straße als
arrived was set he fast that the street as
had concluded he

finsterer Sack vor einem zerbröckelnden, lichtlosen
(a) dark bag before a crumbling lightless

Palazzo endete, und daß sie in eine Seitengasse abgebogen
palazzo ended and that she in a side alley curved off

sein mußte. Und so, als er sich nach rechts wandte,
be must And so as he himself to (the) right turned

wo aus der Kneipe die blutrünstigen Septimakkorde
where from the pub the bloodthirsty septic chords

eines elektrischen Klaviers zu hören waren: so fand er sie
of an electrical piano to hear were so found he her

endlich. Dicht vor der Kneipe stand sie. Nicht allein,
finally Close before the pub stood she Not alone

sondern mit irgendeinem männlichen Wesen. Dem
but with some male being The

männlichen Wesen aber war eine seidene Dame aus der
male being however was a silk lady from the

Oberwelt der großen Hotels gerade recht gekommen. Das
over-world of the large hotels just right come The

männliche Wesen hatte den Domino am Arm gefaßt.
male being had the domino (mask) at the arm taken

Das männliche Wesen erwies sich als ein Farbiger in
The male being proved herself as a colored person in

zerrissenem französischem Waffenrock: es war Zeit, daß die
torn French coat of arms it was time that the

Division Cradock das Schlachtfeld erreichte ...
division Cradock the battlefield reached

Die Präliminarien zwischen beiden Parteien aber, sie
The preliminaries between both parties however they

waren knapp und erinnerten nur wenig an die Formen
were scarce and remembered only little on the forms

der europäischen Diplomatie. »Let her go!« sagte der
of the European diplomacy Let her go said the

lange Cradock, und »shut up!« brüllte die Gegenpartei und
long Cradock and »shut up!« roared the counterparty and

streifte	sich	schon	die	Ärmel	hoch.	»Shut	up!«	aber
touched	himself	already	the	sleeves	high	»shut	up!«	but

heißt	bekanntlich	»Halt's	Maul!«	und	ließ	im
is called	as known	Hold your	mouth	and	let	in the

vorliegenden	Falle	durchaus	darauf	schließen,	daß	die
present	case	throughout / at all	thereupon	conclude	that	the

Gegenpartei	nicht	gewillt	war,	gutwillig	ihre
counterparty	not	willing	was	good-willing / willingly	her (Gegenpartei fem.)

Frauenbeute	herauszugeben.	Da	lagen	sie	sich
women's booty	to issue	There	lay	they	themselves

im	nächsten	Augenblick	denn	auch	schon	in	den	Haaren.
in the	next	moment	then	also	already	in	the	hairs / hair

Boxen	ist	an	sich	eine	wunderschöne	Kunst	–
Boxing	is	by	itself	a	beautiful	art	–

Voraussetzung	ist	eben	nur	(weil	man	sonst
Requirement	is	just	only	because	one	otherwise

furchtbare	Prügel	bekommt),	daß	auch	der	Gegner	boxen
terrible	beatings	gets	that	also	the	opponent	box

kann	und	zu	boxen	gewillt	ist.	Der	Kapitän	Cradock	war
can	and	to	boxing	willing	is	The	Captain	Cradock	was

kein	Dilettant	in	solch	schweren	Raufereien	und	wußte,
no	dilettante	in	such	heavy	brawls	and	knew

daß man sich in diesem Falle nicht auf legitime
that one himself in this case not on legitimate

Kampfmittel versteifen durfte. Er wählte somit
ordnance stiffen was allowed he chose consequently

eine Technik, mit der er einmal in Saigon einen
a technology with which he once in Saigon an

amerikanischen Klipperkapitän seinen schwer betrunkenen
American clipper captain his heavy drunk

»Ersten« hatte erledigen sehen: hebe den Gegner
first had take care of see would lift the opponent

hoch, mein Junge, dreh' ihn um und laß ihn fallen und
high my young turn him around and let him fall and

laß für alles weitere die Pflastersteine sorgen.
let for everything further the paving stones worry

Er hatte Untergriff. Als er den anderen hoch hob, sah er
He had under-grasp As he the other high lifted saw he

unter der Hundestirn zwei traurige Augen, und in diesem
under the forehead two sad eyes and in this

Augenblick tat dem Cradock den betrunkenen Seemann
moment did the Cradock the drunk sailor

eigentlich leid. Dann, als er ihn so hielt, begann der
actually pity Then as he him so held began the

Seemann zu grölen, und er sah ein breites, höchst
sailor to bawl and he saw a broad most high
most

ordinäres Marseiller Matrosenmesser über sich gezückt.
ordinary of Marseille sailor knife over himself whipped out

Da drehte Cradock den betrunkenen Seemann nach
There turned Cradock the drunk sailor to

unten und ließ es fallen. Es gab einen dumpfen Laut, und
under and let it fall It gave a dull sound and

da rührte sich den Seemann bis auf weiteres nicht
there stirred itself the sailor until on additional not

mehr.
(any)more

Hart sind die Schädel der Senegalleute, und zerbrechlich
Hard are the skulls of the Senegalese and fragile

im Vergleich zu diesen Schädeln die Trottoirplatten
in the comparison to these skulls the sidewalks

der europäischen Städte. »Lassen Sie den Unsinn!« schrie
of the European cities Leave you the nonsense cried
You stop with

der Cradock den Domino an, der sich karitativ mit
the Cradock the domino (mask) to who herself charitably with

dem Seemann zu beschäftigen gedachte. Dann machten sie,
the sailor to employ thought Then made they

daß sie herauskamen aus der Rue Solferino, in der
that they came out from the road Solferino in which

länger zu verweilen nicht sehr ratsam war. Ziemlich
longer to linger not very advisable was Rather

schnell vollzog sich dieser Rückzug. Vorüber an Dirnen,
fast took place itself this retreat Past by whores

an Krüppeln mit sagenhaft verunstalteten Fratzen ... vorbei
by cripples with fabulous defaced grimaces past

an dem Fuhrmann, der seine Mula nun endlich auf den
by the wagoner who his mules now finally on the

Gipfel der Gasse geprügelt hatte, und vorüber an dem
top of the street beaten had and past on the

Betrunkenen, der nun ganz zufrieden auf dem
drunk who now completely satisfied on the

Kehricht saß und von dort aus ein fröhliches, aber
garbage sat and from there out a merry but

männlich-starkes und nicht unter allen Umständen für die
masculine strong and not under all circumstances for the

Ohren seidener Dominos bestimmtes Lied in die
ears (of the) silky domino (mask) meant song in the

Frühlingsnacht hinaussandte. Und dann, etwas echauffiert
spring night sent out And then something feverish

und zwischen guter und schlechter Laune, standen sie
and between good and bad mood stood they

wieder auf der Rue du commerce.
again on the road of the Commerce

»Promenieren Sie immer in solchen Straßen?« knurrte
Walk around you always in such streets growled

böse der Cradock. »Immer, wenn der Kapitän Cradock
angry the Cradock Always when the Captain Cradock

mein Begleiter ist«, wollte sie eigentlich sagen und ließ es
my escort is wanted she actually say and let it

dann doch lieber bleiben und sagte dann nur, daß sie auf
then indeed rather stay and said then only that she on

dem kürzesten Wege ins Hotel zurückgewollt und sich
the shortest road in the Hotel wanted back and herself

schmählich verlaufen habe. Da nahm der Cradock,
shamefully run away / have There took the Cradock
gotten lost had

während sie schon die Rue du cinquième avril
while she already the road of the Fifth (of) April

hinabgingen, ihren Arm und begann, ihr eine scharfe
went down her arm and began, her a sharp

Predigt zu halten.
sermon to hold
give

Daß sich in Kairo dicht beim Fischmarkt eine ganz
That itself in Cairo close to the fish market a completely

ähnliche Geschichte ereignet habe mit der Gattin des
similar story occurred have with the wife of the
had

französischen Konsuls, und erst nach Wochen sei Madame
French consul and first after weeks be madame
was

Lagrange aufgetaucht in Alexandria. An einem wenig
Lagrange duck-up in Alexandria At a little
surfaced not very

repräsentablen Orte, in einem wenig repräsentablen
representative place in a little representative
not very

Zustand und mit einem wohltätigen Gedächtnisverlust für
condition and with a charitable memory loss for
fortunate

alles, was sich inzwischen ereignet hatte mit
everything what itself In the meantime occurred had with
that

Madame. Daß diese alten Teile der Mittelmeerstädte
madame That this old parts of the Mediterranean cities

schlimme Menschenfallen seien, und daß gar ein Seemann
bad human traps are and that at all a sailor

wie der Oger aus dem Märchen kleine schwarzseidene
like the oger from the fairy tales little black silk

Dominos mit Haut und Haaren verspeise. So
Domino's with skin and hair eat So
with domino's masked women

schwadronierte er im üblichen Überseejargon und war
swaggered he in the usual overseas jargon and was

ihr dabei, ohne daß sie dabei einen nennenswerten
her there-by without that she there-by a noteworthy

Widerstand leistete, nähergerückt und holte sich dann
resistance accomplished approached and got himself then

(das war schon unter den dunklen Arkaden kurz vor
that was already under the dark arcades short before

dem Café Flamingo) seinen Retterlohn.
the coffee shop flamingo his rescuer reward

Indem er sie nämlich ohne alles Federlesen auf
While he her namely without everything feather reading on
Because without further ado

den Nacken küßte.
the neck kissed

Zwei- oder dreimal. Was er übrigens für sein gutes
Two or three times What he by the way for his good

Recht hielt, und was sie sich selbst gefallen ließ mit
right held and what she herself -self- pleased let with

einem etwas verlegenen Lächeln.
a somewhat embarrassed smile

Dann, an der Ecke der Rue de la Paix, wo in der
Then on the corner of the road of the Peace where in the

Auslage des Hauses Lebas auf schwarzem Samt der
display of the house Lebas on black velvet the

Schmuck des Hauses Romanow leuchtete, fragte er sie,
jewel of the house of Romanow lit asked he her

wo und wann sie sich im Kasino treffen
where and when they each other in the Casino meet

würden ...
would

Daß er heute noch im Kasino spielen würde, war für
That he today still in the Casino play would was for

ihn, da er nun einmal hier war, eine
him there he now once here was a

Selbstverständlichkeit, und ebenso selbstverständlich
self-understood-ness/self-evidence and likewise self-understandably
self-evidently

erschien es ihm, daß für den Rest dieses Abends dieser
appeared it him that for the rest of this evening this

Domino ihm gehörte. Da sagte denn der seidene
domino (mask) him belonged to There said then the silk

Domino, daß sie ihn um neun Uhr abends im
domino that she him around nine hour in the evening in the
at

Palmensaal des Kasinos erwarte, und dann trennten sie
palm hall of the casino expected and then separated they

sich, und der Cradock sah ihr nach, wie sie ihren
themselves and -the- Cradock saw her after how she her
stared after her

Nacken durch das Gewühl der Rue de la Paix trug.
neck through the busy the road of the Peace carried

Einen königlichen Nacken ... blütenstengelzart und kühn
A royal neck delicate as a flower stem and bold

und anmutig zugleich ... eine Herrlichkeit unter den
and graceful at the same time a splendour between the

Nacken der Shopkeepertöchter von New York und
necks of the shopkeeper-daughters from New York and

Chicago: es war selbstverständlich, daß auf diesen Nacken
Chicago it was self-understandably that on this neck
self-evidently

und nur auf diesen die Perlen des Hauses Lebas
and only on this the Pearls of the house Lebas

gehörten. Da beeilte er sich denn, noch zur rechten
belonged There hurried he himself then still at the right

Zeit zu kommen ...
time to come
    arrive

Bei Lebas freilich wollten sie schon schließen – man war
At Lebas indeed wanted they already close – one was

schon im Aufbruch und wurde erst höflich, als der
already in the breaking up and became first polite as the

verspätete Käufer nach dem Perlenkollier in der Auslage
late buyer to the pearl necklace in the display

fragte. Der Cradock ließ die Perlen, die einmal einer
asked The Cradock let the Pearls which once an

Kaiserin gehört hatten, ziemlich nachlässig durch die
empress belonged to had rather careless through the

Hand gleiten und befahl dann, ohne nach dem Preise zu
hand slide and ordered then without after the price to

fragen, daß man ihm den Schmuck um neun Uhr
ask that one him the jewel at nine hour(s)

abends in den Palmensaal des Kasinos schicken
in the evening in the palm hall of the Casino to send

solle, wo auch der Betrag zu erheben sei. Der
should where also the amount to raise be The
    receive

spitzbärtige Verkäufer, zusammenklappend wie ein
goatee seller collapsing like a

Rasiermesser, wollte etwas sagen, wurde aber dahin
razor wanted something say became however there to

beschieden, daß der Schmuck fest gekauft sei, und daß er,
decided that the jewel fast bought be and that he
surely

der Kapitän Cradock, pünktlichste Ausführung seines
the Captain Cradock most punctual execution of his

Auftrages erwarte und es im übrigen sehr eilig habe.
order expected and -it- in the rest very hurried had
for the was

Dann ging er.
Then went he

Eine halbe Stunde später, als er in seiner Kabine vor
A half hour later as he in his cabin before

dem Spiegel seine Krawatte knüpfte, fiel es ihm wohl ein,
the mirror his tie tied fell it him well in

daß er ja keine Ahnung von dem Preise habe.
that he yes no idea from the price have
indeed had

Gleich darauf dachte er schon an ganz andere
Immediately thereupon thought he already on completely other

Dinge: seit wann fragte denn auch ein Kavalier nach dem
things since when asked then also a cavalier to the

Preise, wenn er eine schöne Frau beschenken konnte,
price when he a beautiful woman gift could

und wozu gab es für einen alten Hasardeur, wenn er
and to which gave it for an old chancer when he
gambler

wirklich Geld brauchen sollte, Rouletten in Monte Carlo?
really money need should roulette in Monte Carlo

An die Preisfrage, wie gesagt, dachte er nicht mehr
On the price question as said thought he not (any)more

und beendete, die Rigolettoarie pfeifend, seine Toilette und
and ended the Rigoletto aria whistling his toilet and

konstatierte befriedigt, daß die Taille noch mehr als
stated satisfied that the waist still more as

tadellos war, und daß sich auch noch kein graues Haar
impeccable was and that himself also still no grey hair

finden ließ an den Schläfen. Durch das Kabinenfenster
find let on the temples Through the cabin window

schienen aber nun schon längst wie schöne helle
seemed however now already long as beautiful bright

Diademe die Lichter des Kasinos, und das »Ascenseur«
tiaras the lights of the casinos and the elevator
(French)

der Liftboys beim Elevator am Bahnhof kam durch
of the liftboys at the elevator at the railway station came through

die laue Nacht.
the lukewarm night

Auf der zweiten Silbe betont... ascénseur... kapriziös und
On the second syllable stressed elevator capricious and
(French)

lockend. Und der Cradock trieb die Bootsgäste zu
enticing And the Cradock drove the boat guests to
boatmen

rascherer   Fahrt   an,   als   er   sich   übersetzen   ließ   nach
faster   ride   on   as   he   himself   overset   let   to
            moving   boat over

Monte   Carlo.
Monte   Carlo

Kapitel III

Was aber Violet Counteß Hensbarrow, ehemalige
What however Violet countess Hensbarrow former

Erzieherin und nunmehrige erste und einzige »Palastdame«
educator and now first and only palace lady

der Hoheit von Labrador, betrifft, so war sie empört.
of the highness from Labrador concerns so was she outraged

Schlechterdings und geradezu empört.
Worst of all and almost outraged
Absolutely

Bis in den Frühlingsabend hinein hatte sie nach der
Until in the spring evening inside had she after the

strapazanten Reise und dem ausgiebigen Frühstück dem
tiring journey and the extensive breakfast the

Laster des Nachmittagsschlafes gefrönt, war um sieben
vice of the afternoon sleeps indulged was around seven
at

Uhr erst erwacht, hatte eine halbe Stunde mit
hour first woken up had a half hour with

bleischwerer Müdigkeit und mit offenen Augen dagelegen,
lead-heavy fatigue and with open eyes laid there
heavy

hatte mit dieser Anwesenheit in Monte Carlo und mit der
had with this presence in Monte Carlo and with the

ganzen Ägyptenreise ihrer Herrin gehadert. Erstens ging
whole Egypt trip her Mistress quarreled First (of all) went

man heutzutage nicht nach Monte Carlo, sondern nach
one these days not to Monte Carlo but to

Cannes. Zweitens fuhr man nach Ägypten nicht auf einem
Cannes second drove one to Egypt not on a
sailed

für die Anwesenheit zweier Damen gar nicht vorbereiteten
for the presence (of) two ladies at all not prepared

Schiff. Drittens aber und viertens und fünftens: man
ship Thirdly however and fourthly and fifth one

ging nach Ägypten nicht auf ein Schiff, das dieser Cradock
went to Egypt not on a ship that this Cradock

kommandierte. Einmal war dieser Cradock kein Brite von
commanded Once was this Cradock no Brit from
For one

Geburt, zweitens war er ein berüchtigter Abenteurer,
birth secondly was he a notorious adventurer

Spieler und Hasardeur, drittens hatte er, was die alte
player and chancer thirdly had he what the old
gambler

Violet durch den heute noch im Flottenamt tätigen
Violet through the today still in the fleet office active

Vetter Percy ganz genau wußte, in Siam heilige
cousin Percy completely precise knew in Siam holy
Thailand

Tempelkatzen mit Baldriantropfen närrisch gemacht.
temple cats with valerian drops foolish made

Schließlich aber hatte man schon vor Jahren über ihn
Finally however had one already before years over him

und die Mary in London allerlei gemunkelt.
and the Mary in London all sorts of (things) rumored

Folglich war dieses ganze Abenteuer und die Fahrt auf
Consequently was this whole adventure and the ride on

dem Kreuzer »Persimon« nur ein Vorwand, einen alten
the cruiser Persimon only a pretext an old
warship

Galan wiederzusehen, und folglich war ein Skandal
beau to see again and consequently was a scandal

im Anzuge. Mit dieser trüben Erkenntnis hatte sich
in the making With this opaque understanding had herself

die Gräfin von ihrem Lager erhoben. Eine halbe Stunde
the countess from her bed arisen A half hour

später, während die ältere und nicht mehr übermäßig
later while the older and not (any)more excessive

schlanke Dame sich vergeblich um das Schließen ihrer
slender lady herself in vain for the closing of her
with

silbergestickten Abendrobe bemühte, war etwas
silver embroidered evening gown occupied was something

geschehen, was die schlimmsten Befürchtungen wahr
happened what the worst fears true

machte.
made

Hereingewirbelt ins Zimmer kam in der Laune eines
Whirled inside into the room came in the mood of a

eben in die Ferien entlassenen Schulmädchens die Hoheit
just in the vacation laid off schoolgirl the highness
freed

von Labrador, setzte sich (was mit den Geboten
from Labrador set herself what with the commandments

des Anstandes unvereinbar war) auf das noch nicht
of the decency incompatible was on the still not

zurechtgemachte Bett ihrer alten Hofdame, schlug die Beine
trimmed bed her old court lady struck the legs

übereinander, paffte eine ihrer unleidlichen Zigaretten
over-one-another puffed one of her insufferable cigarettes

ins Zimmer und erzählte, nachdem die alte Violet die
in the room and told after the old Violet the

Zofe schleunigst hinausgeschickt hatte, daß sie – die
maid immediately sent out had that she – the

regierende Fürstin-Witwe von Labrador – soeben als
ruling princess-widow from Labrador – just now as

Domino maskiert den Karnevalskorso besucht habe und
domino (mask) masked the carnival parade visited have and
had

mit dem Kapitän Cradock zusammengetroffen sei.
with the Captain Cradock met be
had

Daß sie mit ihm ein amüsantes Abenteuer in der Altstadt
That she with him an amusing adventure in the old town

bestanden habe und von ihm dreimal geküßt worden
existed have and from him three times kissed become
had had

sei. Zweimal auf den Nacken und einmal auf den Hals –
be Twice on the neck and once on the throat –

»Kuß auf den Mund« wurde trotz strenger Inquisition
kiss on the mouth became despite severe inquisition

geleugnet. An diese Mitteilung hatte sich eine ernste,
denied At this sharing had itself a serious
telling

längere Aussprache beider Damen angeschlossen.
longer pronunciation of both ladies connected
discussion

Zu erinnern ist daran, daß die alte Violet vor nun
To remember is there-to that the old Violet before now
this

schon zwanzig Jahren die Erziehung ihrer jetzigen Herrin
already twenty years the education of her current Mistress

überwacht hatte, daß sie sich
supervised had that they each other

unter vier Augen duzten, und daß diese Beziehungen der
under four eyes you-d and that these relations the
were informal together

alten Dame in solcher Aussprache einen durchaus
old lady in such pronunciation a throughout
discussion at all

degagierten Ton gestatteten. Ob sie denn wenigstens
disengaged tone allowed Whether she then at least
more relaxed

diesen ungeheuren Verstoß sofort entsprechend
this tremendous violation immediately correspondingly
(the kisses)

geahndet habe, fragte die alte Violet: da hatte die Mary
punished have asked the old Violet there had the Mary
had

sich geschüttelt vor Lachen und geantwortet, daß er sie
herself shaken for laugh and answered that he her
shook of laughter

ja gar nicht erkannt habe, und daß sie ihn
indeed at all not recognized have and that she him
had

selbstverständlich nach dem Dinner – maskiert natürlich –
self-understandably after the dinner – masked of course –
self-evidently

im Palmensaal des Kasinos treffen werde. Ob sie
in the palm hall of the casino meet will Whether she

sich denn nicht ihrer Stellung, ihrer fürstlichen Würde
herself then not her position her princely would

bewußt sei, hatte die empörte alte Dame gefragt: da
conscious be had the indignant old lady asked there

war die Hoheit in den Harnisch geraten und hatte sogar
was the highness in the harness gotten and had even

mit dem Fuß gestampft und sehr energisch erklärt, daß
with the foot stamped and very energetic explained that

es genug sei, mit achtzehn Jahren an einen abgelebten
it enough be with eighteen years on a worn out

Greis verheiratet und mit fünfundzwanzig Witwe zu
old man married and with twenty five widow to

werden und das ganze Jahr über
become and the whole year over
through

Landesmutter zu spielen.
country-mother to play
mother of the nation

Daß sie jetzt nicht Staatsoberhaupt, sondern ein
That she now not head of state but a

schwarzseidener Domino sei, erklärte nachdrücklich die
black silk domino (mask) be explained emphatically the

Mary. Und daß auch sie einmal das Recht habe, in
Mary And that also she (this) once the right have in
had

Karnevalsstimmung zu sein, erklärte sie ebenfalls. Ob
carnival mood to be explained she likewise Whether

sie übrigens, da Susan nun einmal fort sei, der alten
she by the way there Susan now once away be the old
since indeed

Violet die etwas schwer zugehende Taille zuhaken
Violet the something heavy to-going waist to hook up
difficult closing

dürfe, fragte sie und fiel plötzlich der alten Dame um
might asked she and fell suddenly the old lady around

den Hals und versicherte, daß gar nichts ... aber ganz
the neck and assured that at all nothing but completely

bestimmt auch gar nichts passieren werde, und daß sie
decidedly also at all nothing pass will and that she
would

sich eben nur einmal einen einzigen Tag austoben
herself just only once a single day let off steam

wolle, und daß die »liebe alte Eio« ganz beruhigt
wanted and that the dear old Eio completely calmed down

sein könne. Als dann aber die »liebe alte Eio« fragte,
be could As then however the dear old Eio asked

ob sie denn etwa diesen entsetzlichen Cradock, diesen
whether she then about maybe this terrible Cradock this

Flaneur, Hasardeur und Baldrianer, noch liebe, da hatte
flaneur chancer/gambler and valerian still love there had

die Hoheit einen trotzigen Mund gezogen und
the highness a defiant mouth pulled and

geschwiegen. Gesprochen wurde von dem »Komplex
remained silent Spoken became from the complex problem

Cradock« bis auf weiteres nicht mehr. Das Dinner
Cradock until on further not (any)more The dinner

verlief mit »Hoheit« und »liebe Gräfin« ziemlich
ran course with highness and dear countess rather

wortkarg, und dann war man – eine halbe Stunde vor
taciturn and then was one/were they – a half hour before

der mit Cradock verabredeten Zeit – ins Kasino
the with Cradock agreed time – in the Casino

gegangen.
gone

Der Karneval aber, der draußen gegen das Kasino
The carnival however which outside against the Casino

brandete, er schickte seine großen und kleinen Wellen
brandished -he- sent his/its large and small waves

bis hierher in die Roulettesäle. Oben in den Räumen
until hereto in the roulette rooms Above in the spaces rooms

des Baccaratklubs hatte man eine Maskenredoute, und als
of the baccarat clubs had one a mask redoubt carnival area and as

Geishas und Pierretten und silbrige Rokokodamen
geishas and Pierrots and silvery rococo ladies

zwitscherten kleine ätherische Amerikanerinnen durch die
chirped little ethereal american women through the

Gänge. Im übrigen war es hier bei der Roulette das
walkways in the rest was -it- here at the roulette the

übliche Bild: ein bekannter Jazzkomponist aus Boston
usual picture a famous jazz composer from Boston

hatte siebenhundertsechzig Dollar gewonnen, ein alter
had seven hundred sixty dollar won an old

schwedischer Gutsbesitzer mit dem bekannten
swedish landowner with the acquaintances

bombensicheren Spielsystem war nun schon so weit, daß
bombproof game system was now already so far that

er sich telegraphisch Geld kommen lassen mußte ... in
he himself telegraphically money come let must In

einem Winkel machte ein Herr aus Basel seiner Gattin
a corner made a gentleman from Basel his wife

erregte Vorwürfe wegen eines Spielverlustes von zwölf
excited reproaches because of of a game loss from twelve

Gulden. Sonst gab es noch die üblichen jungen Polen
guilders Otherwise gave it still the usual young Poles
(money) was there

mit edler Schwermut im Antlitz und kleiner Hochstapelei
with noble melancholy in the face and (a) little high-stacking
trickery

in der Vergangenheit ... dann einen indischen Talmifürsten,
in the past then an Indian Talmi princes

zwei japanische Studenten, einige Sachsen mit heimlicher
two Japanese students some Saxon with secret

Netzwäsche hinter dem Smokinghemd. Endlich aber und
mesh wash behind the dress shirt Finally however and

vor allem ältliche fette Russinnen, die in der Bar
before all elderly fat Russian women who in the bar

zuviel »Ginfizz« getrunken hatten und sich nun
too much ginfizz drunk had and themselves now

zuviel degagiert benahmen. Pause war eben bei der
too much disengaged behaved Pause was just at the
loose

Roulette, und die Croupiers rechneten ab vor dem
roulette and the croupiers counted off before the
made final calculation

Schichtwechsel, und das ganze, wirklich etwas spießige
shift change and the whole really somewhat bourgeois

Publikum dieses aus der Mode gekommenen Kasinos
audience this from the fashion come casino

flutete für eine Stunde hinaus in die Bar, in die warme
streamed for an hour out in the bar in the warmth

Nacht, auf die Terrasse und auf den Korso. Es wurde
night on the terrace and on the corso it became

leer im Saal, die beiden Damen hatten sich die
empty in the hall the both ladies had themselves the

Cocktails hinter der Palmengruppe servieren lassen.
cocktails behind the palm group serve let

Die kleine Mary war aufgestanden und auf die Terrasse
The little Mary was gotten up and on the terrace
had

gegangen, träumte hinaus in die laue Frühlingsnacht.
gone dreamed out in the lukewarm spring night

Unten die Bucht lockte mit Mondlicht und kleinen
Under the bay lured with moonlight and small

goldenen Kräuselwellen. Der kleine silberne Kreuzer, der
golden ripple waves The little silver cruiser which
warship

dort unten vor seinen Ankern schwamm, schickte die
there under before its anchor swam sent the

schöne volle Stimme seiner Sirene über das Wasser, und
beautiful full voice of its siren over the water and

das kleine Boot, das sich nun loslöste von seinem Leibe,
the little boat which itself now detached from its body

das mochte schon ihn tragen. Ihn, den berüchtigten,
that might already him carry him the notorious

schlimmen Cradock. Den Abenteurer Cradock. Den
bad Cradock the adventurer Cradock The

Gottseibeiuns Cradock ... Ein kühlerer Luftzug kam plötzlich
God-be-with-us cradock a cooler air-pull came suddenly
draft

von den Bergen her, fiel auf die nackten Schultern,
from the mountains away fell on the naked shoulders

reizte die noch immer angegriffenen Lungen. Bitterböser
roused the still always attacked lungs Bitter

Husten kam. Die alte Violet brachte den Umhang und
coughing came The old Violet brought the cape and

bestand darauf, daß sie wieder in dem heißen Saal unter
insisted thereupon that she again in the hot hall under

den Palmen Platz nahm.
the palm trees place took

Sie saß verdrossen vor ihrem Glase, sie schwieg trotzig.
She sat annoyed before her glass she was silent defiant

So lustig war es gewesen, eine kleine Inkognito-Fürstin auf
So merry was it been a little incognito princess on
had

Ferien, ein unbekannter Domino zu sein. Dann war
vacation an unknown domino (mask) to be Then was

die alte Violet gekommen mit ihrer Moralpauke und ihrer
the old Violet come with her moral timpani and her

Schicksalsfrage, ob man diesen Cradock liebe, und
fate question whether one this Cradock love and

seither hatte man eigentlich die ganze Unbefangenheit
since had one actually the whole uninhibitedness

verloren: an die nutzlos verwehte Jugend mußte sie
lost on the useless blown away youth must she
of

denken, an diese alberne Ehe mit einem schütteren
think on this silly marriage with a doddering
of

Lebegreis, an die lächerliche Operette des kleinen
live-gray on the ridiculous operetta of the small
elderly man of

Balkanstaates, an das »Palais«, das eigentlich nicht viel
Balkan state on the palace which actually not much
of

mehr als ein umgebauter Pferdestall war. An die
(any)more as a rebuilt horse stable was An the
Of

schäbigen Livreen ihrer Bedienung, an ihren
shabby liveries of her service on her
lackeys of

»Oberstzeremonienmeister« mit den blankgescheuerten
over-master of ceremonies with the brightly scrubbed

Hosen, an ihre alte dicke Violet mit dem permanenten
pants on her old fat Violet with the permanent
of

Tröpfchen an der Nasenspitze ...
little drop on the tip of the nose

Daran mußte sie denken. Schwermut war gekommen. Das
There-on must she think Melancholy was come The
Of that had

Gefühl eines ungenützt verstreichenden Lebens, die
feeling of an unused passing life the

allererste Vorahnung vorzeitigen Alterns. Dreiviertel neun
very first premonition of premature aging Three quarters nine

war es und mithin noch eine Viertelstunde vor der
was it and therefore still a quarter of an hour before the

verabredeten Zeit, als sie draußen in der Bar zwei laute
agreed time as she outside in the bar two loud

Männerstimmen hörte. Die eine – der tiefe Baß eines
male voices heard The one – the deep bass of a

wahrscheinlich ältlichen und wohlbeleibten Menschen – war
probably elderly and well-embodied / large human / man – was

ihr unbekannt. Die zweite mit dem unbekümmerten und
her unknown The second with the carefree and

etwas jungenhaften Lachen, die gehörte ihm, dem
somewhat boyish laughing that belonged to him the

langen Cradock. »Hierher«, flüsterte sie der alten Violet zu
tall Cradock Here whispered she the old Violet to

und zog sie hinter die grüne Wand der Palmen. »Daß
and pulled her behind the green wall of the palm trees That

du mir nicht das Spiel verdirbst«, zischte bitterböse die
you me not the play spoil hissed bitterly evil the

Hoheit und setzte die Maske auf. Als sie sich eben
highness and set the mask on As she herself just

verkrochen hatte in den großen Ledersessel, ging
hidden had in the large leather armchair went

drüben die Tür auf. Mit seinem Schiffsarzt Crofts
over there the door up / open With his ship doctor Crofts

kam der Kapitän Cradock.
came the Captain Cradock

Der Doktor hatte noch immer im Café de Paris
The doctor had still always in the coffee shop of Paris

über dem »Manchester Guardian« gesessen, hatte sich
over the Manchester Guardian sat had himself
(newspaper)

dann seinem Kapitän etwas unerwünschterweise
then his Captain somewhat undesirably

angeschlossen und war augenblicklich damit beschäftigt,
joined and was immediately there-with occupied

Land und Leute in diesem verfluchten Hafen einer heftigen
land and people in this cursed harbor a violent

Kritik zu unterziehen. Die Monegassen, das waren nach
criticism to undergo The Monegasques that were after
give

Ansicht des Doktor Crofts Bauern... Bauern mit einer
opinion of the doctor Crofts farmers Farmers with a

etwas abweichenden Title, aber eben Bauern. Das
somewhat deviating title but just farmers Thee

frühlingsfrohe Land ringsum war mit seinen Blumendüften
spring joyful land all around was with its floral scents

ein Friseurladen, die ganze blütenselige Riviera eine ewige
a barber shop the whole flowery Riviera an eternal

Fruchtsauce, und der Cocktail, der
fruit sauce and the cocktail which

hier   serviert   wurde,   war   »amerikanisches
here   served   became   was   American

Klapperschlangengift«.   Der Kellner endlich, der, leise eine
rattlesnake venom   The waiter   finally   who   softly a

Verdikoloratur trällernd, den Cocktail gebracht hatte, das
Verdi-accent   warbling   the cocktail brought   had   that

war ein verdammter Operntenor, und die Bewohner der
was a   damned   opera tenor and the residents of the

Riviera im   besonderen und die   von   Italien im
Riviera in the special   and those from Italy   in -the-
                especially

allgemeinen waren in   ihrer Gesamtheit eine »Nation von
general   were   in   their entirety   a   nation   of

Heldentenören«. Nach dieser homerischen Schilderung von
hero tenors   After this   Homeric   description   from

Land und Leuten fragte der Doktor Crofts, was   das
land and people asked   the doctor Crofts   what that

eigentlich für ein seidener Domino   (und der alte, nicht
actually   for a   silky   domino (mask) and the old   not

sehr frauenfreundliche Herr sagte »halbnacktes Biest«
very women friendly   Mr   said   half-naked   beast

statt   Domino)   gewesen sei, mit   dem   er heute seinen
instead domino (mask) been   be   with which he today his

Kapitän gesehen habe.
Captain seen   have
                  had

Für einen alten Aventurier war der lange Cradock
For an old aventurier was the tall Cradock

eigentlich ungewöhnlich erregt, als er die Geschichte dieses
actually unusually excited as he the story of this

Nachmittags zu erzählen begann – ging auf und ab mit
afternoon to tell began – went on and off with

langen Schritten, trank ziemlich hastig, blieb stehen und
long strides drank rather hastily remained stand and

trank wieder. Ob Crofts wisse, wie das sei, wenn
drank again Whether Crofts knew how that be when

einen angehenden Vierziger Erinnerungen an allererste
a budding forty year old memories on (the) very first

Liebesgeschichten befielen, fragte der lange Cradock.
love stories befell asked the tall Cradock
attacked

Das wußte der alte dicke Crofts nicht mehr.
That knew the old fat Crofts not (any)more

»In Port Said«, sagte der lange Cradock und wollte mit
In Port Said said the tall Cradock and wanted with

seiner Midshipman-Geschichte und der kleinen Araberin
his midshipman story and the small Arab woman

Kaina beginnen. Da knurrte der alte Crofts, daß Port
Kaina begin There growled the old Crofts that Port

Said der unpassendste Ort der Welt sei, und daß alle
Said the most inappropriate place of the world be and that all

von   dorther   kommenden   Liebesgeschichten
from   over there   coming   love stories

notwendigerweise   unpassende   Geschichten   seien.   Nach
necessarily   inappropriate   stories   are   After

diesen   Vorhalten   konnte   der   Cradock   dann   endlich   mit
this   hold up   could   the   Cradock   then   finally   with

seiner   Beichte   beginnen ...
his   confession   begin

So   also,   in   ihren   Lederstuhl   geschmiegt,   hörte   die   kleine
So   thus   in   her   leather chair   nestled   heard   the   little

Mary   die   Ereignisse   dieses   Nachmittags,   wie   sie   sich
Mary   the   events   of this   afternoon   as   they   themselves

spiegelten   im   Gedächtnis   ihres   alten   Galans.   Daß   ihr
reflected   in the   memory   of her   old   galant (lover)   That   her

Nacken   ihn   eben   doch   nur   an   ein   kleines   Arabermädchen
neck   him   just   indeed   only   on   a   little   Arab girl
                                     of

aus   Port   Said   und   an   einen   allerersten,   wenn   auch
from   Port   Said   and   on   a   very first   when   also
                                                       if

harmlos   verlaufenen   Kadettenflirt   erinnert   habe.   Daß   er
harmless   ran   cadet flirt   reminded   have   That   he
           passed   had

sich   zunächst   einfach   in   ihren   Nacken   verliebt   habe,
himself   first   simply   in   her   neck   fallen in love   have
                                                                     had

und   daß   es   immer   eine   höchst   gefährliche   Sache   sei,
and   that   it   always   a   most high   dangerous   thing   be
                                   most   is

wenn Männer jenseits der allerersten Jugend
when men on the other side of the very first youth

überfallen würden von den Erinnerungen an allererste,
ambushed became from the memories on (the) very first

wenn auch harmlos verlaufene Liebesgeschichten ... Das also
when also harmless ran love stories That also
passed

bekam die kleine Mary zu hören. Dann kam das Abenteuer
became the little Mary to hear Then came the adventure
got

in der Rue de la Paix ... dann die drei Küsse (zwei auf
in the road of the Peace then the three kisses two on

den Nacken und einer auf den Hals) und dann kam das,
the neck and one on the throat and then came that

was sie freilich noch nicht wußte: der Ankauf dieses
what she indeed still not knew the purchase of this

einzigartigen göttlichen Halsbandes ...
unique divine collar

Angekauft, weil dem Cradock gerade der einzige zu
Bought because the Cradock just the only to

diesem Halsband passende Frauennacken begegnet war.
this collar suitable woman's neck encountered was
had

Angekauft, weil der lange Cradock den Gedanken einfach
Bought because the tall Cradock the thought simply

nicht ertragen hätte, daß dieses Halsband jemals in den
not endure had that this collar ever in the
could

Besitz einer anderen Frau, als der gerade von ihm
possession of an other woman as/than the just from him

bevorzugten, gekommen wäre.
favored come/landed were/had

Angekauft, weil man eben, wenn man wirklich einmal
Bought because one just when one really (for) once

einer ganz schönen Frau begegnete, auch die
a completely beautiful woman met also the

kavaliermäßigen Konsequenzen tragen mußte.
cavalier-like consequences carry must

Das war ja nun ein bodenlos leichtsinniger, ein
That was yes/indeed now a bottomless/without reason reckless a

jungenhafter, ein unerhört ritterlicher, ein echter
boyish an outrageously chivalrous a real

Cradockstreich – die kleine Hoheit hinter ihren Palmen
Cradock prank – the little highness behind her palm trees

hätte eben kein Weib sein müssen, wenn in ihr nur ein
had just no wife be must when in her only an

anderer Impuls als dieser gewesen wäre: die alte Violet
other pulse as this been were the old Violet

hinausschicken, den dicken Doktor zum Teufel schicken,
send out the fat doctor to the devil to send

alles Störende fortschicken und alle landesmütterlichen
everything disruptive send away and all country mother

Pflichten vergessen und dem langen Cradock um den
duties forgotten and the tall Cradock around the

Hals fallen … in diesem Augenblick geschah jenseits
neck fall in this moment happened on the other side

dieser Wintergarten-Botanik etwas, was den Dingen eine
of this winter garden botany something what the things a
that

ganz andere Wendung gab. –
completely other turn gave

Ein Diener kam und fragte nach dem Kapitän Cradock und
A servant came and asked after the Captain Cradock and

führte hinter sich einen Herrn im Cutaway herein.
led behind himself a gentleman in the cutaway in

Der Cutaway kam und sagte, daß er Jarras heiße und
The cutaway came and said that he Jarras was named and

im Auftrage der Firma Lebas käme und sowohl dies
in the assignment of the company Lebas came and both this

wie das hier zu überbringen habe. Dann gab er das
as the here to deliver have Then gave he the
had

Päckchen mit dem Schmuck dem Kapitän Cradock, und
little package with the jewel to the Captain Cradock and

die Rechnung überreichte er demjenigen, der gerade
the bill over-reached he that one who just
(gave)

danach griff. Nämlich dem Doktor Crofts.
there-after grabbed Namely the doctor Crofts
for it

Bemerkt muß werden, daß der Doktor Crofts um gute
Noticed must become that the doctor Crofts around good

zwanzig Jahre älter und an Bord derjenige war, von dem
twenty years older and on board that one was from whom

der Cradock sich ganz gehörig und väterlich den
the Cradock himself completely proper and fatherly the

Kopf waschen ließ, wenn es (was ja wirklich vorkam) ein
head wash let when it what yes really happened a

wenig »Holterdipolter« ging in seinem Leben. Im
little holterdipolter went in his life In the
wrong

vorliegenden Falle war es mit den beiden so, daß der
present case was it with the both so that the

Kapitän beseligt mit den eingehandelten Perlen spielte und
Captain blessed with the traded Pearls played and

der Doktor sehr wenig beseligt in die Rechnung starrte.
the doctor very little blessed in the bill stared

»Weißt du, was das Ding kostet?« fragte der Doktor. Daß
Know you what the thing costs asked the doctor That

er das doch unmöglich wissen könne, sagte der Cradock.
he that indeed impossibly know could said the Cradock

»Man fragt doch nach dem Preis«, sagte der Doktor.
One asks indeed after the price said the doctor

»Man fragt, wenn man einer schönen Frau eine Freude
One asks when one a beautiful woman a joy

machen kann, niemals nach dem Preis«, sagte der Cradock.
make can never after the price said the Cradock

Nach dieser Sentenz seines Kapitäns, gegen die sich
After this sentence of his captain against the himself

vorderhand ja nichts machen ließ, sagte der Doktor
forehand yes nothing make let said the doctor

Crofts zu Herrn Jarras von der Firma Lebas, daß er,
Crofts to Mr Jarras from the company Lebas that he

ehe der Schmuck bezahlt werde, noch einmal unter vier
before the jewel paid become still once under four

Augen mit dem Kapitän sprechen müsse. Dann schob er
eyes with the Captain speak must Then pushed he

Herrn Jarras zur Tür hinaus, und dann begann zwischen
Mr Jarras to the door out and then began between

ihm und dem Kapitän ein Gespräch, das an
him and the Captain a conversation that on
which

Überraschungen und dramatischen Wendungen nicht gerade
surprises and dramatic turns not just

arm war. –
poor was

»Kassenstand?« knurrte der alte Crofts. »Wieviel hast du
Cash register level growled the old Crofts How much have you

bei dir?« Da drehte der Kapitän wortlos die linke
with you There turned the Captain wordless the left

Hosentasche um, und es fielen zu Boden neben einigen
pocket around and it fell to ground beside some

Gegenständen, die in Herrentaschen sich immer
objects which in men's pockets themselves always

vorfinden und deren Benennung den Geboten der
find and whose designation the commandments of the
are found

Schicklichkeit widersprechen würde: es fiel also zu Boden
decency disagree would it fell thus to ground

die private Barschaft des Kapitäns Cradock.
the private cash of the captain Cradock

Elf Pfund, sieben Schilling, sechs Pence. »Zweitausend
Eleven pound seven shilling six pence Two thousand

Pfund, du Windkutscher, kostet der Schmuck«, schrie der
pound you wind coachman costs the jewellery cried the

Doktor. Da drehte der lange Cradock die andere
doctor There turned the tall Cradock the other

Hosentasche herum, und da fiel zu Boden die
pocket around and there fell to ground the

Schiffskasse des Kreuzers »Persimon«.
ships cash (box) of the cruiser Persimon
warship

Zweitausendvierhundert Pfund. Regierungsgelder. Gelder für
Two thousand four hundred pound Government funds Funds for

Mannschaftslöhnung, für dringend benötigte Kohlen.
crew's wages for urgent needed coals

»Damit willst du zahlen?« stöhnte der Doktor. Der
There-with / With that — want — you — pay — groaned — the — doctor — The

Cradock, hingelümmelt mit langausgestreckten Beinen in
Cradock — slouched down — with — elongated — legs — in

seinen Stuhl, nickte höchst gleichmütig. »Defraudant!«
his — chair — nodded — most hightly — indifferent — Fraud

schrie der Doktor. Der Cradock schwieg. Defraudant war
cried — the — doctor — The — Cradock — was silent — Fraud — was

ein allzu bilderreiches Wort, auf das ein Kavalier nicht
an — all too — rich in images — word — on — that / which — a — cavalier — not

antwortete. »Deine Ahnen«, stöhnte der Doktor, »werden
answered — Your — ancestors — groaned — the — doctor — will

sich im Grabe herumdrehen!«
themselves — in the — grave — turn around

Da antwortete der Cradock, daß seine Ahnen im
There — answered — the — Cradock — that — his — ancestors — in the

Gedanken an ihren Nachfahren schon seit geraumer Zeit
thoughts — on — their — descendants — already — since — some — time

mit sechzig Umdrehungen pro Minute um ihre
with — sixty — revolutions — per — minute — around — their

Längsachse rotierten in ihren Gräbern. Als aber der
longitudinal axis — rotated — in — their — graves — As — however — the

Doktor fragte, wie er denn eigentlich diese
doctor — asked — how — he — then — actually — this

Regierungsgelder wieder ersetzen wolle, da machte der
government funds again replace wanted there made the

Cradock mit dem Kopf eine nicht mißzuverstehende
Cradock with the head a not misunderstood

Bewegung nach dem Spieltisch hinüber und sagte nur das
movement to the game table over and said only the

eine Wort »Roulette«. Und als der Doktor die Hände rang,
one word roulette And as the doctor the hands rank

was denn eigentlich werden solle, wenn er an dieser
what then actually become should when he on this
happen

Roulette alles verlöre, da sagte der Cradock das,
roulette everything lose there said the Cradock that

was er in allen kitzlichen Situationen seines Lebens sich
what he in all ticklish situations of his life himself
difficult

gesagt hatte.
said had

Neunzehnhundertneunzehn, als bei dem bewußten
Nineteen nineteen when at the conscious
mentioned

Kaffernputsch neunzig brüllende Wilden seine Farm
kaffir putsch ninety roaring savages his farm

umstellt hatten. Und zwei Jahre später, als er beim
surrounded had And two years later as he at the

Lizard mit gebrochener Großschote vor dem Oststurm
lizard with broken mainsheet before the east storm

ins   offene Meer hinausgetrieben worden war ...
in the open   sea   driven out   become   was

»Ich verliere nie«, sagte der Cradock und gähnte
I   lose   never said the Cradock and yawned

gelangweilt und hob die Gelder auf und versorgte sie in
bored   and lifted the funds up and took care them in
put back

beide Hosentaschen. Die Privatgelder in die linke und die
both   pockets   The private money in the left and the

Regierungs- und Kohlengelder in die rechte. Nach diesem
government and coal money in the right After this

schönen männlichen Bekenntnis, an dem alle
beautiful male confession on which all

Überredungskünste des Doktor Crofts scheiterten, trat
arts of persuasion of the doctor Crofts failed stepped

eine neue Komplikation der Lage ein ...
a new complication the situation in

Der erste Mann, der diese Bühne betrat, war der Leutnant
The first man who this stage entered was the lieutenant

Williams, und der Leutnant Williams hatte ein eben auf der
Williams and the lieutenant Williams had a just on the

»Persimon« eingegangenes Telegramm in der Hand, hatte
Persimon received telegram in the hand had

den Kapitän bereits überall gesucht, beteuerte, daß es
the Captain already everywhere sought asserted that it

ein — an
dringendes, — urgent
ein — a
ganz — completely
außerordentlich — extraordinary
wichtiges — important

Staatstelegramm — state telegram
sei: — be was
der — the
Leutnant — lieutenant
Williams — Williams
wurde — became
im — in the

Drange — urge
der — of the
weiteren — further
Ereignisse — events
übersehen — overlooked
und — and
dann — then
mit — with

harten — hard
Worten — words
und — and
allen — all
Protesten — protests
zum — to the in
Trotz — despite
dahin — there to

beschieden, — decided
daß — that
er — he
sich — himself
samt — together with
seinem — his

Staatstelegramm — state telegram
in — in
die — the
Hölle — hell
scheren — shear
solle. — should

Der — The
zweite — second
Mann — man
aber — however
war — was
der — the
Barkeeper, — barkeeper
und — and
der — the

Barkeeper — barkeeper
meldete, — reported
daß — that
draußen — outside
der — the
Herr — Mr
Jarras — Jarras
von — from
der — the

Firma — company
Lebas — Lebas
unmöglich — impossibly
länger — longer
warten — wait
könne — could
und — and

nötigenfalls — if necessary
das — the
bewußte — mentioned
Paket — package
zurückerbitte — please return
und — and
in — in

jedem — each
Fall — case
nun — now
endlich — finally
Bescheid — information
oder — or
Geld — money
haben — have

müsse. — must

113

»Rückgängig machen!« schrie der Doktor Crofts und meinte
Undone   make   cried the doctor Crofts and meant

den Perlenkauf.
the pearl purchase

»Esel«, sagte sanft der Kapitän Cradock und meinte den
Ass   said   softly the Captain Cradock and meant   the

Doktor   Crofts   und   schob   den   Leutnant   Williams
doctor   Crofts   and   pushed   the   lieutenant   Williams

samt   seinem Telegramm zur   Seite und ging, um
together with his   telegram   to the side   and went   for

Herrn Jarras zu besänftigen, zur   Tür   hinaus. Es
Mr   Jarras to soothe   to the   door   out   It
                                 through the

geschah   schon   in seiner Abwesenheit, daß   hinter der
happened already in his   absence   that behind the

Palmengruppe zwei Damen   hervortraten und   sich
palm group   two   ladies emerged   and   themselves

durchaus   in   diese Angelegenheit mischen wollten. Eine
throughout in   this   matter   mix   wanted   An
totally

ältliche unmaskierte, die dem ratlos   in   seinem Sessel
elderly   unmasked   who the at a loss in   his   seat

verbliebenen   Crofts   wie   ein   »ganz   angenehmes
remaining   Crofts   as   a   all   pleasant

silbergesticktes   altes Krokodil« vorkam.   Und   dann   eine
silver embroidered old   crocodile appeared   And   then   a

jüngere, die nach Ort, Stunde und Maske niemand
younger (one) who after place hour and mask nobody

anderes sein konnte, als das »halbnackte Biest« des
else be could as the half-naked beast of the

heutigen Nachmittags. Da schnurrte denn das einmal in
today's afternoon There hummed then the once in
(blabbed) now

Gang gekommene Räderwerk weiter.
course come wheel works further

Sie, die kleine Mary, hatte hinter ihren Palmen natürlich
She the little Mary had behind her palm trees of course

die Entwicklung der Dinge sofort begriffen: das
the development the things immediately understood the

Halsband war für sie gekauft worden, weil ihr Nacken
collar was for her bought become because her neck

an den eines kleinen Arabermädchens aus Port Said
on that of a small Arab girl from Port Said
to

erinnierte. Die Schiffskasse mit den Kohlengeldern sollte
remembered The ships cash (box) with the coal money should

geplündert werden, weil das Halsband für die legitimen
looted become because the collar for the legitimate

Mittel eines Kapitäns aus ihrer Kriegsmarine zu teuer
means of a captain from her navy too expensive

war. Und gespielt endlich sollte werden, weil man doch
was And played finally should become because one indeed

irgendwie das Loch in der Schiffskasse wieder flicken
somehow the hole in the ships cash (box) again patch

mußte. –
had to

Zuerst hatte sie sich natürlich geärgert. Dann war sie
First had she herself of course annoyed Then was she
had

neugierig geworden. Wenn nämlich dieser Cradock gesagt
curious become When namely this Cradock said

hatte, daß er für eine schöne Frau alles wage, dann
had that he for a beautiful woman everything dare then

mußte man eben sehen, ob es wirklich noch solche
must one just see whether it really still such
there

Ritter gab in dieser etwas unritterlich gewordenen Welt.
knight gave in this somewhat unchivalrous become world
were

Und wenn er gesagt hatte, daß er niemals verlöre, dann
And when he said had that he never lose then

lockte eben an seiner Seite das Wagnis. Das
lured just to his side the risk The

Ungewöhnliche und das Abenteuer waren zu der kleinen
unusual and the adventure were to the little

Mary gekommen nach so und soviel toten Jahren, und
Mary come after so and so many dead years and

da war sie denn aufgetaucht aus ihrem Palmenversteck
there was she then duck-up from her palm hiding place
surfaced

und hatte die Bühne der Männer betreten.
and had the stage of the men entered

Das aber, was nun begann auf dieser Bühne, das war
That however what now began on this stage that was

ein Spiel, das die Akteure einigermaßen
a play that the actors somewhat
   theater

durcheinanderhetzte und für die nächsten vierundzwanzig
through each other rushed and for the next twenty four

Stunden wirklich einiges Leben brachte in dieses verstaubte
hours really some life brought in this dusty

und tote Monte Carlo. Der Kapitän Cradock, wie gesagt,
and dead Monte Carlo The Captain Cradock as said

war inzwischen hinausgegangen, um den in der Bar
was In the meantime went out for the in the bar
had

wartenden Herrn Jarras von der Firma Lebas zu
waiting Mr Jarras from the company Lebas to

beruhigen – aus der Bar hörte man einen Wortwechsel,
calm down – from the bar heard one a word exchange
   conversation

der Schlüsse auf mancherlei Meinungsdifferenzen
of which conclusions on many differences of opinion

zuließ. Der kleine Williams aber hielt noch immer sein
allowed The little Williams however held still always his

Telegramm in der Hand, und der alte Crofts saß als tief
telegram in the hand and the old Crofts sat as deeply

gebrochener Mann in seinem Sessel. »Ist Ihr Kapitän
broken man in his seat Is your Captain

immer so feurig?« fragte der Domino. »Bei Seewind
always so fiery asked the domino (mask) By sea wind

sanft wie der Erzbischof von Canterbury«, stöhnte der
soft as the archbishop from Canterbury groaned the

Doktor Crofts. Und dann, als draußen der Wortwechsel
doctor Crofts And then as outside the word exchange
conversation

zwischen dem Kapitän und der Firma Lebas zu einem
between the Captain and the company Lebas to a

ansehnlichen Fortissimo anschwoll, da sagte er, daß
handsome fortissimo swelled there said he that

heute leider etwas Seewind sei. Windstärke
today unfortunately some sea wind be Wind force

einhundertvierundzwanzig. Dann nahm er dem armen
one hundred twenty-four Then took he the poor

Williams endlich sein Telegramm aus der Hand und
Williams finally his telegram from the hand and

öffnete. Im selben Augenblick trat, ohne die etwas
opened In the same moment stepped without the somewhat

abseits stehenden Damen zu bemerken, in bester Laune
offside standing ladies to notice in (the) best mood

der Kapitän Cradock ins Zimmer und erklärte, daß man
the Captain Cradock into the room and explained that one

mit solchen Leuten wie mit diesem Cutaway doch nur
with such people as with this Cutaway indeed only

ein freundliches Wort zu reden brauche, und das Halsband
a friendly word to talk need and the collar

habe er natürlich sofort bezahlt und ... Da hielt ihm
have he of course immediately paid and There held him
had

wortlos der Doktor Crofts das Telegramm hin.
wordless the doctor Crofts the telegram away
before

Das Telegramm aber war von derjenigen Behörde, die
The telegram however was from of that authority that

sich in Labrador etwas stolz »Marineministerium«
itself in Labrador somewhat proud Ministry of navy

nannte, und es teilte dem Kapitän der »Persimon« mit,
called and it shared the Captain the Persimon with

daß morgen, am ersten März, Ihre Hoheit,
that tomorrow at the first (of) March her highness

gegenwärtig von Mailand unterwegs, mit kleinstem
currently from Milan on the way with smallest

Gefolge in Monte Carlo mit dem Nachmittagsexpreß
entourage in Monte Carlo with the afternoon express

eintreffen und den Kreuzer »Persimon« zur Überfahrt
arrive and the cruiser Persimon for the crossing
warship

nach Ägypten benutzen werde. Direktester Kurs sei
to Egypt use will Most direct course be

sofort nach Eintreffen auf Alexandria zu nehmen,
immediately to arrive on Alexandria to take

jedwede besondere Vorbereitung auf allerhöchsten Wunsch
any special preparation on supreme wish

zu vermeiden.
to avoid

Das stand in dem Telegramm. Hinten bei dem
That stood in the telegram In the back at the

verwaisten Spieltisch gab es mit schwarzer Maske und
orphaned game table gave it with black mask and

seidenem Domino eine Dame, die den Inhalt des
silk domino (mask) a lady which the content of the

Telegrammes sich ganz gut zusammenreimen konnte
telegram herself completely good rhyme together could

und hinter der Maske mühsam das Lachen verhielt. »Die
and behind the mask with trouble the laughing kept in The

grundgütige Landesmutter kommt«, stöhnte der
ground-goody country-mother comes groaned the
principal kind mother of the nation

weiberfeindliche alte Crofts. »Die freudlose Witwe« sagte,
hostile to women old Crofts The cheerless widow said

unhörbar glücklicherweise für den Domino, der lange
inaudibly fortunately for the domino (mask) the tall

Cradock und ballte den Fetzen zusammen und
Cradock and clenched the shred (of paper) together and

schleuderte ihn auf die Erde. Eine etwas beklommene
hurled him/it on the ground A somewhat uneasy

Stille war im Saal. –
silence was in the room

Er rannte auf und ab. Er war wütend. Seit jener Hochzeit
He ran on and off He was furious Since that wedding

in London hatte er eigentlich nur miserable Bilder von ihr
in London had he actually only miserable images from her

gesehen, wußte nicht einmal, ob sie nicht am Ende
seen knew not once whether she not at the end

gar schon verkümmert und ein böser alter Mann in
at all already withered and an angry old man in

Weiberröcken geworden war. Der Domino aber von
women skirts become was The domino (mask) however from

heute nachmittag, der war jedenfalls nicht verkümmert
today afternoon that (one) was in any case not withered

und böse und alt, und auf drei Hafentage hatte man ja
and angry and old and on three port days had one yes

wohl eigentlich rechnen können, und mindestens drei
well actually count can and at least three

Spielnächte brauchte er doch wohl auch, um ohne allzu
game nights needed he indeed well also for without all too

gewagtes Spiel die fehlenden zweitausend Pfund an der
daring play the missing two thousand pound on the

Roulette wieder zu verdienen! »Nun wird die grundgütige
roulette again to earn Now will the ground-goody
principal kind

Landesmutter wohl zu Fuß nach Ägypten pilgern
country-mother well at foot to Egypt (make) pilgrimage
mother of the nation

müssen, wenn du ihre Kohlengelder stiehlst«, fauchte in
must when you her coal money steals hissed in

seinem Sessel der alte Crofts. »Weiberwirtschaft«, stöhnte
his seat the old Crofts Women economy groaned

wütend der Cradock und beförderte mit einem Fußtritt
furious the Cradock and promoted with a kick

das ministerielle Telegramm in die Ecke. Und in diesem
the ministerial telegram in the corner And in this

Augenblick, als er gerade am Spieltisch vorüberkam, rief
moment as he just at the game table came over called

sie ihn an. »Kapitän Cradock ...«
she him on captain Cradock

Die beiden abseits stehenden Damen hatte er in der
The both offside standing ladies had he in the
to the side

Erregung bislang nicht bemerkt – dazu hatte ihn wohl
excitement so far not noticed – there-to had him well

das Telegramm allzusehr beschäftigt. Daß sie ihn nun
the telegram all-to-much occupied That she him now

unter Nennung seines Namens anrief, das beachtete er
under mention of his name addressed that noticed he

im Augenblick nicht – dazu war er viel zu erfreut
in the moment not – there-to was he much too pleased

über das Wiedersehen. »Untröstlich, mich anscheinend
over the see again Inconsolable me apparently

verspätet zu haben«, sagte der Cradock und beugte sich
delayed to have said the Cradock and bowed himself

(die alte Violet ignorierte er als eine unerwünschte Statistin
the old Violet ignored he as an unwanted statistical

vollkommen) über ihre Hand. »Unannehmlichkeiten?« fragte
perfectly over her hand Inconveniences asked

teilnahmsvoll der Domino, und man konnte natürlich
sympathetically the domino (mask) and one could of course

nicht sehen, wie sie hinter der Maske mit dem Lachen
not see how she behind the mask with the laughing

kämpfte bei dieser Frage ...
struggled at this question

Der lange Cradock aber sagte sich, daß es nach
The tall Cradock however said himself that it after

diesem Telegramm doch wohl allerlei Notwendiges zu
this telegram indeed well all kinds of necessary to
important

ordnen gab an Bord. Daß er für das Spiel um Kopf und
order gave on board That he for the game for head and

Kragen nur eine einzige Nacht übrig hatte, daß es besser
collar only one single night left had that it better

war, wenn man diesen Kopf vorher frei machte von allen
was when one this head before free made from all

Geschäften und Sorgen. Daß ihn leider allerlei
affairs and worry That him unfortunately all kinds of

dringlichste und unaufschiebbare dienstliche Angelegenheiten
most urgent and undelayable official affairs

für eine knappe Stunde an Bord zurückgerufen hätten,
for a scarce hour on board called back had

sagte der Cradock zu Madame.
said the Cradock to madame

Daß ihm diese dringlichen und unaufschiebbaren
That him this urgent and indelayable

Dienstgeschäfte hoffentlich nicht allzuviel Kopfschmerzen
official business hopefully not too much headaches

machen würden, antwortete Madame.
make would answered madame

Ob er sie denn wenigstens ganz bestimmt hier
Whether he her then at least completely definitely here

vorfinden würde, fragte der Kapitän.
find would asked the Captain

Daß sie ihn selbstverständlich hier erwarte, sagte Madame
That she him self-understandably here expected said madame
self-evidently

und reichte ihm die Hand zum Kuß. Und damit
and reached him the hand to the kiss And there-with
handed

trennten sie sich einstweilen.
separated they themselves for the time being

Der lange Cradock aber war, als er nach diesem
The tall Cradock however was as he after this

Gespräch das Kasino verließ, völlig wiederhergestellt in
conversation the Casino left totally restored in

seiner Laune.
his mood

Dem alten Crofts, der melancholisch über der ersten
The old Crofts who melancholically over the first

Flasche Chateau d'Yquem saß, erklärte er, daß er ein
bottle Chateau d'Yquem sat explained he that he an

unverbesserlicher Hypochonder und Schwarzseher und ein
incorrigible hypochondriac and doomlookers and a
doomsayers

humorloser Talgmops sei.
humorless tallow mop be

Dem kleinen Williams, der in der Bar ganz bescheiden
The small Williams who in the bar completely modest

seinen »Deap Sea« trank, gaukelte er noch zwischen Tür
his Deep Sea drank juggled he still between door

und Angel mit »alter Junge« und jovialem
and fishing rod with old boy and jovial

Schulterschlag als Folge des fürstlichen Besuches
tap on the shoulder as consequence of the princely visit

an Bord den Sonnenorden von Labrador oder vielleicht
on board the North of the sun from Labrador or perhaps

gar ein selbständiges Kommando vor.
at all an independent command before

Sich selbst aber sagte er, daß die Dinge doch
Himself self however said he that the things indeed

schließlich niemals so schlimm abliefen, wie es anfänglich
finally never so bad ran off / ended as it initially

schiene. Daß er bis morgen ja schließlich auch von
seem That he until morning yes finally also from / by

James Vanderbilt zum Universalerben eingesetzt oder in
James Vanderbilt to the universal heir used or in

Mergentheim der Erbonkel James Cradock von seinen
Mergentheim of the Heir uncle James Cradock from his

fünf Prozent Zucker geholt sein konnte. Daß ihn das
five percent sugar kept be could That him the

Spielglück bisher noch nie verlassen habe, daß bis
game-fortune until-here / until now still never left have / had that until

morgen noch lange zwölf Stunden waren, und daß diese
morning still long twelve hours were and that these

Stunden ein buntes Abenteuer mit einer schönen Frau
hours a colorful adventure with a beautiful woman

bedeuteten.
meant

Das alles sagte sich der lange Cradock, als er das
That everything said himself the tall Cradock as he the

Kasino verließ. Er pfiff den Sussexmarsch und drückte
Casino left He whistled the Sussex march and squeezed

dem Bootsführer als Trinkgeld alle seine Silberschillinge in
the boat driver as drink-money all his silver shillings in
tip

die Hand. Und war als unverwüstliches Glückskind
the hand And was as indestructible child of fortune

überhaupt in der Laune jenes berühmten Mannes, dem
at all in the mood of that famous man whom

die Götter in der Wiege bescherten, alle Tage Geburtstag
the Gods in the cradle bestowed all days birthday

zu haben.
to have

Kapitel IV

An Bord erwartete ihn der Funker Bengtson mit
On board expected him the radio operator Bengtson with

einem zweiten Telegramm. Es war (wohl
a second telegram It was well
sure

des Inkognitos wegen!) schlicht mit »Mary«
of the incognitos because of only with Mary
because of the incognitos

unterzeichnet. Es verbat sich für morgen nochmals alle
undersigned It forbade itself for (the) morning again all
any

besonderen Vorbereitungen und war vor zwei Stunden in
special preparations and was before two hours in

Mailand aufgegeben. Und der Kapitän konnte es natürlich
Milan given up And the Captain could it of course
created

nicht wissen, daß im Auftrage der
not know that in the assignment of the

unternehmungslustigen Hoheit von Labrador der Mailänder
enterprising highness from Labrador the Milan

Konsul dieses Telegramm aufgegeben hatte ... daß man
consul this telegram given up would have that one

ihn düpieren und in völlige Sicherheit wiegen wollte!
him dupe and in complete security weigh wanted
financially harm

Er zerriß es in siebenunddreißig Fetzen und sprach
He ripped it in thirtyseven shreds and spoke

zunächst einmal mit dem Chefingenieur. Der Chefingenieur
then once with the chief engineer The chief engineer

Pavlicek erklärte, daß mit den noch in den Bunkern zu
Pavlicek explained that with the still in the bunker to
coal hold

findenden Kohlen allenfalls ein armer Mann einen mäßigen
find coals at most a poor man a moderate

Osterkuchen backen, die »Persimon« aber unmöglich
eastercake bake (could) the Persimon however impossibly

weiter als allenfalls bis Cap d'Antibes kommen könne.
further as at most until Cap d'Antibes come could

Keine gute Auskunft. Er sah, daß ihm das Messer doch
No good notice He saw that him the knives indeed

ziemlich dicht an der Kehle saß. Da ging er denn in
rather close on the throat sat There went he then in

seine Kabine und schloß sich ein.
his cabin and locked himself in

Für seine Privatschatulle, soweit er sie nicht in der
For his private (cash) case so far he her not in the

Westentasche bei sich trug, hatte der lange Cradock
vest pocket at himself carried had the tall Cradock

neuerdings ein ganz originelles System der
recently a completely original system of the

Geldaufbewahrung eingeführt, das er in Südafrika von
money storage introduced the he in South Africa from

einem dorthin verwehten russischen Offizier gelernt hatte:
a there-to blown away Russian officer learned had

man wechselte die jeweilige Monatsgage in einzelne
one exchanged the respective monthly salary in single

Pfundstücke ein, man nahm die Hand voll Goldmünzen und
pound pieces in one took the hand full (of) gold coins and

schleuderte sie auf gut Glück gegen die Decke der
hurled them on good fortune against the ceiling of the

Kabine. Man behielt auf diese Weise nur ganz wenig
cabin One kept on this manner only completely little

in der Tasche zurück, man kam sich als armer Mann
in the pocket back one came himself as poor man

vor und gab nicht (was sonst unfehlbar
before and gave not what otherwise infallible
(gab aus: spent)

geschehen wäre!) alles gleich am ersten Tage
happened would be everything immediately at the first days

aus. Man hatte einen grundehrlichen Waliser zum
out One had an honest Welsh (guy) to the
as

Burschen, und man suchte, wenn man Geld brauchte, das
lad and one searched when one money needed the
servant

Notwendige auf Schränken, in Dielenritzen und unter dem
necessary on the shelves in floor cracks and under the

Bette sich zusammen: auch in den verzweifeltsten
bed oneself together also in the most desperate

Situationen fand sich dann immer noch etwas ...
situations found oneself then always still something

Im vorliegenden Falle fanden sich (am Letzten des
In the present case found itself at the last of the

Monats, wollen Sie gütigst bedenken) noch sieben Pfund.
month want you kindly think still seven pound
be so good to think

Die sieben Pfund ergänzten den Inhalt der linken
The seven pound increased the content of the left

(privaten) Westentasche auf rund achtzehn Pfund. In der
private vest pocket on around eighteen pound In the

rechten (staatlichen) Westentasche befanden sich, nachdem
right of the state vest pocket found itself after

man zweitausend für ein Perlenhalsband hatte ausgeben
one two thousand for a pearl collar had give out
spend

müssen, noch vierhundert Pfund Regierungsgelder.
must still four hundred pound government funds

Vierhundert Pfund Regierungsgelder wanderten jetzt aus
Four hundred pound government funds roamed now from

der staatlichen in die private Westentasche, wurden
the state in the private vest pocket became

dadurch bis auf weiteres Cradocksche Privatgelder
there-through until on further Cradock private moneys
through that

und ergänzten das Betriebskapital in willkommener Weise
and increased the working capital in more welcome manner

auf vierhundertachtzehn Pfund. Dieser Kassasturz (wofern
on four hundred eighteen pound This checkout what

ich mir diesen alten k. u. k. österreichischen Fachausdruck
I myself this old k. u. k Austrian technical term

für »Bilanz« zu eigen machen darf) ergab also ein »Haben«
for balance to own make may gave thus a have
                                                       have now

von vierhundertachtzehn Pfund und ein »Soll« von
of four hundred eighteen pound and a should of
                                        should earn

zweitausendvierhundert Pfund, die binnen vierundzwanzig
two thousand four hundred pound, that within twenty four

Stunden ersetzt und demgemäß in den zehn Stunden
hours replaced and accordingly in the ten hours

dieser Nacht an der Roulette verdient werden mußten,
of this night on the roulette earned become must

wofern nicht wirklich die Hoheit von Labrador zu Fuß
in so far not really the highness of Labrador to foot

nach Ägypten pilgern sollte. Die Situation war
to Egypt (make) pilgrimage should The situation was

ernst. Die Pistole auf dem Tisch sah den langen Cradock
serious The pistol on the table saw the tall Cradock
                                        looked

an mit einem bösen schwarzen Auge, und das böse
on with a bad black eye, and the evil
at

schwarze Auge sagte, daß nach altem ehrwürdigem Kodex
black eye said that after old venerable code

ein Gentleman sich totzuschießen habe, wenn er der
a gentleman himself to shoot have when he the

Defraudation von Staatsgeldern überführt worden sei. Da
defraudation from state funds transferred become be There

aber der Gedanke an den Tod ein Kommißgedanke für
however the thought on the death an acting thought for

romantische Fähnriche war, so schickte man den Gedanken
romantic ensigns was so sent one the thoughts

an den Tod zum Teufel und ging zur Tat über. Man
on the death to the devil and went to the deed over One
action

depeschierte also an jenen einzigen noch vorhandenen
dispatched thus on that single still existing

Cradock-Onkel in Mergentheim, daß man sofort
Cradock uncle in Mergentheim that one immediately

zweitausendfünfhundert Pfund brauche (eigentlich nur der
two thousand five hundred pound need actually only the

Form halber und ohne die mindeste Hoffnung auf Erfolg,
form half and without the least hope on success

da dieser Mergentheimer Onkel geiziger als der reiche
there this Mergentheimer uncle stingier as the rich

Mann im Evangelium war). Dann aber, als das
man in the gospel was Then however as the

Telegramm expediert war, tat der Cradock das, was an
telegram expedited was did the Cradock that what on

seiner Stelle alle Spieler von Ruf und Erfahrung getan
his spot all players from call and experience done

hätten; er stellte für die heutige Nacht sich ein
had he set for the today night himself a

Spielsystem zusammen. –
game system together

Die Roulette nämlich, wollen Sie bedenken, ist nur
The roulette namely want you (well) think is only

scheinbar ein aus Galalith, Zelluloid und Messing
apparently one from galalith celluloid and brass
(material)

zusammengesetztes totes Ding – die Roulette hat, wie alle
together put dead thing – the roulette has as all

scheinbar toten Dinge, ihren geheimen Rhythmus und ihre
apparently dead things her secret rhythm and her

geheimen Gesetze, die man eben zu ergründen und zu
secret laws that one just to fathom and to

berücksichtigen hat. Es ist in Monte Carlo vor drei
consider has It is in Monte Carlo before three

Jahren passiert, daß die Kugel siebzehnmal
years happened that the bullet seventeen times

hintereinander auf der Zahl Null haltmachte. Und in
behind each other on the number zero stopped And in

demselben Monte Carlo hatte – das war kurz vor dem
the same Monte Carlo had – that was short before the

Krieg – ein Herr hundert Gulden auf elf gesetzt,
war – a gentleman hundred guilders (money) on eleven set

gewann den fünfunddreißigfachen Betrag, ließ ihn stehen,
won the thirty five times amount let it stand

gewann wieder das Fünfunddreißigfache, ließ (er verhielt
won again the thirty five times let he related

sich seit der dritten Volte auffallend still), ohne ein
himself since the third turn strikingly quiet without a

Wort zu sagen, den ungeheuer angewachsenen Betrag zum
word to say the monstrously grown amount to the

zweitenmal auf elf stehen, gewann auf elf noch
second time on eleven stand won on eleven still

fünfmal, und erst vor der sechsten Volte wurde
five times and first before the sixth turn became

festgestellt, daß er – inzwischen einen Herzschlag
detected that he – In the meantime a heartbeat

erlitten hatte und tot war. Die Roulette hat ihre
suffered had and dead was The roulette has her

geheimen Gesetze, und es war einfach selbstverständlich,
secret laws and it was simply self-understandable self-evident

daß der Cradock seinen Kriegsplan sich zusammenstellte.
that the Cradock his war plan himself put together

Als er aber erst mit seinen Berechnungen fertig war,
As he however first with his calculations ready was

da war er auch, wie in solchem Falle alle Spieler,
there was he also as in such case all players

einfach nicht mehr zu erschüttern in der Überzeugung,
simply not (any)more to shake in the conviction

daß diese Schlacht gut ausgehen werde. Elf Uhr war
that this battle good go out will Eleven hour(s) was
       end   o'clock

es, als er das Kasino wieder erreichte. –
it as he the Casino again reached

Zwischen den beiden Damen hatte es während seiner
Between the both ladies had -it- while his

Abwesenheit eine ziemlich erregte Auseinandersetzung
absence a rather excited confrontation

gegeben. »Man unterschlägt keine Staatsgelder«, hatte die
given One embezzles no state money had the
occurred

alte Violet gesagt. Da hatte ihre Herrin erwidert, daß es
old Violet said There had her Mistress replied that it

ja nicht eigentliche Staatsgelder, sondern, zum größten
yes not actual state funds but for the greatest
indeed

Teile wenigstens, Mittel aus ihrer eigenen Privatschatulle
part at least means from her own private (cash) box

seien. »Man unterschlägt überhaupt keine Gelder«, hatte
be One embezzles at all no funds had

die alte Dame gesagt. Da hatte die Mary erwidert, daß
the old lady said There had the Mary replied that

es ein Riesenunterschied sei, ob man die
it a huge difference be whether one the

unterschlagenen Gelder in die eigene Tasche stecken oder
embezzled funds in the own pocket stick or

damit eine schöne Frau beschenken wolle. – »Du
there-with a beautiful woman gift wanted – You

bist frivol!« hatte die alte Violet gescholten. »Heute ist
are frivolous had the old Violet scolded Today is

Karneval«, hatte die regierende Fürstin-Witwe von Labrador
carnival had the ruling princess-widow of Labrador

erwidert. Und da ihre Hofdame und einstige Lehrerin alle
replied And there her court lady and former teacher all
since

die anderen Geschütze der Überredungskunst schon
the other guns of the persuasion already

abgefeuert hatte, so versuchte sie es mit der letzten
fired had so tried she it with the last

großkalibrigen Kanone. Daß diesem schrecklichen Cradock
large caliber canon That this horrible Cradock

alles zuzutrauen sei, und daß er das verbriefte Recht
everything to entrust be and that he the lettered right
certified

habe, ohne Hosen bei ihr zu erscheinen und sie in
had without pants by her to appear and she in
before

diesem Zustande um Gnade zu bitten und ...
this condition for mercy to ask and

Die Gräfin Hensbarrow rang die Hände. »Kein
The countess Hensbarrow wrung the hands No

europäischer Thron würde heute diese Hosenlosigkeit
european throne would today this pantlessness

überstehen«, jammerte die alte Dame. Da rang bei
survive wailed the old lady There struggled at

der Vorstellung, daß der Cradock ohne Hosen und im
the image that the Cradock without pants and in the

Frack (womöglich hier, im Palmensaal des Kasinos)
tailcoat possibly here in the palm hall of the casino

einen Fußfall tun könne, die Mary vor Lachen nach Luft.
a foot-fall do could the Mary for laughing after air
prostration of

»Ich sehe deinen Thron wanken«, schluchzte die alte
I see your throne waver sobbed the old

pathetische Dame und erreichte damit doch nur, daß
pathetic lady and attained there-with indeed only that

die böse Hoheit sich übermütig hin und her warf
the evil highness herself over-courageous here and there threw
cocky

in ihrem Sessel und erklärte, daß dieser hier eigentlich
in her seat and explained that this here actually

noch ganz fest stünde. Da war es zuviel, und
still completely fast stood There was it too much and
concluded was

da | bekam | ihre | Hofdame | einen | roten | Kopf. | »Ich | bitte
there | became | her | court lady | a | red | head | I | ask

Ew. | Hoheit | um | die | Erlaubnis, | mich | zurückziehen
et. | highness | for | the | permission | me | to withdraw
(ewige: eternal)

zu | dürfen«, | sagte | in | tiefer | Verbeugung | und | in
to | allow | said | in | deep | bow | and | in

tiefgekränktem | Ton | die | Gräfin | Hensbarrow. | Wogegen
deeply hurt | tone | the | countess | Hensbarrow | Where-against

die | Mary | absolut | nichts | einzuwenden | hatte, | und
the | Mary | absolutely | nothing | in to turn to object | had | and

woraufhin | die | alte | Dame | schwerbeleidigt | aus | dem | Saal
whereupon | the | old | lady | seriously offended | from | the | hall

gerauscht | war. | Fast | im | selben | Augenblick | war | Cradock
rushed | was had | Almost | in the | same | moment | was had | Cradock

eingetreten. –
in-stepped
entered

Die | Bar, | in | der | er | vorher | haltgemacht | hatte, | zu | einer
The | bar | in | which | he | before | stopped | had | for | a

letzten | Vorbereitung | aufs | Gefecht, | war | überfüllt | gewesen.
last | preparation | on the for the | battle | was had | overfilled | been

Wie | Tiere | am | Trog | drängten | sich, | Ellbogen | an
As | animals | at the | trough | pressed | themselves | elbows | on

Ellbogen, | mit | geröteten | Gesichtern | und | feisten | Rücken
elbows | with | flushed | faces | and | big | backs

diese Gäste … bleiche, übernächtige Mixer musterten
these guests pale overnight mixer eyed

geringschätzig dieses etwas provinzielle Publikum,
contemptuous this something provincial audience

verteilten hochmütig, als spendeten sie Libationen, die
distributed haughtily as donated they libations the

Geister der tausend auf den Regalen aufmarschierten
spirits of the thousand on the shelves marched up

Flaschen: den »Sol y Sombra«, den die Brasilianer
bottles the sun and shadow which the Brazilians
(Spanish)

eingeschleppt haben in Europa …, Bambus-Cocktail und den
in-dragged have in Europe bamboo cocktail and the
brought in

»Blenton« der englischen Kriegsmarine, und seltenen
Blenton the English navy and rare

bitteren »Gibson« mit seiner kleinen weißen Zwiebel.
bitter Gibson with its small white onion

Ventilatoren summten, halbe und Vierteleleganz machten
Fans buzzed half and quarter elegance made

sich breit … Glatzen spiegelten sanft die Lampen
themselves wide Bald reflected softly the lamps

wider, und an den Tischen lösten zwischen Glas und Glas
against and on the tables solved between glass and glass

behäbige Smokingbesitzer unbeschwert die großen Probleme
sluggish smoking owners carefree the great problems

des Erdballes: die Verschuldung Europas und die
of the globe the indebtedness (of) Europe and the
earth

Nöte des mittelenglischen Industriestreiks und die
hardships of the middle English industrial strikes and the

Gefahren, die sich aus der Sowjetpropaganda in
dangers which themselves from the Soviet propaganda in

Südafrika ergaben. –
South Africa gave up
came out

Er, der Kapitän Cradock, ehrfurchtsvoll begrüßt von diesen
He the Captain Cradock awesome greeted of these
by

Kellnern, die ihn aus dem Londoner »Ritz« und aus San
waiters who him from the London Ritz and from San

Sebastian und von Ostende her kannten ... er saß
Sebastian and from Oostende away knew he sat
(Belgium town)

zusammen mit Williams, abseits an einem kleinen Tisch,
together with Williams offside at a small table

trank einen Schwedenpunsch, schickte, um die brennende
drank a Swedish punch sent for the burning

Alkoholwunde zu besänftigen, einen sanfteren »Chocolate«
alcohol wound to soothe a gentler chocolate

hinterdrein. Dann stand er brüsk auf. Er ärgerte sich
back there in Then stood he brusquely up He annoyed himself

über das Geschwätz der fetten Spießer ringsum, und
over the babble of the fat philistines all around and
rabble

zum ersten Male geschah es hier, daß ein ganz toller
to the first time happened it here that a completely great

Gedanke durch sein Hirn fuhr: dieses ganze gräßliche
thought through his brain drove this whole hideous

Kasino vom Erdboden fortzuradieren, irgendeinen
Casino from the earth-floor away to erase some
ground

unausdenklichen Schrecken zu jagen über diese
inconceivable fright to chase over this

selbstzufriedenen Bourgeois, sich zu weiden an dem
complacent bourgeois himself to devote to the

Einsturz ihrer Philisterwelt ...
collapse of their philistine world

Das war vorderhand ein ganz momentanes Aufzucken,
That was forehand a completely momentary flinch

und ich glaube nicht, daß diese Idee schon in jener
and I believe not that this idea already in that

Bar-Viertelstunde feste Formen annahm im Hirn
quarter of an hour at the bar fixed forms took up in the brain

des langen Cradock. Immerhin nahm er sich, als er
of the tall Cradock After all took he himself as he

schon an der Tür des Spielsaales stand, den Leutnant
already on the door of the gambling halls stood the lieutenant

Williams beim Rockknopf und gab ihm einen letzten
Williams at the rock button and gave him a last

Befehl: dreißig Mann von der »Persimon« waren sofort
order thirty man from the Persimon were immediately

hierher zu beordern, hatten sich (Zivil, ohne Waffen
hereto to order had himself civil without weapons

und natürlich ganz unauffällig) hier vor dem Kasino
and of course completely inconspicuous here before the Casino

einzufinden und nebenan im Café de Paris Weiteres
to find and next-to in the coffee shop of Paris additional
to the side

zu erwarten. Ein etwas dunkler, in seinen Zielen
to expect A something dark in its aim

rätselhafter Befehl, den der Kapitän, schon mit dem
puzzling order which the Captain already with the

Türdrücker in der Hand, erteilte. Irgendwelche Aufklärungen
door handle in the hand issued Any enlightenment

gab er jedenfalls nicht. Er hatte Eile. Er verabschiedete
gave he anyhow not He had haste He said goodbye to

den Leutnant Williams mit einem flüchtigen Kopfnicken
the lieutenant Williams with a fleeting head-nod

und trat ein. Und da saß also ... dieses Mal ohne
and stepped in And there sat then this time without

die in seinen Augen völlig überflüssige
the in his eyes totally superfluous

Altdamenbegleitung ... unter der Palmengruppe der
old lady escort under the palm group the

Domino.
domino (mask)

»Kapitän Cradock ...«
Captain Cradock

Dieses Mal aber, als er von ihr mit seinem Namen
This time however as he from her with his name

angeredet wurde, stutzte er. »Sie kennen mich,
addressed became stopped short he You know me

Madame, woher?«
madame where from

Da lachte sie sehr übermütig. »Wer kennt Ihren Namen
There laughed she very cocky Who knows your name

denn nicht, Sie Baldrianeur heiliger Tempelkatzen,
then not you valerian holy temple cats

Banksprenger von San Sebastian, Held aller Ozeane,
bankruptcy from San Sebastian hero of all oceans

Brecher aller Frauenherzen, Abenteurer, berüchtigter
crusher of all women's hearts adventurer notorious

Seeräuber ...«
sea-robber
pirate

Das klang spöttisch, kokett, ließ natürlich die
That sounded mocking flirtatious let of course the

Vermutung zu, daß hinter dem Domino (obwohl der
suspicion to that behind the domino (mask) although the

Kapitän sich ganz vergeblich den Kopf zerbrach)
Captain himself completely in vain the head broke

irgendeine Londoner oder Kapstädter Bekannte
some from London or from Cape town known acquaintance

versteckt war. »Wer sind Sie, Madame?« Und dieses Mal
hidden was Who are you madame And this time

versuchte er, der Mann des schnellen Angriffes, der
tried he the man of the quick attack the

Maske sich zu bemächtigen, und mußte es doch
mask himself to seize and must it indeed

erleben, daß sie lachend hinter den Stuhl flüchtete und
live to see that she laughing behind the chair fled and
experience

ihm entkam ...
him escaped

»Defraudant labradorischer Schiffskassen..,« Dieses Mal
Defrauding Labrador ship's accounts This once

war's zuviel, und auf der Stirn Cradocks war eine
was it too much and on the forehead Cradocks was a

steile Falte zu sehen. Sagte sie »Defraudant labradorischer
steep wrinkle to see said she defrauding Labrador

Schiffskassen«, so war es klar, daß sie vorhin die ganze
ship's account so was it clear that she before the whole

Auseinandersetzung mit dem alten Crofts mitangehört
confrontation with the old Crofts listened to

hatte. Daß sie um das Perlenhalsband wußte, daß sie
had That she about the pearl collar knew that she

ihm die Freude verdorben hatte, daß sie auch wußte,
him the joy spoiled had that she also knew

womit der Schmuck bezahlt worden war ...
where-with the jewel paid become was
with which

»Sie haben gelauscht, Madame?«
You have listened madame?

»Da ich vorhin zeitig und pünktlich am verabredeten
There I before in time and punctually at the agreed
Since

Orte zur Stelle war!«
place at the spot was

»Und wissen jetzt natürlich alle meine Geheimnisse.«
And know now of course all my secrets

»Da diese Geheimnisse vorhin nicht gerade leise
There this secret before not just softly
Since

besprochen wurden!«
discussed became

Da lachte er bitter ...
There laughed he bitter ...

»Während Sie im sicheren Versteck sitzenblieben und
While you in the assured hiding place sit-remain and

lauschten!« Sein Gesicht war noch finsterer geworden, er
listened His face was still darker become he
had

begann erregt auf und ab zu gehen.
began excited on and off to go

Eine Weile sprachen sie beide nicht. Drei Saaldiener
A while spoke they both not Three room attendants

kamen, rückten Stühle zurecht, verschwanden; ein
came moved up chairs to (their) right (place) disappeared a

Croupier kam, machte sich an der Roulette zu schaffen,
croupier came made himself on the roulette to create work

ordnete Jetons, rechnete, bemühte sich, im Saale
ordered chips calculated occupied himself in the hall

nichts zu sehen außer seinem Handwerkszeug. Erste
nothing to see except his hand tool First

Spieler fanden sich ein ... drei ältere Französinnen,
players found themselves in three older french women

ein ägyptischer Baumwollhändler, ein sehr alter russischer
an egyptian tree-wool-handler a very old Russian
cotton dealer

Staatsrat: drückten sich im leeren Raum herum,
state council pressed themselves in the empty space around

empfanden es peinlich, die Ersten zu sein, lorgnettierten
experienced it (as) painful the first to be lorgnetted

nach den beiden unter den Palmen hinüber ...
to the both under the palm trees away over

Der lange Cradock war schließlich stehengeblieben. Da
The tall Cradock was finally stand-remained There
had halted Since

Madame es für gut befunden habe, zu lauschen, so habe
madame it for good found have to listen so have
thought had had

er seinerseits nicht den mindesten Grund, etwas zu
he in turn not the least reason something to

verheimlichen. Die Schiffskasse geplündert: Madame
conceal The ship's account plundered Madame

zuliebe. Fremde Gelder defraudiert: für Madame. Ein
for the sake of Foreign funds defrauded for madame A

Halsband gekauft, um Madame zu erfreuen: mit
collar bought for madame to delight with

gestohlenen Geldern ...
stolen money

»Mit Geldern«, sagte vorwurfsvoll der Domino, »mit
With money « said reproachfully the domino (mask) with

denen Ihre arme kranke Fürstin nach Ägypten fahren
which her poor sick queen to Egypt go

wollte!« Da sagte der Cradock, daß eine abwesende
wanted to There said the Cradock that an absent

Frau ein Gespenst sei, und daß eine anwesende Frau
woman a ghost be and that a present woman

alles verlangen könne; daß er folglich das Gespenst
everything desire could that he consequently the ghost

bestohlen und die anwesende Frau – übrigens
robbed and the present woman – by the way

unter   erheblicher   Gefahr   für   seinen   eigenen   Hals   –
under   more significant   danger   for   his   own   neck   –

beschenkt   habe ...
gifted   have

»Und   wenn   nun   morgen«,   sagte   der   Domino,   »ich   nicht
And   when   now   tomorrow   said   the   domino (mask)   I   not

mehr   da   bin   und   Ihre ...   übrigens   immer   noch   sehr
(any)more   there   am   and   your   by the way   always   still   very

schöne   Landesherrin   anwesend   sein   wird?«
beautiful   sovereign   present   be   will

Dann   werde   er,   sagte   gleichmütig   der   Cradock,
Then   will   he   said   indifferent   the   Cradock

selbstverständlich   gegen   die   anwesende   schöne   Hoheit
self-understandably   against   the   present   beautiful   highness
self-evidently

galant   sein   und   Madame,   da   sie   ja   nicht   mehr
gallant   be   and   madame   there   her   yes   not   (any)more
                                                    indeed

anwesend   sein   werde,   vergessen   haben.   »Ungetüm!«
present   be   will   forgotten   have   Monster

klagte   angesichts   dieser   unfaßlichen   Philosophie   der
complained   in face   of this   incomprehensible   philosophy   the

Domino   und   meinte   mit   »Ungetüm«   den   langen
domino (mask)   and   meant   with   Monster   the   tall

Cradock.   Ob   sie   die   Perlen   nun   annehmen   wolle   oder
Cradock   Whether   she   the   Pearls   now   on-take   wanted   or
                                            accept

nicht? fragte der Cradock und hatte die Miene eines
not asked the Cradock and had the expression of a

Ambassadeurs, der ein Ultimatum überbringt. Da wußte
ambassador who an ultimatum delivers There knew

sie, daß sie vor der Wahl stand, diesem Abenteuer
she that she before the choice stood this adventure

endgültig ein Ende zu machen und wieder zu ihrer alten
finally an end to make and again to her old
give

Violet hinaufzugehen; oder mit diesem gefährlichen Partner
Violet to go up or with this dangerous partner

ein nicht ganz ungefährliches Spiel weiterzuspielen: so
a not completely harmless play to continue playing so

oder so mußte das Ding jetzt zur Entscheidung kommen.
or so must the thing now to the decision come

Der Saal füllte sich: zwei zweifelhafte Großfürsten, ein
The hall filled itself two dubious great princes an

englischer Kokainhändler, ein Heldenbariton von der
English cocaine dealer a hero baritone from the

Kottbusser Oper, ein Zwickauer Kinderwagenfabrikant ...
kottbusser opera a from Zwickau stroller manufacturer

drei abgetakelte Kokotten aus Brüssel ... ein alter
three stripped away cocots from Brussels an old

polnischer Jude mit weißem Vollbart und tieftraurigen
Polish Jew with white full beard and deep sad

Ahasveraugen. Sie hielt unschlüssig das Halsband der
Ahasver eyes She held undecided the collar of the
(the wandering Jew)

Romanows in den Händen.
Romanovs in the hands
(Russian royal line)

Die Glastür wurde geöffnet, ein kalter Luftzug traf ihre
The glass door became opened a cold air-pull struck her
draft

nackten Schultern – sie fröstelte. Ein Geiger von der
naked shoulders – she shivered A violinist from the
bare

Barkapelle, ein offensichtlich todkranker Mensch mit
bar chapel an obviously terminally ill human with

abgezehrtem Schädel kam vorbei, blieb einen Augenblick
emaciated skull came past remained a moment

stehen, sah sie an mit den leeren Augen: da
stand saw her on with the empty eyes there
looked at

schauderte sie zusammen. Die Perlen, die sie in den
shivered she together The Pearls which she in the

Händen hielt, hatten einmal einer unglücklichen Fürstin
hands held had once an unhappy queen

gehört, die Perlen schienen eiskalt. Der Mann aber, der
heard the Pearls seemed freezing The man however who

vor ihr stand und ihr ein Ultimatum stellte, war ein
before her stood and her an ultimatum set was a

Desperado, der um Kopf und Kragen spielte und sie
desperado which for head and collar played and her

selbst hineinreißen konnte in den Strudel seines Lebens ...
self tear into could in the swirl of his life

»Ich habe doch Angst, Cradock«, sagte die Mary.
I have indeed fear Cradock said -the- Mary

Er zuckte die Achseln.
He shrugged the shoulders

»Sie wollen, um alles zu ersetzen, spielen?«
You want for everything to replace play

Er zuckte, als gäbe es auf solche Selbstverständlichkeiten
He shrugged as gave it on such evident facts

keine Antwort, abermals.
no answer again

»Und wenn Sie verlieren?«
And when you lose

»Ich verliere nie.«
I lose never

»Und wenn Sie trotzdem verlieren.«
And when you nevertheless lose

»Dann breche ich mir das Genick, und Sie, Madame,
Then break I myself the neck and you madame

brechen das Ihre mit mir. Und Sie kommen in ˎden
break the yours with me And you come in the

Himmel und ich in die Hölle. Und Sie, Madame, singen
heaven and I in the hell And you madame sing

zur　Harmoniumbegleitung　heilige　Lieder　und　werden　ein
to the　accompaniment　holy　songs　and　become　a

Cherub　mit　silbernen　Flügeln. Und　ich　brate　in　heißem　Öl
cherub　with　silver　wings　And　I　fry　in　hot　oil

und　mache　nur　manchmal　in　den　Himmel　hinein　einen
and　make　only　sometimes　in　the　sky　inside　a

kleinen　Vorstoß　und　reiße　Ihnen　eine　Schwanzfeder　aus.«
small　advance　and　tear　them　a　tail feather　out

Sie　lachte. Er　blieb　hartnäckig. Ambassadeur,　der　ein
She　laughed　He　remained　persistent　Ambassador　who　an

Ultimatum　überbringt. »Ja　oder　nein?«　fragte　der　Cradock.
ultimatum　delivers　Yes　or　no　asked　-the-　Cradock

Da　sah　sie　ihn　an　und　dachte　an　das　herbstliche
There　looked　she　him　at　and　thought　on of　the　autumnal

Buchenlaub　im　Park　von　Hampton　und　an　den
bux foliage　in the　park　from　Hampton　and　on of　the

Oktobermorgen　von　damals　und　an　die　Küsse　dieses　ein
October morning　from　that time　and　on of　the　kisses　of this　a

wenig　frechen,　noch　immer　knabenhaften　Mundes. War
little　cheeky　still　always　boyish　mouth　Was

dieser　ein　Rasta,　so　war　er　jedenfalls　ein　Rasta,　dem　man
this　a　rasta　so　was　he　anyhow　a　rasta　who　one

nicht　widerstehen　konnte;　und　wenn　man　zusammen　mit
not　resist　could　and　when　one　together　with

ihm das Genick brach, so war dieser Bruch jedenfalls
him the neck broke so was this break anyhow

immer noch besser als schicksalsloses Vertrocknen.
always still better as fateless to dry up
without future

»Ja«, sagte die Mary.
Yes said -the- Mary

»Kameraden auf Gedeih und Verderb?« fragte der Cradock.
Comrades on thrive and spoil asked -the- Cradock

»Auf Gedeih und Verderb«, sagte die Mary. »Bis morgen«,
On thrive and spoil said the Mary Until tomorrow
For good for bad

sagte die Mary. Da war der Pakt besiegelt, und da
said the Mary There was the pact sealed and there

gingen sie zum Spieltisch. –
went they to the game table

Das Publikum aber, das sich inzwischen eingefunden
The audience however that itself In the meantime found

hatte, es war womöglich noch unerträglicher als das in
had it was where-possible still more unbearable as that in
possibly

der Bar. Eine ganz seltene amerikanische Sekte war
the bar A completely rare American sect was

erschienen mit ihrem Prediger, um an Ort und Stelle das
appeared with her preacher for on place and spot the

Roulettelaster von Monte Carlo zu studieren ... Frau
roulette button from Monte Carlo to study Mrs.

Senator Harms aus Bremen wollte eben nur mal sehen,
senator Harms from Bremen wanted just only once see

nöch, was die S-p-ieler für Gesichter machten, wenn sie
still what the player for faces made when they

ihr ganzes Geld verlören ... ein vollblütiger Agrarier
their whole money lost a more thoroughbred agrarian farmer

aus dem Kreise Treptow an der Rega klagte einem
from the circle Treptow on the Rega complained (to) a

Berufsgenossen, daß seit der Revolution aller Respekt beim
profession-fellow colleague that since the revolution all respect at the

Teufel sei, und daß neulich eine seiner
devil be and that newly the other day one of his

Kartoffelgräberinnen bei einem Schäferstündchen ihn sogar
potato diggers at a shepherd's hour him even

geduzt habe ... eine ältere Dame aus Boston mit
dozed have an older lady from Boston with

Hornbrille, Pferdegebiß und der Stimme einer
horn-rimmed glasses horse teeth and the voice of a

wildgewordenen Steppenstute schrie nach einem
gone wild steppe mare cried to a

Maraschino ... ein Patrizier aus Basel war fest
maraschino a patrician from Basel was firmly

entschlossen, höchstens zwei Francs fünfundsiebzig
decided at most two francs seventyfive

Centimes zu verlieren, und trug durch den Saal die
centimes to lose and carried through the hall the

Haarwand eines zahnbürstenfarbenen Vollbartes, in dem
hair wall of a toothbrush colored full beard in which

man, wofern es schon Hochsommer gewesen wäre, die
one where-far it already midsummer been would be the
in so far

Bienen hätte summen hören können. Was sonst da
bees had zooming hear can What otherwise there

war, war eigentlich nur Komparserie für diese spießige
was was actually only extra series for this bourgeois
extras

Korrektheit: ein sehr junger Hochstapler aus Madrid, ein
correctness a very young imposter from Madrid a

Bordellbesitzer aus Smyrna, ein junger, auffallend schöner
brothel owner from Smyrna a young striking beautiful

Maler aus München. Sonst noch ein Dutzend
painter from Munich Otherwise still a dozen

niedergebrochener Offiziere aus den unterschiedlichen
broken down officers from the different

Armeen des Weltkrieges. –
armies of the world war

Hinter ihnen her flüsterte es. Ein alter Major vom
Behind them away whispered it An old major from the

Coldstreamregiment meinte, daß die Dame an Cradocks
coldstream regiment thought that the lady on Cradocks

Seite bestimmt eine Nichte des Londoner Vanderbilt sei,
side identified a niece of the London Vanderbilt be
was

und daß Cradock selbst sich seit seinen Londoner
and that Cradock himself himself since his London

Tagen in den seither verstrichenen zehn Jahren überhaupt
days in the since elapsed ten years at all

nicht verändert habe. Ein Pariser Frauenarzt, der den
not changed have A Parisian women-doctor who the
had gynecologist

Kapitän in San Sebastian hatte spielen sehen, wollte
Captain in San Sebastian had play see wanted

wissen, daß Cradock das damals gewonnene Geld zum
to know that Cradock the at that time won money to the

größten Teil in zwei Wochen ... so gewissermaßen aus
great part in two weeks so (in) certain measure from
so to speak

der Hosentasche heraus ... an die ersten besten Bettler,
the pocket out on the first best beggar

Kriegskrüppel, Landstreicher und niedergebrochenen
war cripple vagrant and broken down

Abenteurer verschleudert habe. Alle aber waren sie
adventurer flung have All however were they
had

sich, als sie den großen Sturmvogel Cradock
themselves as they the large Storm-bird Cradock
petrel

auftauchen sahen, darüber einig, daß dieses ein wenig
duck up saw about it agreed that this a little
appear

eingeschlafene Monte Carlo nun doch noch einmal einen
asleep Monte Carlo now indeed still once a

großen Tag haben werde ...
great day have will
would

Elf Uhr war's. Er hatte sie nun doch gebeten, ihn
Eleven hour was it He had her now indeed asked him
o'clock

eine Viertelstunde allein zu lassen – er hatte zunächst
a quarter of an hour alone to let – he had first

mit seinen Spielexperimenten und dem Ertasten der
with his game experiments and the groping of the
feeling

besten Phase zu tun. Die Jetons waren eingehandelt, die
best phase to do The chips were in-dealt/obtained the

Armee (vierhundertundachtzehn Pfund) noch einmal
army four hundred and eighteen pound still once

gemustert; er saß, das altmodische, breitschienige Monokel
inspected he sat the old fashioned broad railed monocle

eingeklemmt, setzte minimale Beträge, verlor dreimal,
in-pinched set minimal amounts lost three times
bet

setzte wieder, schrieb lange Zahlenkolonnen auf einen
set again wrote long columns of numbers on a
bet

Zettel, rechnete ...
note calculated

Die einfachen Chancen zuerst ... Pair und Impair mit
The simple opportunities first ... Pair and impair with

minimalen Beträgen: er verlor. Er stieg höher zu »Kolonne
minimal   amounts   he lost He rose higher to   column

von zwölf Nummern« (ein noch ganz kleinliches Spiel
from twelve numbers a still completely petty play

mit doppelter Gewinnchance): er verlor. Pfund um Pfund
with double chance of winning he lost Pound for pound

wurden seine Avantgarden geschlagen. Er rechnete. Er
became his avant-gardes struck (down) He calculated He

setzte wieder. »Transversale von sechs Nummern«, ein
set   again   Transversal from six   numbers   an
bet

immerhin nicht mehr ganz niedriges Spiel: drei
after all not (any)more completely low   play three
                                    minor

weitere Pfunde wanderten hinüber zum Croupier, und
further pounds walked   over   to the croupier and

wenn es so weiterging ...
when it so went on

Er stand auf, gönnte sich eine Zigarette, sah den
He stood on granted himself a cigarette saw the

Domino hinter sich stehen ... blaß, erregt, in dem
domino (mask) behind himself stand pale excited in the

bekannten Zustande des Laien, der zum ersten Male
familiar to-stand of the lay person who for the first time
         condition

ein Spiel sieht. »Sie verlieren?« fragte sie. »Bitte Sie
a game sees You lose asked she Beg you

aufrichtig, mir nicht auf die Finger zu sehen beim Spiel«,
sincerely me not on the fingers to see at the game

sagte Cradock. Dann konnte man ihn sehen, wie er ging,
said Cradock Then could one him see as he went

um neue Jetons zu kaufen: das Glück blieb aus, und
for new chips to buy the fortune remained out and
away

üble Sterne schienen aufgegangen zu sein über diesem
bad stars seemed gone up to be over this

Abend ...
evening

Weiter. »Kolonne zu vier«, ein Spiel schon von
Further column to four a play already of

beträchtlichem Wagnis und achtfachem Gewinn: Verlust,
considerable risk and eight times profit loss

Gewinst, Verlust. Wieder rechnete er. Wenn das Glück
won loss Again calculated he When the fortune

nämlich nicht hier, in den hohen Gängen des Spieles zu
namely not here in the high courses of the game to

finden war, so war es heute für ihn überhaupt nicht zu
find was so was it today for him at all not to

sprechen. Und wenn es heute für ihn nicht zu sprechen
speak And when it today for him not to speak
manage manage

war, so gab es ein »Morgen« für ihn nicht mehr. Dann
was so gave it a tomorrow for him not (any)more Then

war er überführt der Unterschlagung fremder Gelder,
was he transferred for the embezzlement of foreign funds

war so deklassiert, daß kein Straßenköter mehr
was so (much) declassed that no street dog (any)more
            demoted

ein Wurstbrot annahm aus seiner Hand! Er atmete
a sausage sandwich took up from his hand He breathed
            would take

tief und trank einen sehr großen Kognak, ging in die Bar
deep and drank a very large cognac went in the bar

hinaus, hörte von Williams, daß die Leute vollzählig
out heard from Williams that the people full-counted
                                    crew all

drüben im Café de Paris säßen, wurde bei der
over there in the coffee shop of Paris sat became at the

Rückkehr in den Spielsaal noch zwischen Tür und Angel
return in the game room still between door and hinge

aufgehalten von dem alten Crofts. Daß er selbst nun bei
halted from the old Crofts That he himself now at

Lebas gewesen, daß Lebas bereit sei, mit zwanzig Prozent
Lebas been (had) that Lebas ready be with twenty percent
                            was

Abstandssumme das Halsband zurückzunehmen, sagte der
distance sum the collar to take back said the

Doktor. Daß er sich in die Hölle scheren solle, sagte
doctor That he himself in the hell shear should said
                                    go

kurz und nicht unfreundlich Cradock und ging, ohne
short and not unfriendly Cradock and went without

sich nach Madame umzusehen, wieder an die Arbeit.
himself to madame around to look again on the work

Was jetzt kam, erregte schon einiges Aufsehen bei diesen
What now came excited already some sensation with these

Leuten, die mit ihren Einsätzen von zehn Gulden
people who with their bets from ten guilders (money)

sich schon als große Spieler vorkamen. »A cheval«
themselves already as great players occurred on horse (French)

nämlich hieß das nächsthöhere Spiel ... à cheval bietet
namely was called the next higher game on horse offers (French)

bei einer Gewinnwahrscheinlichkeit von fünf Prozent die
with a probability of winning from five percent the

Gewinnchance des siebzehnfachen Einsatzes. »A cheval«,
chance of winning of the seventeen times (the) bet On horse

mit den letzten zwei Pfunden seiner Avantgarde besetzt,
with the last two pound his avant-garde occupied

gewann einmal, verlor, gewann beim dritten Male, gewann
won once lost won at the third time won

nach Abzug von vierhundertundsechzig verlorenen
after deduction from four hundred sixty lost

Schilling insgesamt sechsundsiebzig auf die Haben-Seite zu
shilling all in all seventy six on the have side to

schreibende Pfund: bei »à cheval« saß das Glück ... das
writing pound with on horse sat the happiness the

Glück verlangte das größere Wagnis von ihm. Da
fortune desired the bigger risk from him There

verließ er, Madame zu holen, den Kreis der Spieler.
left he madame to get the circle of the players

Für diese Volte kamen sie gerade noch zur Zeit.
For this return came she just still at the on time

»Faites vot' jeu« hatte, bei schon laufender Kugel der
Make your play (French) had at already going moving bullet roulette ball the

Croupier eben gesagt, und »Rien ne va plus« wollte
croupier just said and Nothing not goes (any)more wanted
(French)

er eben sagen und sah dann im letzten Augenblick noch
he just say and saw then in the last moment still

einmal fragend zu Cradock hinüber. »Hundert à cheval,
once questioning to Cradock over Hundred on horse

zwölf zu dreizehn« sagte, über die Köpfe der Zuschauer
twelve to thirteen said over the heads of the spectators

hinweg, der Cradock. »Machen Sie's halbwäje!« sagte
away the Cradock Make you it halfway said

halblaut ein sächsischer Herr ... der Pariser Gynäkologe
halfloud a Saxon gentleman the Parisian gynecologist

flüsterte dem Coldstreammajor zu, daß Cradock nun doch
whispered the coldstream major to that Cradock now indeed

endlich in Bewegung käme. Sie, die beiden
finally in movement would come They the both

Kampfgenossen dieses Gefechtes, standen in dieser Minute
comrades-in-arms of this battled stood in this minute

ein wenig abseits an der Peripherie des Spielerkreises. So,
a little offside on the periphery of the player group So

daß sie das Spiel selbst nicht übersehen konnten.
that they the play itself not overlook could

So aber ist es nun einmal, daß wir alle, je mehr unser
So however is it now once that we all the more our

tägliches Leben umgeht mit toten Mechanismen, immer
everyday life goes around with dead mechanisms always
deals

abhängiger werden von jenen Dämonen, die unsichtbar
more dependent become from those demons who invisibly

wohnen in Maschinen, Zahlen und – Rouletten. Techniker
live in machinery numbers and – roulette Technicians

sind in Berufsdingen bekanntlich abergläubischer als
are in professional matters as known more superstitious as

Marseiller Fischweiber, große Architekten sind nun schon
from Marseille fishwives great architects are now already

längst so weit, daß sie die Sterne befragen, ehe sie in
long so far that she the stars ask before they in

das Eisengebälk eines Wolkenkratzers die erste Niete
the iron beams of a skyscraper the first rivet

schlagen lassen.
hammer let

Der Cradock, während die Kugel schon gegen die Nägel
The Cradock while the bullet already against the nails
roulette ball

des Roulettetellers prallte, tat etwas, was er im
of the roulette plates bounced did something what he in the

Vorpostengefecht sich aufgespart haben mochte für die
outpost battle himself saved have might for the
skirmish

entscheidende Stunde der Schlacht.
decisive hour of the battle

Er nahm seine Brieftasche. Aus der Brieftasche ein
He took his letter-bag From the letter-bag a
wallet wallet

Päckchen Seidenpapier. Aus dem Seidenpapier einen
little package (of) tissue paper from the tissue paper a

kleinen Fetzen Tüll mit eingewebten Silberfäden, die
small shred (of) tulle with woven silver threads which

nun schon ganz rot angelaufen waren. Ein Ding, das
now already completely red on-run were A thing which
turned had

der Fetzen eines Schleiers sein mochte. Ein Ding, das man
the shred of a veil be might A thing that one

einmal getragen hatte als lebensfrisches, junges Geschöpf
once carried had as fresh from life young creature

und zum Andenken verschenkt hatte an einen leider
and to the memories given away had on an unfortunately
to

etwas vergeßlichen Gefährten ...
somewhat forgetful companion

»Glückstalisman?« fragte die Mary, fühlte, daß etwas in
Lucky talisman asked the Mary felt that something in

ihre Augen wollte, was in dieser Stunde in die Augen
her eyes desired what in this hour in the eyes

nicht gehörte.
not belonged

»Glückstalisman«, sagte gleichmütig der Cradock und
Lucky talisman said indifferent the Cradock and

steckte das Ding in den linken Schuh. Da aber hatte
stuck the thing in the left shoe There however had

es sich in dem Kreise dieser gaffenden, flirtenden,
it himself in the circle this gaping flirting

médisanten Menschen entschieden, das Spiel ...
médisant people decided the game

»Dreizehn«, sagte auf seinem überhöhten Stuhl der
Thirteen said on his inflated chair the

Croupier. »Dreizehn für Sie«, sagte, sich zu Cradock
croupier Thirteen for you said himself to Cradock

umdrehend, freundlich der Coldstreammajor. Gewonnen
turning around friendly the coldstream major Won

siebzehnhundert Pfund. Getuschel, Geflüster, Bewegung
seventeen hundred pound Whisper whisper movement

ringsum. Das Geld nahm er in tadelloser Haltung. Wohl
all around The money took he in impeccable stature Well

aber, was ihr nicht entging, mit Händen, deren Finger
however what her not escaped with hands whose finger

doch ein wenig zitterten. Dann, wie es nach einem
indeed a little trembled Then as it after a

größeren Coup zu gehen pflegt, war er umgeben von
great coup to go uses was he surrounded of
by

fremden Menschen. Von den alten Habitués der
strange people Of the old habitués of the
unfamiliar By

europäischen Spielsäle, von niedergebrochenen Kameraden,
European game rooms of broken down comrades

von Roués, die sich anzüglich nach ihr ... nach dem
of roués who themselves suggestively to you to the

Domino erkundigten. Sie ging allein zu der
domino (mask) inquired She went alone to the

Palmengruppe zurück.
palm group back

Hier war es still, und man war allein. Die Tränen, die
Here was it quiet and one was alone The tears which

kamen nun erst recht, und sie wütete gegen sich selbst
came now first right and she raged against herself self
truly

und ihren Kummer. Ein Fetzen Seidentüll war ja
and her sorrow A shred of silk tulle was yes
indeed

schließlich nicht mehr als eben ein Fetzen Seidentüll,
finally not (any)more as just a shred of silk tulle

und eingerichtet war es doch nun einmal so, daß
and furnished was it indeed now once so that

Männergedächtnis kürzer reicht als Frauenliebe. Aber daß
men's memory shorter reach as women love But that

es wehe tut, wenn man selbst eine Liebe bewahrt, und
it pain does when one himself a love preserved and

der andere vergißt es – das war nebst Weibertränen und
the other forgets it – that was next (to) women tears and

verletzter Eitelkeit nun einmal ebenfalls vorgesehen im
injured vanity now once likewise intended in the

Plane der Weltenschöpfung. Ja, sie weinte wirklich. Sie
plan the world creation Yes she cried really she

bot natürlich die letzte Selbstbeherrschung auf und
offered of course the last self-control on and

trocknete rasch die Tränen und setzte die Maske wieder
dried quickly the tears and set the mask again

auf. Da aber hatte er sie schon wieder aufgespürt
on There however had he her already again tracked down

in ihrem Versteck ...
in her hide-out

»Was, Madame, haben Sie eigentlich?«
What madame have you actually

Keine Antwort. Da wollte er ernstlich wissen, was
No answer There wanted he seriously know what

ihr   fehle …
(with) her   was wrong

Sie bat um eine Zigarette. Ihre Haltung hatte sie wieder.
She bade for a cigarette. her stature had she again

»Ihr Talisman?« fragte die Mary und wies auf seinen
Your talisman asked the Mary and pointed on his

linken Schuh.
left shoe

»Er bewährt sich, denke ich.«
He proofs himself think i
It

»Brautschleier?«
Bridal veil

»Brautschleier«, nickte Cradock.
Bridal veil nodded Cradock

»Von wem?«
Of whom

»Die Roulette, Cradock, geht nicht ohne Sie«, rief von
The roulette Cradock goes not without you called from

drüben ein Herr. »Faites vot' jeu«, sagte von
over there a gentleman Make your play said from
(French)

drüben der Croupier und sah fragend zu Cradock
over there the croupier and saw questioning to Cradock

herüber. »Hundert à cheval, zwölf zu dreizehn«, rief der
over Hundred on horse twelve to thirteen called the
(French)

Cradock zurück. »Das Glück, Madame«, sagte er und hatte
Cradock back The fortune madame said he and had

noch immer ihre Frage nicht beantwortet, »das Glück ist
still always her question not answered the fortune is

eine große Dame, die man nicht antichambrieren lassen
a great lady who one not antichambrate let

darf.« »Rien ne va plus«, sagte der Croupier.
may Nothing not goes (any)more said the croupier
(French)

»Madame ...«, sagte der Cradock und reichte ihr den Arm.
madame said the Cradock and reached her the arm
handed

Da war es, das serienweise kommende und serienweise
There was it the in series coming and in series

sich versagende Glück, das ihnen begegnete, ohne daß
itself failing fortune that them met without that

sie sein eigentliches Spielen auch nur gesehen hatten.
she his actual play also only seen had

Die kleine Kugel aus Galalith nämlich, sie hat auch in
The little bullet from galalith namely she has also in
roulette ball (plastic)

der Dauer ihres Tanzes ihre Launen – sie kann in einem
the duration of her dance her whims – she can in a

Anlauf das Fach wählen, sie kann, die Nerven
start the compartment choose she can the annoy
roulette number

marternd, ein scheinbar schon gewähltes
torturing an apparently already chosen

Fach verlassen, zurücktaumeln, das Spiel mit den
compartment leave stumble back the play with the
roulette number

Prellnägeln noch einmal beginnen und zum Schluß eine
bruising nails still once begin and at the end a

Nummer beglücken, an die niemand mehr gedacht
number delight on which nobody (any)more thought

hat ...
has

Dies hier, die zweite große Volte, war ein rascher Schuß ...
This here the second great turn was a fast shot

»Espagnol«, wie's die Croupiers nennen. »Dreizehn.« Die
Spanish how it the croupiers call Thirteen The
(French)

Glücksnummer kam ihnen, während sie auf den Spieltisch
lucky number came them while they on the game table
to

zugingen, gewissermaßen entgegengelaufen.
to-went (in) certain measure ran towards
went so to speak

»Tausendsiebenhundert für Cradock.« In Pfundnoten, in
(a) thousand seven hundred for Cradock In pound notes in

Holländergulden, in plumpen, seltenen Hundertdollarstücken.
Dutch guilders in clumsy rare hundred dollar pieces

Mit dem Ergebnis der ersten Volte zusammen
With the result of the first turn together

dreitausendvierhundert Pfund. Mit dem Rest des
three thousand four hundred pound With the rest of the

Betriebskapitals zusammen fast dreitausendsechshundert.
working capital together almost three thousand six hundred

Genug, um die Hoheit von Labrador zweimal nach
Enough for the highness from Labrador twice to

Ägypten zu schicken. Genug beinahe, um zweimal das Loch
Egypt to send Enough almost for twice the hole

in der Schiffskasse zu flicken. Schon lange nicht war er
in the ships cash (box) to patch Already long not was he
had

so reich gewesen.
so rich been

Dreitausendvierhundert Pfund. Gratulanten und
Three thousand four hundred pound Congratulations and

Schmarotzer. Kokotten, die das Geld witterten, und
parasites cocots the the money sniffed and

angebliche alte Bekannte, die man nie gesehen hatte,
supposed old known the one never seen had
acquaintances

und die nach einigem Stottern einen kleinen Anleiheversuch
and the to some stutter a small bond attempt

starteten. Er schob alles beiseite. Für heute hatte er
started he pushed everything to the side for today had he

genug von dieser Atmosphäre von Talmieleganz und
enough from this atmosphere from valley elegance and

Niederbruch und Spießertum. Unter keinen Umständen
downfall and philistinism under no circumstances

wollte er weiterspielen. Er reichte ihr den Arm. »Und nun,
wanted he keep playing he reached her the arm And now
handed

Madame?«
madame? «

Da übersah sie seinen Arm: »Sie sind mir eine Antwort
There overlooked she his arm You are me an answer
ignored

schuldig.«
guilty

»Ich stehe zur Verfügung.«
I stand to the disposal

»Von wem haben Sie den Fetzen?«
Of whom have you the shred

Da lachte er. »Eifersüchtig auf Vorgängerinnen?« höhnte
There laughed he Jealous on predecessors sneered

der Cradock.
the Cradock

»Von wem der Talisman?«
Of whom the talisman

»Wenn Sie's wissen wollen – von der freudlosen Witwe ...«
If you it know want – from the cheerless widow

»Freudlosen Witwe ...«
Cheerless widow

»Von der Hoheit und freudlosen Witwe von Labrador.«
Of the highness and cheerless widow from Labrador

Und so erzählte er in aller Kürze seine Geschichte. Daß in
And so told he in all brevity his story That in

London einmal eine kleine Prinzessin einem kleinen
London once a little princess a small

Flottenleutnant gut gewesen sei und ihm auf ihrer
fleet lieutenant good been be and him on her
was

Hochzeit dann einen Fetzen ihres Brautschleiers geschenkt
wedding then a shred of her bridal veil given

habe. Die Prinzessin von damals, das sei nun die
have The princess from that time that be now the
had was

regierende Fürstin-Witwe von Labrador ... dieselbe, die
ruling princess-widow from labrador the same who

morgen komme. Der Flottenleutnant aber ...«
tomorrow comes The fleet lieutenant however

»Was aus dem Flottenleutnant geworden ist, will ich
What from the fleet lieutenant become is want I

Ihnen sagen, Cradock! Der Flottenleutnant von damals ist
you say Cradock The fleet lieutenant from that time is

ein herzloser Bursche, der Frauenliebe schmäht, indem er
a heartless lad the women love reviles while he

ihre Andenken mit Füßen tritt. Der Flottenleutnant von
her memories with feet treads The fleet lieutenant from

damals ist nun ein Rasta mit gefrorenem Herzen ...«
that time is now a rasta with frozen heart

»Vielleicht ...«
Perhaps

»Ein vereinsamender böser Abenteurer ...«
A turning lonely angry adventurer

»Vielleicht ...«
Perhaps

»Der undankbar empfangene Liebe vergißt ...«
The ungrateful received love forgets

»Das Leben, Madame, geht weiter!«
The life madame goes further

»Ein alternder Desperado, ein alternder professioneller
An aging desperado an aging professional

Spieler, dessen Herz keinen unberührten Winkel hat, der
player whose heart no untouched corner has who
gambler

sich an fremdem Gelde vergreift ...«
himself on stranger money over-grabs
others' seizes

»Madame!«
Madame

»Und dessen Hände nun schon zu zittern beginnen, wenn
And whose hands now already to tremble begin when

er, um seine Defraudationen zu cachieren, sich an den
he for his defraudations to hide himself on the

Spieltisch setzt!«
game table   sets

Da   sprang er auf ...
There jumped he up   ...

»Dann werden Sie   sich   also   davon   überzeugen, wie
Then   will   you yourself thus there-from convince   how

sehr Sie mir Unrecht getan haben! Mehr als Unrecht! Daß
much you me wrong   done have   More as   wrong   That

Sie   nach einem Grunde suchten, mich zu verletzen, daß
you   after a   ground search   me   to hurt   that
      for   reason

Sie   um   einen dürftigen Vorwand besorgt   sind, mich
you   for   a   poor   pretext concerned are   me

wieder an   der Roulette zu sehen! Ich werde spielen,
again on   the roulette to see   I   will   play

Madame ...«
  madame

»So spielen Sie also!«
So   play   you so
                  then

Da   riß er aus der Tasche seine ganze Barschaft.
There   ripped he from the pocket his   whole cash (amount)

Dreitausendsechshundert   Pfund ... abgegriffene Pfundnoten,
Three thousand six hundred pound   tapped   pound notes

Holländergulden,   klobige Hundertdollarstücke: aber der
dutch guilders   chunky   hundred dollar pieces but   the

Gegenwert für Ehre und Existenz eines Mannes. »Spiel
equivalent for honor and existence of a man Play

mit dem ganzen Einsatz, Madame! Spiel bis zum
with the whole commitment madame Play until to the

Genickbruch, da Sie es so wünschen! Es gibt ein Spiel,
broken neck there you it so wish It gives a game
There is

heißt Paroli ...«
is called paroli

»Es gibt ein Spiel, heißt Genickbruch ...«
It gives a game is called broken neck

»Und man verliert alles und hat die gleiche Aussicht
And one loses everything and has the same view

auf Gewinn, wie ein Londoner Liftboy auf den Posten des
on profit as a London liftboy on the post of the

Vizekönigs von Indien. Ein Spiel um Kopf und Ehre ...«
viceroy from India A game for head and honor

»So spielen Sie es doch!«
So play you it then

»Und wenn man verliert ...«
And when one loses

»So wagen Sie es also!«
So dare you it then

Da nimmt er ihre Hand. »Was habe ich Ihnen getan?«
There takes he her hand What have I you done

Sie zuckt die Achsel und schweigt, hängt sich in den
She shrugs the shoulders and is silent hangs herself in the

gebotenen Arm, läßt sich an den Spieltisch führen.
offered arm lets herself on the game table lead

Empörung im Herzen, verletzte Frauenliebe, verletzte
Indignation in the heart injured women love injured

Eitelkeit. Blinder Haß, der ihn gedemütigt sehen, und
vanity Blind hate that him humiliated see and

heimliche Reue, die am liebsten in der letzten Sekunde
secret repent which at the dearest in the last second

noch alles rückgängig machen möchte. So steht's in
still everything undone make may So stands it in

dieser Stunde um die Mary. Die Vorgänge der nächsten
this hour for the Mary The operations of the next

entscheidenden Minuten werden zu einem Nebel, aus dem
decisive minutes become to a fog from which

wie Inseln einzelne Bilder ragen. -
as islands single images protrude

Ganz leise Geigen, eine Uhr, die Mitternacht schlägt,
Completely soft violin a clock that midnight strikes

ein Dampfer, der unten im Hafen mit seiner Sirene
a steam boat which under in the harbor with its siren

heult, Menschen, die hinter ihnen eifrig tuscheln, zwei
howls people who behind them zealously whisper two

Saaldiener, die sich tief verbeugen ...
room attendants who themselves deep bow down

Erster Coup. »Faites vot' jeu!« sagt der Croupier und sieht,
First coup Make your play says the croupier and sees

wie eigentlich alles ringsum, auf den Kapitän
how actually everything all around on the Captain

Cradock ... der Heldenbariton, der eben sechshundert Pfund
cradock the hero baritone who just six hundred pound

verloren hat, findet keine Aufmerksamkeit mehr.
lost has finds no attention (any)more

»Dreitausendvierhundert auf dreizehn«, sagte Cradock ...
Three thousand four hundred on thirteen said Cradock

»Dreitausendvierhundert auf dreizehn«, wiederholt der
Three thousand four hundred on thirteen repeats the

Croupier und dreht.
croupier and turns

Kugel tanzt, Kugel wird müde, prallt gegen die
(The) bullet dances (the) bullet becomes tired bounces against the

Nägel und schießt ... dieses Mal mit der Unbeirrbarkeit
nails and shoots this time with the unwavering

eines Projektils ... auf dreizehn.
of a projectile on thirteen

Bleibt. Steht. Bewegung ringsum. »Dreizehn«, dienert
Remains stands Movement all around Thirteen serves

höflich der Croupier. »Dreizehn«, tuschelt's im Raum
polite the croupier Thirteen whispers in the space

ringsum. Fünfunddreißigmal dreitausendvierhundert. Nicht
all around Thirty five times three thousand four hundred Not

mehr auszudenken. Der Croupier bedauert, nicht
(any)more to think of The croupier regrets not

gleich zahlen zu können, wird aber sofort die
immediately count to be able will however immediately the

Bank anweisen ... »Madame?« sagt mit leichter Verbeugung
bank instruct Madame says with (a) light bow

und einiger Ironie in der Stimme der Cradock. »Und was
and some irony in the voice the Cradock And what

weiter?« gibt sie ebenso blasiert zurück und möchte doch
further gives she likewise blase back and may indeed

dabei so gerne heraus aus ihrer Bitterkeit. Möchte. Kann
there-by so gladly out from her bitterness May Can

nicht. Muß ihn weiterhetzen, bis er das Genick bricht.
not Must him rush on until he the neck breaks

Zweiter Coup ...
Second coup

Zunächst wird ein Scheck präsentiert. Zwei Pariser
Next became a check presented Two Parisian

Journalisten hat man aus der Bar herbeigerufen, ein
journalists had one from the bar summoned a

gerade anwesender Illustrator von »Harpers Magazin«
just present illustrator from Harper's Magazine

skizziert die Szene ... zwei junge Amerikanerinnen starren,
outlined the scene two young American women stare

während der Scheck übergeben wird, den langen Cradock
while the check overhanded became the tall Cradock

an mit einer Indiskretion, zu der nachgerade noch
at with an indiscretion to which after-immediately still

ein Fernrohr mit Stativ fehlt. »Hundertundneunzehntausend
a telescope with tripod lacks One hundred and nineteen thousand

bleiben stehen«, sagt leise und freundlich der Cradock.
remain standing says softly and friendly the Cradock

»Hundertundneunzehntausend bleiben stehen«, notiert
One hundred and nineteen thousand remain standing written down

der Croupier. »Wahnsinn«, sagt hinten jemand. »Bei
the croupier Madness says in the back someone By

dem rappelt's wohl«, sagt der Kinderwagenfabrikant aus
that one rattles it well says the stroller manufacturer from
indeed

Zwickau. »Wird ohne einen Cent in der Tasche den Saal
Zwickau Will without a cent in the pocket the hall

verlassen«, bedauert der Coldstreammajor. »Rien ne va
leave regrets the coldstream major Nothing not goes

plus«, sagt der Croupier. Da schwirrt wieder die
(any)more says the croupier There whirs again the

Kugel.
bullet
roulette ball

Kugel schwirrt, tanzt um Ehre und Leben des
(The) bullet whirs dances for honor and life of the

langen Cradock, Kugel prallt an Hohlkehle und
tall Cradock (the) bullet bounces on grooves and

Prellnagel ... man kann's nun nicht mehr ansehen ...
bounce nails one can it now not (any)more look at

schließt die Augen ...
closes the eyes

Wenn man so die Augen geschlossen hält, möchte man
When one so the eyes closed holds may one

wieder gut zu ihm sein und ihn um Verzeihung bitten.
again good to him be and him for forgiveness ask

Wenn man aber die Augen öffnet, steht da so ein
When one however the eyes opens stands there so a

provozierend überlegenes männliches Ungetüm ... eine
provocative superior masculine monster a

Mannsherrlichkeit, die man erniedrigt und auf den Knien
man's glory who one humiliates and on the knees

sehen möchte. Und dann endlich hört man seine
see may And then finally hears one his

hochmütige Stimme, wie er, während um Leben und Ehre
haughty voice as he while for life and honor

des Kapitän Cradock die Kugel schnurrt, nebenan den
of the Captain Cradock the bullet whirs next-to the
roulette ball to the side

französischen General mit dem weißen
French general with the white

Vercingetorix-Schnauzbart nach dem Schicksal des
Vercingetorix mustache after the fate of the

Polo-Ponys »Ponsonby« (von Bellorophon aus der Astarte)
polo ponies Ponsonby from bell orophone from the Astarte

fragt. Da kocht ihr vor dieser betonten Sicherheit
asks There cooks her before this emphasized assuredness

das Blut: man kann, wenn man ihn so sprechen hört, auf
the blood one can when one him so speak hears on
in

keinen Fall gut und zart mit ihm sein ... man muß ihn
no case good and tender with him be one must him

demütigen und auf den Knien sehen. Wieder schließt sie
humble and on the knees see Again closes she

die Augen. Da geschieht etwas Seltsames ...
the eyes There happens something strange

Ganz nahe, begleitet vom Surren und Prellen der
Completely close accompanied from the whir and bounce the

Kugel, hört sie Geigenmusik ... ein aufdringliches Fiedeln,
bullet hears she violin music a pushy fiddle

das an den Nerven zerrt. Als sie die Augen öffnet, sieht
the on the annoy tugs as she the eyes opened sees

sie dicht hinter dem Kapitän Cradock den Geiger von
she close behind the Captain Cradock the violinist from

vorhin stehen.
a while ago stand

Der Geiger ist ein armer Teufel mit Magenkrebs oder
The violinist is a poor devil with stomach cancer or

sonstigem Marasmus, hält sich am Ende noch
other malnutrition holds himself at the end still

mühselig, um seinen Leuten noch eine letzte Monatsgage
laborious for his people still a last monthly

zusammenzufiedeln, mit Morphium aufrecht. Fiedelt
to fiddle together with morphine upright Fiddles

Rigoletto. Hat ein Gesicht, das abgemagert ist wie das
rigoletto Has a face that emaciated is as that

einer Mumie ... grünliche Bartstoppeln beginnen die Haut zu
of a mummy greenish beard stubbles begin the skin to

durchbohren. »Cradock« sagt, tief erschrocken, die Mary
pierce Cradock says deep frightened the Mary

und faßt seine Hand. Der Cradock, auf das Gefiedel
and grabs his hand The Cradock on the fiddled

aufmerksam geworden, dreht sich um, sieht den
attentive become turns himself around sees the

Geiger, zuckt die Achseln, bläst ihm den Rauch seiner
violinist shrug the shoulders blows him the smoke his

Zigarette ins Gesicht. Im selben Augenblick steht auf
cigarette · in the · face · In the · same · moment · stands · on

dem Rouletteller die Kugel stille. »Null«, sagt
the · roulette plate · the · bullet / roulette ball · quiet · Zero · says

freundlich der Croupier. »Pech«, sagt leise der Franzose
friendly · the · croupier · Bad luck · says · softly · the · frenchman

mit dem weißen Vercingetorix-Bart. Verloren. –
with · the · white · vercingetorix beard · Lost

Verloren, bis auf ein paar Pfund, alles. Rechte und
Lost · up to · on · a · few · pound(s) · everything · Right · and

linke Westentasche, Cradock- und Regierungskasse, Existenz
left · vest pocket · Cradock · and · government fund(s) · existence

und Ehre. »Fatum«, sagt der Pariser Doktor. »Hab's
and · honor · Doom (Latin) · says · the · Parisian · doctor · (I) have it

kommen sehen«, sagt der Major. »Mußte leider so
come · see · says · the · major · Must · unfortunately · so

kommen«, sagt der Franzose mit dem Gallierbart, geht
come · says · the · frenchman · with · the · Gaul beard · goes

seufzend einen Vermouth trinken. Im Saal zuerst das
sighing · a · vermouth · drink · In the · hall · first · the

große Schweigen, das immer den großen Spielkatastrophen
great · silence · that · always · the · large · gambling disasters

folgt. Dann erst halblaute Bemerkungen ... bedauernd,
follows · Then · first · half-loud · remarks · regretful

mokant,	schadenfroh.	Und	endlich, ...	noch	ehe	man
mocking	mischievous	And	at last	still	before	one

überall	weiß,	was	eigentlich	geschehen	ist ...	der	lange
everywhere	knows	what	actually	happened	is	the	tall

Cradock,	der	mit	einer	wortlosen	Handbewegung	den
Cradock	who	with	a	wordless	hand movement	the

Croupier	von	seinem	Stuhle	herunternötigt,	auf	den	Stuhl
croupier	from	his	stool	coerces	on	the	chair

klettert	und	um	Ruhe	bittet.
climbs	and	for	rest	asks
			silence	

Da	also	steht	er.	Ohne	Spur	von	Erregung.	Verbindlich
There	thus	stands	he	Without	trace	from	excitement	Obligingly

lächelnd.	Braucht	nicht	erst	um	Aufmerksamkeit	zu	bitten ...
smiling	Needs	not	first	for	attention	to	ask

der	Saal	ist	still	wie	eine	Kathedrale.	Da
the	hall	is	quiet	as	a	cathedral	There

fängt	er	denn	an.
catches	he	then	on
starts he			

Tausendvierhundert	Pfund	habe	er	aus	eigenen	Mitteln
Thousand four hundred	pound	has	he	from	own	means

verloren	–	auf	die	verzichte	er	selbstverständlich	gerne.
lost	–	on	that	forgo	he	self-understandably	gladly
						self-evidently	

Die	restlichen	zweitausend	Pfund	aber	(und	nur	hier
The	remaining	two thousand	pound	however	and	only	here

hob er ein wenig die Stimme) ... die restlichen zweitausend
lifted he a little the voice the remaining two thousand

Pfund also könne er beim allerbesten Willen und bei
pound thus could he at the very best will and at

jedwedem Verständnis für die Interessen der Bank nicht
anyone's understanding for the interests of the bank not

entbehren. Müsse die Bank bitten, die erwähnten
dispense with Must the bench ask the mentioned

zweitausend Pfund bis morgen früh um sieben Uhr an
two thousand pound until morning early around seven hour on
at

Bord seines Schiffes zurückzuerstatten ... müsse sie bis
board of his ship to refund must she until

spätestens sieben Uhr unbedingt haben, widrigenfalls ...
no later than seven hour absolutely have otherwise

Bei diesem Worte »widrigenfalls« scheint der lange Cradock
At these words otherwise seems the tall Cradock

plötzlich länger zu werden, auf »widrigenfalls« kommen
suddenly taller to become on otherwise come

aus dem Kreise der Zuhörer die ersten Reaktionen ...
from the circle of the listeners the first reactions

»Aha«, sagt ein Hamburger Herr, setzt sich, um den
Ah says a Hamburger gentleman set himself for the

Kapitän besser zu sehen, den Klemmer auf die Nase.
Captain better to see the (glasses) clasp on the nose

»Wollen wir doch erst mal sehen«, sagt der
Want we indeed first once see says the

Kinderwagenfabrikant und schiebt drohend den Bauch
stroller manufacturer and pushes menacing the belly

vor.
in front

»A moi«, sagt eine reif erblühte Pariser Dame und fällt
To me says a ripe blossomed Parisian lady and falls
(French: help)

in Ohnmacht.
in impotence

Widrigenfalls er zu seinem tiefen Bedauern gezwungen sei,
Otherwise he to his deep pity compelled be

das Feuer seiner Artillerie morgen Punkt sieben Uhr auf
the fire of his artillery tomorrow point seven hour on
exactly

das Kasino im besonderen und auf diesen paradiesischen
the Casino in the special and on this heavenly

Ort im allgemeinen zu richten, sagt freundlich und
place in the general to aim says friendly and

bestimmt der lange Cradock, verläßt seelenruhig seinen
decidedly the tall Cradock leaves soul-calm his
calmly

Rednerstuhl, geht mit wiegendem Seemannsschritt nach der
speaker chair goes with swaying sailor step to the

Bar, öffnet die Tür. »Williams«, sagt, in der Tür stehend,
bar opens the door Williams says in the door standing

der Kapitän. »Kannst jetzt die Leute kommen lassen«, sagt
the Captain (You) can now the people come let says

der Cradock und nickt freundlich und wendet sich
the Cradock and nods friendly and turns himself

wieder dem Saale zu. Die Lage hatte sich kompliziert in
again the hall to The situation had itself complicated in

seiner Abwesenheit.
his absence

An jedem Spieltisch in Monte Carlo gibt es einen
On each game table in Monte Carlo gives it a

verborgenen Glockenkontakt, er ist ein Überbleibsel aus
hidden bell contact he is a leftover from
it

jenen Zeiten, wo das inzwischen etwas provinziell
those times where that In the meantime something provincial

gewordene Monte Carlo noch öfters seinen großen Tag –
become Monte Carlo still often its big day –

einen echten Verzweiflungsausbruch, eine Kollision mit den
a real outbreak of despair a collision with the

Croupiers, gar einen Selbstmord bei währendem Spiel mit
croupiers at all a suicide by ongoing play with

Blitz und Knall und Gehirnspritzern auf Damenkleidern
lightning and bang and brain splashes on women's dresses

zu verzeichnen hatte. Diesen Kontakt, der Alarm läutet und
to record had This contact the alarm rings and

den amtierenden Direktor herbeiruft, hatte bereits vor
the incumbent director summons had already before

dem Worte »widrigenfalls« der Croupier en chef
the words otherwise the croupier in boss
(French: managing)

gehandhabt, die Glocke hatte den Direktor Samanon in der
handled the bell jar had the director Samanon in the

Lektüre des »Méridional« aufgestört: da war der
reading of the Meridional disturbed there was the
(newspaper)

Direktor, um nach dem Rechten zu sehen, sofort
director for to the right to see immediately

aufgebrochen mit drei Saaldienern. Der Cradock aber,
broken up with three room servants The Cradock however

der von der Bar auf das eigentliche Schlachtfeld
who from the bar on the actual battlefield

zurückkehrte, sah sich drei schütteren alten Männchen
returned saw himself three doddering old little men

in Uniform und einem stattlichen, fleischigen Herrn mit
in uniform and a stately fleshy gentleman with

braunbierfarbenem Vollbart gegenüber. Lachte dem bärtigen
brown beer colored full beard opposite Laughed the bearded

Herrn ins Gesicht, schob die alten Männchen
gentleman in the face pushed the old little men

beiseite und stieg wieder auf seinen Stuhl. –
to the side and rose again on his chair

Daß er in diesem fröhlichen Herrn (und er weist auf
That he in this joyful gentleman and he points at

den Direktor Samanon) den Vertreter der Bank
the director Samanon the representative of the bank

vermuten dürfe, sagt der Cradock. Daß er ihm noch
suspect might says the Cradock That he him still

einmal seine außerordentlich bescheidenen Forderungen –
once his extraordinary humble demands –

zweitausend bis morgen früh um sieben Uhr – ans
two thousand until morning early around seven hour – to the
at

Herz lege und im übrigen auf das Elfzentimeter-Kaliber
heart lie and in the rest on the eleven centimeter caliber
to

der »Persimon« verweisen müsse.
of the Persimon refer must

Daß er den Herrn Direktor freundlichst bitte, ihn jetzt
That he the gentleman director kindest asks him now

nicht zu unterbrechen. Daß er jeden Widerstand für
not to interrupt That he every resistance for

unzweckmäßig halte, daß er sich um ein
inappropriate holds that he himself for a

zuvorkommendes, rücksichtsvolles Verhandeln bemühe, daß
courteous considerate negotiating strives that

er aber für alle Fälle doch vorgesorgt habe ... in
he however for all cases indeed prepared has in
in

diesem Augenblick betritt mit seinen Leuten der kleine
this moment enters with his people the little

Williams den Saal.
Williams the hall

Die aber, die hinter dem Leutnant Williams
Those however who behind the lieutenant Williams

hereinkommen, das sind keine schütteren Greise –
inside come that are no doddering old man –

herrliche Burschen aus allen europäischen Ländern sind es
lordly lads from all European countries are it
great they

– Preisboxer und Ringkämpfer von Weltruf ...
– price boxers and wrestlers from world reputation

Albanesen und levantinische Fischer und Inselgriechen und
Albanians and Levantine fisherman and island Greek and

ein paar Neger sogar und sonst noch alles,
a few black people even and otherwise still everything

was seine Muskeln und sein Fell dem Staate Labrador
what his muscles and his hide the state (of) Labrador

verkauft hat für drei Lei am Tage. Solch herrliche
sold has for three Lei at the day Such lordly
(coins) per great

Kolosse kommen zur Tür herein, hübsch manierlich und
colossi come to the door in handsome mannerly and

beinahe feierlich und jedenfalls ohne jede Rüpelei. Der
almost partylike and anyhow without any brawl The

Direktor Samanon versucht zu reden, kommt nicht zu
director Samanon tries to talk comes not to

Wort. Ein paar Damen bewahren beste Haltung und lachen,
word A few ladies preserve best stature and laugh

ein paar Herren bewahren weniger gute Haltung und
a few gentlemen preserve less good stature and

retirieren durch die Glastür ins Freie. Der
retire through the glass door in the free (space) The

Herr aus Sachsen schreit durch den Saal, daß er
gentleman from Saxon cries through the hall that he

sich beim deutschen Konsul beschweren werde.
himself at the German consul complain will

Ruhig, verbindlich, höflich bleibt der Cradock. Daß er
Calm obliging polite remains the Cradock That he

dringend bitte, nicht zu erschrecken, und daß keinem aus
urgently asks not to scare and that no one from

dieser erlesenen Gesellschaft auch nur das Allergeringste
this exquisite company also only the very least

geschehen werde, sagt der Cradock. Daß andererseits
happen will says the Cradock That on the other hand

im Falle des ja hoffentlich überflüssigen
in the case of the yes hopefully superfluous
indeed

Bombardements doch immerhin mit einer möglichen
bombings indeed After all with a possible

Beschädigung der Hotels gerechnet werden müsse, daß
damage of the hotel counted become must that

der erste Zug diesen schönen Fleck Erde leider
the first train this beautiful spot (of) Earth unfortunately

erst morgen früh um neun Uhr und dreiunddreißig
only tomorrow early around nine hour and thirty three
at o'clock

Minuten verlasse, daß mithin die unterschiedlichen
minutes leaves that therefore the different

Herrschaften nur eigene Interessen wahren würden, wenn
gentlemen only own interests guard would when

sie, gegebenenfalls durch eine Deputation bei der Bank,
they possibly through a deputation at the bank

seine außerordentlich bescheidenen Forderungen
his extraordinary humble demands

unterstützen wollten.
support wanted

Das also sagt der Kapitän. Läßt die Flügeltür öffnen und
That thus says the Captain Lets the wing door open and

sagt, daß es nun wohl das beste sei, wenn alle friedlich
says that it now well the best be when all peacefully

und ruhig den Saal verlassen und zu Hause sich noch
and calm the hall leave and to house themselves still

besonders seine letzten Worte – Unterstützung seiner
particularly his last words – support his

Forderung bei der Bank – recht genau überlegen wollten.
demand at the bank – right precise consider wanted
really

Dann winkt er dem Leutnant Williams, und damit
Then beckons he the lieutenant Williams, and there-with

rücken die Leute – Hand in Hand wie bei einem
back the people – hand in hand as at a

Broadway-Krawall eine New-Yorker Polizistenkette – langsam
broadway riot a New Yorker police chain – slowly

auf die Saaltür zu. Alles vollzieht sich in bester
on the hall door to Everything takes place itself in most best

Ordnung ... hie und da lacht man sogar ... ein paar
order here and there laughs one even a few

junge Franzosen sprechen, an das heutige Datum erinnernd,
young Frenchmen speak on the today date reminiscent

sogar von einem Karnevalsscherz.
even from a carnival joke

Alles wickelt sich ab, wie diese Cradocksche Rede
Everything wraps itself off as this Cradockian speech

gewesen ist: ruhig, sauber, ohne Flegelei. Draußen auf der
been is calm clean without whine Outside on the

Terrasse beginnen die Damen mit den Matrosen zu
terrace begin the ladies with the sailors to

scherzen, und der einzige, der protestiert und noch immer
joke and the only who protests and still always

eine Rede zu halten versucht, ist der Direktor Samanon.
a speech to hold tries is the director Samanon

»Tragt den Herrn hinaus«, sagt der Cradock. »Wir
Carry the gentleman out says the Cradock We

werden Sie hinaustragen«, sagen die Matrosen und nehmen
will you carry out say the sailors and take

(ganz behutsam und beinahe vorsorglich) den Direktor
completely carefully and almost as a precaution the director

Samanon auf den Arm und tragen ihn in sein Büro zurück.
Samanon on the arm and carry him in his office back

Die Saaldiener gehen voran und zeigen den Weg.
The room attendants go in front and demonstrate the way

Der Saal ist leer, die Terrasse draußen ist leer: keine
The hall is empty the terrace outside is empty no

zehn Minuten sind vergangen seit dem letzten Spiel. –
ten minutes are lapsed since the last game

Alles, was geschehen ist, hat sie von der Bank unter
Everything what happened is has she from the bench under

den Palmen mitangesehen. Die Empörung, die Bitterkeit …
the palm trees watched along The indignation the bitterness

alles das ist nun nicht mehr da. Da steht
everything that is now not (any)more there There stands

Cradock plötzlich vor ihr.
Cradock suddenly before her

»Sind Sie zufrieden, Madame?« fragt der Cradock.
Are you satisfied madame asks the Cradock

Sie schweigt.
She is silent

»Belieben Sie zu antworten?« fragt der Cradock.
Deign you to reply asks the Cradock

Da steht sie auf. »Augen zu!« kommandiert sie. »Sind
There stands she up Eyes closed commands she Are

zu«, sagt der Cradock. »Auf Ehre?« fragt sie. »Habe keine
closed says the Cradock On honor asks she Have none

mehr«, brummt der Cradock. Da nimmt sie die Maske
(any)more mutters the Cradock There takes she the mask

ab und küßt ihn.
off and kisses him

Eigentlich genau so wie vor zehn Jahren. So mit der
Actually exactly so as before ten years So with the

ganzen mädchenhaften Inbrunst der kleinen Mary von
whole girlish fierceness of the small Mary from

damals, und wenn es nicht so ein vergeßliches und
that time and when it not so a forgetful and

undankbares Mannsbild wäre: er müßte sie nun
ungrateful man picture would be he must her now

eigentlich an diesen Mädchenküssen erkennen. Jawohl, an
actually on this girl kissing recognize Yes indeed on

diesen für ihn, den alten Sünder aufgesparten
this for him the old sinner saved

Mädchenküssen.
girl kissing

Er erkennt sie nicht. Ein alter Sünder ist er. Ein
He recognizes her not An old sinner is he A

schlimmer Abenteurer ohne Gedächtnis.
worse adventurer without memory

Die Tür ist aufgeblieben.
The door is open remained

»Wo gehen wir hin?« fragt der lange Cradock, und er
Where go we to asks the tall Cradock and he

denkt, daß er in diesem Lande ja nun wohl geächtet
thinks that he in this land yes now well outlawed
indeed

und verbannt ist aus der Gemeinschaft der Menschen.
and banished is from the community of the people

»Müssen ja nicht wissen, wohin«, sagt die Mary und
Must yes not know where says the Mary and
indeed

denkt an die alte Märchenweisheit, daß man die ganz
thinks on the old fairytale wisdom that one the completely

großen Wunder immer nur entdeckt, wenn man nicht
large miracle always only discovers when one not

weiß, wohin man geht.
knows where-to one goes

So also gehen sie denn hinaus. Eng aneinandergeschmiegt
So thus go they then out Close nestled together

und völlig losgelöst von allen Wirrnissen.
and totally detached from all confusion

Es gibt, wenn man den häßlichen Ort erst hinter sich
It gives when one the ugly place first behind himself

hat und nach der Corniche zu geht, verschwiegene Wege
has and to the corniche to goes discreet roads

in Monte Carlo.
in Monte Carlo

Von dieser Nacht aber kann ich bezeugen, daß sie die
From this night however can I testify that she the

erste sanfte und ganz gelinde Frühlingsnacht jenes
first soft and completely mild spring night of that

Jahres war. Voll verbuhlter Süßigkeit und behangen mit
year was Full fated sweetness and hung with

ganz großen frühlingshellen Sternen.
completely large spring light stars

Der rötliche Arkturus brannte und Spika mit dem blauen
The reddish arctus burned and spika with the blue

Feuer ... der böse Aldebaran und Vega, von der man sagt,
fire the evil aldebaran and vega from which one says

daß sie ein mildes Auge wirft auf heimatlose Liebespaare.
that she a mild eye throws on homeless lovers

Kapitel V

Ein einziges einsames Licht brannte in dieser Nacht in den
A single lonely light burned in this night in the

Steinmassen des Kasinos: das Licht brannte im Zimmer
stone masses of the casino the light burned in the room

des Direktors Samanon.
of the director Samanon

Ich für mein Teil glaube (und die weiteren Ereignisse
I for my part believe and the further events

geben diesem Glauben recht), daß die Bank
give this believe right that the bank
truth

klug daran getan hätte, zum bösen Spiel des Kapitäns
sensibly to it done had to the bad play of the captain
would have been sensible

Cradock gute Miene zu machen und ihm zweitausend
Cradock good expression to make and him two thousand
gesture

Pfund auszuhändigen und diese zweitausend Pfund auf das
pound to hand over and these two thousand pound on the

Reklamekonto der Bank zu buchen: ganz Europa
advertisement account of the bank to book all of Europe

hätte (was es dann später sowieso tat) gelacht. Ganz
had what it then later anyway did laughed. All of

Europa hätte sich bei der einschlägigen Nachricht daran
Europe had itself at the relevant message to it

erinnert, daß neben Cannes und Nizza und Ventimiglia
reminded that beside Cannes and Nice and Ventimiglia

noch immer das einmal hochberühmte, jetzt aber ein
still always the once highly famous now however a

wenig vergessene Monte Carlo existiert ... alle alten
little forgotten Monte Carlo exists all old

Aventuriers hätten eingesehen, daß Monte Carlo gar nicht
aventuriers had seen that Monte Carlo at all not

so verstaubt sein konnte wie sein Ruf. Daß heute noch so
so dusty be could as its call That today still so
fame

berühmte Spieler wie der große Cradock an seinen Tischen
famous players as the great Cradock on its tables

säßen. Daß auch heute Monte Carlo noch seinen großen
sat That also today Monte Carlo still its large

Tag haben könnte.
day have could

So wäre es gewesen, wenn die Bank klug gehandelt
So would be it been when the bank sensibly handled
acted

hätte. Die Bank handelte nicht klug. Die Bank handelte
had The bank acted not sensibly The bank acted

ausgesprochen töricht. Der von Westen her über den
expressedly foolish The from the West away over the
quite

Ozean flutende Puritanismus bringt es wohl mit sich,
ocean flooding puritanism brings it well with himself

daß man in einer so weltmännisch-weitblickenden Handlung
that one in one so cosmopolitan-far-sighted action

und einer so klugen Verbuchung von zweitausend Pfund
and a so sensible booking from two thousand pound

so etwas wie eine Störung kosmischer Gesetze
so something as a disturbance (of) cosmic laws

erblickt: eher könnte man durch ein Trinkgeld von
beholds before could one through a drink-money from
tip

sechs Pence den vor dem Paradies Posten stehenden
six pence the before the paradise post standing

Cherub zur Wiederaufnahme des Menschengeschlechtes
cherub to the resumption of the human gender

in das bekannte Gartenetablissement bewegen ... eher
in the known garden establishment move before

könnte die Hölle gefrieren und eher ein Schweizer
could the hell freeze and before a Swiss

Eidgenosse seinem Lieblingssohn Geld ohne Zinsen
confederate his favorite son money without interest

leihen, ehe die Bank von Monte Carlo zur Rückgabe
lend before the bank from Monte Carlo to the return

eines Spielgewinnes bereit gewesen wäre. In
of a game win ready been would be In

dem Zimmer, wo noch so lange in jener unvergeßlich
the room where still so long in that unforgettable

schönen Frühlingsnacht Licht brannte, saß jener schöne,
beautiful spring night light burned sat that beautiful

vollbärtige Herr: Jean Baptiste Samanon, amtierender und
full bearded Mr Jean Baptiste Samanon incumbent and

bevollmächtigter Direktor der Bank von Monte Carlo,
plenipotentiary director of the bank of Monte Carlo

brütete über schlimmer Rache. Jean Baptiste Samanon
brooded over worse revenge Jean Baptiste Samanon

schrieb ein Telegramm an die französische Flottenstation in
wrote a telegram on the french fleet station in

Cap d'Antibes. Daß die Bank von einem frechen Erpresser
Cap d'Antibes That the bank of a cheeky blackmailer
                              by

bedroht werde, daß die Menschenrechte in Gefahr seien,
threatened became that the human rights in danger be

daß man um allerschnellste Hilfe bäte: das telegraphierte
that one for very fastest help begged that telegraphed

in dieser Stunde der Direktor Samanon nach Cap d'Antibes.
in this hour the director Samanon to Cap d'Antibes

Ich bin, wie gesagt, nicht der Ansicht, daß dieses
I am as said not of the opinion that this

Telegramm mit den Grundsätzen der Diplomatie und der
telegram with the principles of the diplomacy and the

geschäftlichen Klugheit in Einklang zu bringen war. –
entrepreneurial wisdom in agreement to bring was

In Cap d'Antibes nämlich lag zur Stunde mit
In Cap d'Antibes namely lay to the hour with

auseinandergenommener Backbordmaschine und einem
more disassembled port machine and a

neulich beim Einlaufen gesetzten Defekt an dem
the other day at the break in set malfunction on the

Ruderapparat der französische Kreuzer »Sadi Carnot«. Die
rowing machine the french cruiser Sadi Carnot The
warship

Offiziere des »Sadi Carnot« tanzten (es war Karneval,
officers of the Sadi Carnot danced it was carnival

wollen Sie gütigst bedenken!) an diesem Abend in
want you kindly think on this evening in
be so good to think

Cannes, der Kommandant Constance lag mit einem vom
Cannes the commander Constance lay with a from the

allzu jähen Frühlingseinbruch gesetzten Gichtanfall
all too hurried spring break set gout attack

stöhnend in seiner Kabine. Als der Kommandant Constance
groaning in his cabin As the commander Constance

um etwa drei Uhr nachts durch das eben eingetroffene
for about three hour night through the just arrived

Telegramm aus dem ersten unruhigen Schlafe geweckt
telegram from the first restless sleep waked

wurde und die seltsame Nachricht von der Bedrohung
became and the strange message from the threat

des Kasinos in Monte Carlo gelesen hatte, da hielt er
of the casino in Monte Carlo read had there held he

begreiflicherweise die Nachricht zunächst für einen
understandably the message first for an

unpassenden Karnevalsscherz und warf brummend das
inappropriate carnival joke and threw growling the

Papier auf die Erde.
paper on the ground

Allein geblieben, dachte der alte Herr dann freilich
Alone remained thought the old gentleman then freely
                                                      of course

doch daran, daß seit dem Kriegsende allerlei Dinge
indeed to it that since the war end all kinds of things

möglich waren, deren ernsthafte Erörterung früher einen
possible were whose serious discussion before a

Mann ins Irrenhaus gebracht hätte. Dachte dann doch
man in the madhouse brought had Thought then indeed

wieder an seine auseinandergenommene Backbordmaschine,
again on his disassembled port machine

an seine in Cannes tanzenden Herren und dachte auch
on his in Cannes dancing gentlemen and thought also

daran, daß man sich mit einem Ernstnehmen dieses
to it that one himself with a take seriously of this

Telegrammes unsterblich blamieren konnte. Von allen
telegram immortal disgrace could From all

diesen Bedenken und Rücksichten wurde er sozusagen
these thoughts and considerations became he so to speak

ebenso geplagt wie von der Gicht, und so beschloß er
likewise pestered as from the gout and so decided he

endlich, auf jeden Fall die Rückkehr seines Ersten Offiziers
finally on every case the return of his first officer

zu erwarten. Ich werde später zu berichten haben, was
to await I will later to report have what

der Panzerkreuzer »Sadi Carnot« dem Direktor Samanon
the armored cruiser Sadi Carnot (to) the director Samanon

für eine Antwort gab. –
for an answer gave
as

In den großen Hotels in Monte Carlo aber war man in
In the large hotels in Monte Carlo however was one in

dieser Nacht etwas früher aufgestanden, als man es
this night something earlier gotten up as one it

sonst zu tun pflegt an dieser paradiesischen Küste. Wer
otherwise to do uses on this heavenly coast Who

einen eigenen Wagen stehen hatte in den Garagen des
an own car stand had in the garages of the

Hotel de Paris und des Hotels Savoy, der hatte schon
Hotel of Paris and of the hotels savoy that one had already

um Mitternacht gepackt und war noch vor der ersten
at midnight packed and was still before the first

Frühdämmerung davongebraust auf den Straßen nach Nizza
dawn rushed away on the streets to Nice

und Ventimiglia. Was aber keinen Wagen besaß, das
and Ventimiglia What however no car possessed that
Who those

raste nun wie besessen die Treppen auf und ab, kniete
raced now as possessed the stairs on and off kneeled

auf Koffern, die sich nicht schließen lassen wollten,
on suitcases that themselves not close let wanted

brüllte kleine übernächtige Hotelpagen an, weil Madames
roared little overnight bellboys to because madame's

Hutschachtel von Zimmer Nummer
hat box from room number

dreihundertsiebenundsechzig noch immer nicht in die Halle
three hundred sixty-seven still always not in the hall

heruntergebracht war; konstatierte zum zehnten Male, daß
brought down was stated for the tenth time that

der erste Zug wirklich erst um neun Uhr dreiunddreißig
the first train really only at nine hour thirty three

ging. Brachte den Manager mit Fragen zur Verzweiflung
went Bbrought the manager with questions to the despair

und sah dann und wann in die spiegelglatte Bucht
and saw then and when in the smooth as glass bay

hinunter zu dem silbergrauen Schiff, dessen zierliche
down to the silver gray ship whose delicate

Kanönchen nun schon deutlich erkennbar waren in der
little canons now already clearly recognizable were in the

grauen Dämmerung. Um vier Uhr waren siebzig Prozent
gray dusk At four hour were seventy percent

sämtlicher Hotelzimmer in Monte Carlo gekündigt, um fünf
of all hotel rooms in Monte Carlo quit at five

Uhr waren sämtliche Portiers und Direktoren
hour were all portiers and directors

sanatoriumsreif: viel klüger wäre es gewesen,
sanatorium-ready much more intelligent would be it been
gone crazy would have

wenn die Bank die von dem Kapitän Cradock verlangte
when the bank the from the Captain Cradock desired

Summe gezahlt und auf ihr Reklame- oder wenigstens
total paid and on her advertisement or at least

auf ihr Verlustkonto gebucht hätte.
on her loss account booked had

Grundsätze der Schicklichkeit und der Diskretion
Principles of the decency and the discretion

verbieten es mir, zu sagen, wo an diesem Morgen der
forbid it me to say where on this morning the

lange Cradock Abschied nahm von Madame. Er tat das
tall Cradock leave took from madame He did that

unter erstickenden Küssen und im Gefühl eines
under suffocating kisses and in the feeling of a

Seehelden, der nun die Schlacht bei Abukir vor sich
sea hero who now the battle at Abukir before himself

hatte, hatte sie auch, da ja womöglich schon in einer
had had she also there yes possibly already in an
indeed

Stunde Pech und Schwefel auf Monte Carlo fallen konnten,
hour pitch and sulfur on Monte Carlo fall could

dringend gebeten, den Ort sofort nach ihrer Rückkehr
urgently asked the place immediately to her return

ins Hotel zu verlassen. Versprochen hatte sie wirklich,
in the Hotel to leave Promised had she really

daß sie sofort ihren Wagen anschirren lassen, und
that she immediately her car harness let and

nach Cannes abreisen werde, und dann, in der letzten
to Cannes leave will and then in the last

Viertelstunde, als es schon grau zu werden begann über
quarter of an hour as it already grey to become began over

den Bergen im Osten, da hatte sie sich wieder
the mountains in the (the) east there had she herself again

die Maske aufgesetzt. Der Cradock aber mußte sich
the mask put on The Cradock however must himself

mißmutig eingestehen, daß er ihr Gesicht eigentlich
sullenly admit that he her face actually

überhaupt nicht gesehen hatte.
at all · not · seen · had

Dreißig Minuten vor fünf war es, als er, etwas
Thirty · minutes · before · five · was · it, · as · he, · somewhat

übernächtig, nebenbei gesagt, das Fallreep seines Schiffes
overnighty / a hangover having · next by / by the way · said · the · gangway · of his · ship

hinaufkletterte. Sein erster Gang galt der Kabine
climbed up · His · first · course · concerned · the · cabin

des Funkers, der ja auch etwaige Telephonate des
of the / of · Funkers · who · yes / indeed · also · any · telephones · of the

Kasinos registriert haben mußte. Der übernächtige
casino · registered · have · must · The · overnighty / a hangover having

Funker Bengtson suchte in seinen Papieren herum,
radio operator · Bengtson · searched · in · his · papers · around

der Kapitän Cradock, draußen in seinem Frack wartend,
the · Captain · Cradock, · outside · in · his · tailcoat · waiting,

fröstelte in der Morgenluft. Antwort weder aus
shivered · in · the · morning air · Answer · neither · from

Mergentheim noch aus dem Kasino von Monte Carlo.
Mergentheim · nor · from · the · Casino · from · Monte · Carlo

Geld weder aus dem Kasino von Monte Carlo noch von
money · neither · from · the · Casino · from · Monte · Carlo · nor · from

Onkel James aus Mergentheim. Weder Geld noch
uncle · James · from · Mergentheim. · Neither · money · nor

Antwort. Der Cradock warf achselzuckend die Zigarette
answer the Cradock threw shrugging the cigarette

fort und ging. Für die dort drüben war er seit
away and went For them there over there was he since

gestern abend ja doch nichts anderes als ein
yesterday evening yes indeed nothing other as a

Erpresser ... einem Erpresser antwortete man nicht, und
blackmailer a blackmailer answered one not and

man selbst hatte ein Fähnlein aufgesteckt, das nun, wohl
one himself had a little flag attached that now well

oder übel, fröhlich weiterflattern mußte im Winde. Er
or bad merrily flutter on must in the winds He

stellte sich unter die Brause und trank einen männlichen
set himself under the shower and drank a manly

Kognak. Er ließ Williams und den Chefingenieur Pavlicek
cognac He let Williams and the chief engineer Pavlicek

wecken und schloß sich mit beiden Herren zu einer
wake and kept himself with both gentlemen to a

Besprechung von zwanzig Minuten Dauer ein. Um fünf
meeting from twenty minutes duration in At five

Uhr aber schmetterten Hornsignale über die Bucht, und
hour however threw horn signals over the bay and
o'clock

unter Pfeifentrillern wurde die Mannschaft geweckt mit
under whistle became the team waked with

der Nachricht, daß das Schiff gefechtsklar zu machen sei.
the message that the ship battle-ready to make be

Ernst wurde es. Ganz erschrecklicher Ernst ...
Serious became it Quite terrifyingly serious

Zuerst waren es nur furchtbare Rauchwolken, die, mit
First were it only terrible clouds of smoke that with

dem letzten zusammengekehrten Kohlenschutt gespeist, aus
the last swept up coal debris fed from

den beiden Schornsteinen der »Persimon« aufstiegen und
the both chimneys (of) the Persimon ascended and

Gottes reine Morgenluft auf das entsetzlichste
God's pure morning air at the most horrific (way)

verpesteten. Dann aber begann es zu laufen und zu
poisoned Then however began it to run and to

wimmeln auf den sauberen Decks, und Aufzüge rasselten,
teem on the clean deck and lifts rattled

und Maate fluchten in sämtlichen Sprachen Europas und
and mates swore in all languages (of) Europe and

des Balkans. Dann flogen Mündungsdeckel von den
of the Balkans Then flew muzzle cover from the

Kanonen, und blinkende Messingkartuschen und schreckliche
cannons and flashing brass cartridges and horrible

Fünfzollgranaten wurden herbeigetragen in ihren Körben.
five inch grenades became brought here in their baskets

Im   Lazarett   sogar begann es auf das furchtbarste
In the military hospital even   began it on the most terrible

nach Jodoform und Karbol zu riechen, und dann pochte
to   iodoform and carbolic to smell and then knocked

die Kriegsfurie sogar an die Tür des Doktor Crofts. Der
the war fury even on the door of the doctor Crofts The

Doktor hatte gestern aus Gram über seinen Kapitän nicht
doctor had yesterday from grief over his Captain not

allzuwenig getrunken, der Doktor wollte schlafen. Die
too little drunk the doctor wanted sleep The

Kriegsfurie aber in Gestalt des Kammerstewards Matteo
war fury however in shape of the chamber stewards Matteo

Bardulescu klopfte an die Tür und sagte, daß Krieg
Bardulescu knocked on the door and said that war

ausgebrochen sei zwischen Labrador und Monte Carlo und
broken out be between Labrador and Monte Carlo and

daß der Doktor unbedingt aufstehen müsse. Da hatte der
that the doctor absolutely get up must There had the

Doktor Crofts zurückgebrüllt, daß er weder selbst verrückt
doctor Crofts yelled back that he neither himself crazy

noch Irrenarzt sei und daß er auch keine Lust habe,
nor mad doctor be and that he also no desire have

Theater zu spielen. Damit hatte er sich
theater to play There-with had he himself

auf die andere Seite gedreht.
on the other side turned

Der Kapitän Cradock aber lief nervös auf der Brücke
The Captain Cradock however ran nervous on the bridge

auf und ab. Es war dreißig Minuten vor sieben Uhr, er
on and off It was thirty minutes before seven hour he
up down o'clock

sah mit dem Glase nach dem Kasino hinüber: nichts.
saw with the glass to the Casino over nothing
binoculars

Kein Boot, kein Signal ... nichts. Die Bank schwieg. Die
No boat no signal nothing The bank was silent The

Bank verhandelte nicht einmal. Die Bank glaubte wohl nicht
bank negotiated not once The bank believed well not

einmal, daß man Ernst machen werde ...
once that one serious make would
become

Dreiviertel sieben. Er hatte inzwischen mit den
Three quarters seven He had In the meantime with the

Offizieren geredet: Abenteurer aus allen Staaten Europas ...
officers talked Adventurers from all States (of) Europe

Landsknechte, die alles taten, was er mit seiner
country-service-men who everything did what he with his
Mercenaries

Verantwortung deckte. Dann hatte er auch die Mannschaft
responsibility covered Then had he also the team

zusammenrufen lassen und eine mehr zündende als
call together let and a more sparkling as
rousing

völkerrechtlich korrekte Ansprache gehalten: kein Zweifel,
international law correct speech held no doubt

daß diese daheim von Strandraub und Fischdiebstahl
that this at home from beach robbery and fish theft

lebenden Levantiner schießen würden. Fünf Minuten vor
living Levantines shoot would Five minutes before

sieben Uhr ... Artilleristen an den gerichteten und geladenen
seven hour Artillerymen on the aimed and loaded
o'clock

Geschützen, Donner und Blitz im Rohr, das Schiff
cannons thunder and lightning in the pipe the ship

gefechtsbereit auf allen Stationen: der Kapitän Cradock lief
ready to fight on all stations the Captain Cradock ran

auf der Brücke auf und ab wie ein eben erst
on the bridge on and off as a just first
up down now

eingefangener Menagerietiger, und es ist zu verzeichnen,
caught in menagerie-tiger and it is to record

daß ihm nicht so übermäßig wohl zumute war.
that (it) him not so excessive well at mood was

Er sah nach der Stadt hinüber. Über den grauen
He looked to the city over Over the gray

Morgenhimmel kam von Marseille her der Morgenflieger,
morning sky came from Marseille away the morning flyer

auf der großen Straße nach Nizza sausten ... brennende
on the large street to Nice whizzed burning

Scheinwerfer noch in fahler Dämmerung ... die großen
headlights still in pale dusk the large

Limousinen, am Bahnhof die Aufzüge gingen nun
limousines at the railway station the lifts went now

schon: die europäische Zivilisation, die er, der Abenteurer,
already the European civilization which he the adventurer

grimmig haßte und von der er doch ein Teil und mit
grim hated and from which he indeed a part and with

der er in Konflikt geraten war ...
which he in conflict gotten was

Er sah seine Kanonen, deren Rohre sich so pathetisch
He saw his cannons whose tubes themselves so pathetically

in den Morgenhimmel bohrten: Operettenkanonen, die beim
in the morning sky drilled operetta cannons that at the

dritten Schuß wahrscheinlich auseinanderfliegen würden. Er
third shot probably fly apart would He

sah die Artilleristen: uniformierte levantinische
saw the artillerymen uniformed Levantine

Hammeldiebe, denen zur Operette nur noch die rote
pickpockets who to the operetta only still the red

Schärpe und eine rote Hutfeder fehlten. Operette
sash and a red hat feather were missing Operetta

waren die Offiziere, Operette schien ihm sein ganzes altes
were the officers operetta seemed him his whole old

wackliges Schiff, Operette war die Ordonnanz, die (nackte
shaky ship operetta was the orderly who bare

Füße und zerrissene Hosen) ihm den zweiten Kognak
feet and torn pants him the second cognac

reichte. Das Glas ansetzend, sah er in der Scheibe des
reached The glass setting-on saw he in the disc of the
handed starting

Kompaßgehäuses sein Spiegelbild: mit Ringen unter den
compass case his mirror image with rings under the
bags

Augen und scharfen Falten zwischen Mund und Nase, ein
eyes and sharp wrinkles between mouth and nose a

nicht mehr ganz junger Abenteurer, der mit der
not (any)more completely young adventurer who with the

europäischen Zivilisation angebunden und nun alle Aussicht
European civilization tied up and now all view

hatte, binnen einer Woche ins Zuchthaus zu wandern.
had within a week in the penitentiary to roam

Da goß er das Glas herunter. Für die da drüben
There poured he the glass down For those there up there

war er seit gestern ja doch gezeichnet und geächtet,
was he since yesterday yes indeed drawn and outlawed

und ein Zurück gab es nicht mehr. Drei Minuten
and a back gave it not (any)more Three minutes

fehlten noch an sieben Uhr, und die Artilleristen
were missing still on seven hour and the artillerymen
of o'clock

hatten schon den Zündstrick in der Hand: da geschah
had already the spark plug in the hand there happened

etwas, was zum Heile aller Beteiligten den Dingen
something what to the well being of all involved the things

eine ganz andere Wendung gab.
a completely other turn gave

Der Kapitän Cradock, beschäftigt mit moralischem
The Captain Cradock occupied with moral

Katzenjammer, mit Reflexionen und Kognak, hatte es
cat whine with reflections and cognac had it

übersehen – der kleine Williams, der achtern die
overlooked – the little Williams who aft the

Geschütze kommandieren sollte, hatte es sofort
guns command should had it immediately

bemerkt. Ein kleines weißes Motorboot, das vor einer
noticed A little white motorboat which before a

Minute erst sich losgelöst hatte vom Kai und nun wie
minute first itself detached had from the quay and now as

ein Strich vor großen Kielwellen durchs Wasser
a brush before large keel waves through the water

preschte. Pfeilgerade auf die »Persimon« zu. Eine
dashed Arrow straight on the Persimon to(wards) A

weiße Flagge sogar wurde geschwenkt, und als der Kapitän
white flag even became moved around and as the Captain

Cradock es entdeckt hatte, da war es schon beinahe
Cradock it discovered had there was it already almost

am Fallreep. Genugtuung war gekommen. Der Direktor
at the gangway Satisfaction was come The director

Samanon war gekommen. Die Bank verhandelte. –
Samanon was come The bank negotiated –

Die Sache war einfach so, daß einerseits die Franzosen
The thing was simply so that on the one hand the Frenchmen

noch nicht geantwortet hatten und daß andererseits das
still not answered had and that on the other hand the

Ultimatum abgelaufen und diesem berüchtigten Cradock
ultimatum expired and this notorious Cradock

doch nun einmal alles zuzutrauen war. Ratsam war
indeed now once everything to entrust was Advisable was
had

es erschienen, im letzten Augenblick diesen rabiaten
it appeared in the last moment this rabid

Menschen auf das bevorstehende Eintreffen der Hilfe und
human on the upcoming arrival of the help and
person

auf die Unmöglichkeit jedes Widerstandes aufmerksam zu
on the impossibility of each resistance attentive to

machen. Zahlen wollte man natürlich so ohne weiteres
make To pay wanted one of course so without additional

nicht, und Schiffsgranaten wollte man erst recht nicht:
not and marine grenades wanted one first right not
really

da wollte man Zeit gewinnen und hatte in letzter
there wanted one time win and had in (the) last

Minute zum Unterhandeln den Direktor Samanon geschickt.
minute to the negotiation the director Samanon sent

Mit zweitausend Pfund in der Tasche, die aber nur
With two thousand pound in the pocket which however only

im alleräußersten Notfall gezahlt werden sollten.
in the most extreme emergency paid become should

Trotz dieser zweitausend Pfund war es eine unangenehme
Despite this two thousand pound was it an uncomfortable

Mission. Die Mission eines Mannes, der einer bißbereiten
mission The mission of a man which a ready to bite

Kobra unter Hinweis auf eine soeben in London
cobra under note on a just now in London

telegraphisch bestellte Flinte das Beißen ausreden will:
telegraphically ordered shotgun the bite talk out wants

der Direktor Samanon war ziemlich blaß, als er das
the director Samanon was rather pale as he the

Fallreep hinankletterte.
gangway climbed up

Oben stand der Doktor Crofts, der, um die schlimmsten
Above stood the doctor Crofts who for the worst

Dummheiten seines Kapitäns zu verhindern, nun doch
stupidities of his captain to prevent now indeed

aufgestanden war. »Gott zum Gruß!« sagte der Doktor
gotten up / was / had — God / to the — greeting — said — the — doctor

mit der Höflichkeit eines Henkers, der am elektrischen
with — the — courtesy — of a — hangman — who — at the — electrical

Stuhl den Delinquenten fragt, ob er nicht gütigst
chair — the — delinquent — asks — whether — he — not — kindly / be so good

Platz nehmen wolle. »God save the queen«, sagte der
place — take — wanted — God — save — the — queen — said — the

Direktor Samanon und hatte wohl die Vorstellung, daß man
director — Samanon — and — had — well — the — image — that — one

auf einem Kriegsschiff, dessen Herrin eine gebürtige
on — a — warship — whose — Mistress — a — native

britische Prinzessin war, so und nicht anders sagen
British — princess — was — so — and — not — (anything) else — say

müsse ...
must

»Da ich selbst mütterlicherseits Brite von Geburt bin«,
There / Since — I — myself — maternal — Brit — from — birth — am

fügte der Direktor Samanon hinzu.
added — the — director — Samanon — there-to

»Da die Samoaner«, sagte freundlich der Doktor Crofts,
There / Since — the — Samoans — said — friendly — the — doctor — Crofts

»ebenfalls Briten von Blut sind, seit ihre Vorfahren vor
likewise — British — from — blood — are — since — their — ancestors — before

hundertfünfzig Jahren den Kapitän Cook aufgefressen
hundred and fifty years the Captain cook eaten up

haben.« So waren die Begrüßungszeremonien, nach deren
have So were the welcome ceremonies to whose

Erledigung der Direktor Samanon vor den Kapitän
completion the director Samanon before the Captain

geführt wurde.
led became

Da also standen sich die feindlichen Parteien
There thus stood himself the enemy parties

gegenüber, und es kam in diesem Augenblick nun auch
opposite and it came in this moment now also

dem Direktor Samanon so vor, als sei dieser Cradock
the director Samanon so before as be this Cradock

heute um mindestens einen Fuß länger als in der
today for at least a foot longer as in the

vergangenen Nacht ...
past night

»Mein Kapitän«, sagte Herr Samanon und tat so, als wolle
My captain said Mr Samanon and did so as wanted

er eine Kammerrede halten.
he a chamber speech hold

»Geld?« fragte lakonisch der Cradock.
Money asked laconically the Cradock

»Zu meinem Bedauern – nein«, sagte der Direktor Samanon
To my pity – no said the director Samanon

und war, da das Gesicht seines Partners sich
and was there the face of his partners himself

verfinstert hatte, einen Schritt zurückgetreten. Nach dieser
darkened had a step back stepped After this

Eröffnung, mit beteuernd aufs Herz gelegten und
opening with affirmingly on the heart laid and

beschwörend in die Luft gestreckten Händen, begann er
conjuring in the air stretched hands began he

etwas, was an Rhetorik und Pathos wirklich an eine
something what on rhetoric and pathos really on a
for all the of

Kammerrede erinnerte.
chamber speech reminded

Er, für sein Teil, sagte Herr Samanon, habe heute nacht
He for his part said Mr Samanon have today night

sich auf das lebhafteste für die Rückgabe des Geldes
himself on the most lively for the return of the money

eingesetzt ... er sei leider auf den lebhaftesten
set-in he be unfortunately on the liveliest
worked for

Widerstand der Bank und deren eherne Grundsätze
resistance of the bank and whose brazen principles

(»ehern«, sagte Herr Samanon) gestoßen. Sogar an eine
brazen said Mr Samanon bumped Even on a

Erlegung des Betrages aus eigenen Mitteln hätte er
capture of the amount from own means had he

angesichts des unheilvollen Konfliktes gedacht, wenn eben
in face of the ominous conflicting thought when just

nicht unglückseligerweise seine Pflichten als Familienvater
not unfortunately his duties as family man

ihm diese Ausgabe verboten hätten. Die Bank aber sei
him this output forbidden had The bank however be

inzwischen leider zu anderen Entschlüssen
In the meantime unfortunately to other resolve

gekommen. Zu Entschlüssen von ganz
come To resolve from completely

außerordentlicher Tragweite, die mitzuteilen er jetzt die
extraordinary scope the with-to-share he now the
to tell

Ehre haben werde und für deren Übermittelung er die
honor have will and for whose transmission he the

Unverletzbarkeit des Parlamentärs ...
immunity of the parliamentary

»Wollen Sie mich mit Redensarten hinhalten?« schrie der
Want you me with sayings hold up cried the
delay

Cradock.
Cradock

»Bin gekommen, Sie, mein Kapitän, im letzten Augenblick
Am come you my Captain in the last moment

vor unheilvollen Entschlüssen zu bewahren und ...«
for ominous decisions to preserve and

»Kein Baby, Sir!« schrie der Cradock.
No infant sir cried the Cradock

»Und mit freudigem Einsatz meines Lebens diesen
And with joyful commitment of my life this

paradiesischen Ort zu schützen«, vollendete der Direktor
heavenly place to protect completed the director

Samanon. Eine kleine Treppe führte auf das Kompaßdeck
Samanon A little stairs led on the compass deck

hinauf, und dieser überhöhte und wenigstens etwas
up and this inflated and at least something

gesicherte Ort erschien für den gefährlichsten Teil seiner
secured place appeared for the most dangerous part his

Mission als der geeignetste. Was er nun noch sagte,
mission as the most suitable What he now still said

wurde nicht mehr im Tone einer Kammerrede
became not (any)more in the tone of a chamber speech

vorgetragen.
presented

Daß die Bank leider die Franzosen in Cap d'Antibes
That the bench unfortunately the Frenchmen in Cap d'Antibes

um Hilfe gebeten habe und daß der »Sadi Carnot«
for help asked have and that the Sadi Carnot
had

unterwegs sei, stotterte der Direktor Samanon.
on the way be stuttered the director Samanon

Daß der »Sadi Carnot« die dreifache Bestückung
That the Sadi Carnot the triple assembly (of cannons)

habe und daß jeder Widerstand unmöglich sein werde ...
have / had and that each resistance impossible be will / would

Daß er im Interesse der Bank und auch im
That he in the interest (of) the bank and also in the

Interesse des Kapitäns und unter Preisgabe der
interest (of) the captain and under disclosure of (the)

eigenen Sicherheit gekommen sei, um im letzten
own security come be / had for in the last

Augenblick eine Katastrophe zu verhüten. An dieser Stelle
moment a catastrophe to prevent on this spot

aber wurde er rauh und unsanft unterbrochen. Der
but became he rough and unsoft interrupted The

Kapitän nämlich hatte – untrügliches Sturmzeichen
Captain namely had – infallible storm sign

schlimmsten Grades – seine Mütze auf den Boden
worst degrees – his hat on the ground

geworfen, hatte (wahrscheinlich eine Erinnerung an
thrown had probably a memory on

afrikanische Boxerlebnisse) die Ärmel aufgeschlagen und
African boxing experiences the sleeves struck up / rolled up and

war – fünf Stufen auf einmal – die Treppe
was – five steps at once – the stairs

hinaufgesprungen. Da war denn der Parlamentär der
jumped up There was then the parliamentary the

Bank von Monte Carlo entflohen. –
bank from Monte Carlo escaped

Augenzeugen dieser Szene stimmen durchaus darin
Eyewitnesses of this scene agree throughout therein
at all

überein, daß die Jagd, die sich aus dieser Flucht und
over in that the hunt which itself from this flight and

diesem Angriffe ergab, etwas an sich hatte, was man
this attack gave something on itself had what one

nur als »gespenstisch« bezeichnen kann. Bemerkt muß
only as ghostly describe can Noticed must

werden, daß sie beide ... der eine in seiner Angst und der
become that they both the one in his fear and the

andere in seinem Zorn ... schwiegen; daß sie beide
other in his anger remained silent that they both

ganz leichte Schuhe trugen und somit fast
completely light shoes carried and consequently almost

geräuschlos liefen und daß von den Unbeteiligten (teils
noiseless ran and that from the uninvolved part

aus grenzenloser Neugierde und teils aus Sportinteresse
from limitless curiosity and part from sports interest

an der Leistung des Herrn Samanon) niemand
on the performance of the gentleman Samanon nobody
at

intervenierte. Die Jagd aber, sie führte auf der anderen
intervened The hunt however she led on the other
to

Seite des Kompaßdecks wieder zur Brücke hinunter, sie
side of the compass decks again to the bridge down she

führte von der Brücke aufs Hauptdeck, sie führte endlich
led from the bridge on the main deck she led finally

(mit Achill, Hektor und den Mauern von Troja verhielt es
with Achilles Hector and the walls from troy related it

sich bekanntlich ganz genau so!) dreimal um das
itself as known completely exactly so three times around the

Haus der Rudermaschine herum. Von dort blieb dem
house of the rowing machine around From there remained the

Verfolgten nur noch der Weg zur Brücke hinauf, und es
pursued only still the way to the bridge up and it

geschah hier, daß sein Schicksal sich doch noch
happened here that his fate himself indeed still

vollendete: der Direktor Samanon hatte eine der dort
completed the director Samanon had a that there

liegenden Kabelleitungen übersehen, er war gestolpert. Und
laying cable line overlooked he was stumbled and
had

da hatte sich denn, da an ein Aufstehen nicht
there had himself then there on a get up not

mehr — zu — denken — war, — die — Jagd — in — der — dritten — Minute
(any)more — to — think — was — the — hunt — in — the — third — minute

zugunsten — des — Verfolgers — entschieden.
in favor of — of the — pursuer — decided

Bei — dem — Kapitän — Cradock — aber — war — der — erste — große
At — the — Captain — Cradock — however — was — the — first — great

Wutparoxismus — (in — dem — Schlimmes — sich — hätte — ereignen
anger paroxism — in — the — bad — himself — had — occur

können!) — längst — verraucht, — und — der — erste — Zorn — hatte — sich
can — long — smoked up — and — the — first — anger — had — itself

verwandelt — in — einen — mit — Sadismus — leicht — versetzten
changed — in — a — with — sadism — easily — moved

Galgenhumor. — »Ganz — außerordentlich — betrübt, — Sie — echauffiert
gallows humor — All — extraordinary — sad — you — heated up

zu — haben«, — sagte — der — Cradock — und — half — seinem — Opfer
to — have — said — the — Cradock — and — helped — his — victim

beim — Aufstehen. — »Schätze, — daß — Sie — der — Ruhe — bedürfen,
with the — getting up — Deems — that — you — the — rest — need

Herr«, — sagte — der — Cradock — und — winkte — den — Quartermeister
sir — said — the — Cradock — and — waved — the — quartermaster

Jackson — heran — und — hatte — sich — auch — schon — einen
Jackson — near — and — had — himself — also — already — a

Racheplan — erdacht: — eine — nette — liebe — kleine — Rache — im
revenge plan — invented — a — nice — lovely — little — revenge — in the

Cradockstil.
Cradock style

Ganz in der Nähe gab es da im Deck einen
Completely in the proximity gave it there in the deck a

Bunkerdeckel ... eigentlich war der darunterliegende Raum
bunker cover actually was the underlying space

kein Kohlenbunker, sondern ein enger und dunkler
no coal bunker but a tighter and dark

Aufbewahrungsraum für die Eimer und Besen der
storage room for the bucket and brooms of the

Storekeeper: es war dieser enge, dunkle Raum, an den
storekeeper it was this narrow dark space on which

der Kapitän sofort gedacht hatte. Wenn nämlich die
the Captain immediately thought had When namely the

Bank um dieser elenden zweitausend Pfund willen den
bank for this miserable two thousand pound's will the
sake

Franzosen alarmiert hatte, so war der internationale
Frenchmen alarmed had so was the international

Skandal da, und man war verloren. War man verloren, so
scandal there and one was lost Was one lost so

mußte man mit Glanz untergehen, mußte sich mit
must one with radiance perish must himself with

dem dreimal so starken »Sadi Carnot« herumschießen
the three times so strong Sadi Carnot shoot around

und in Splitter gehen. Ging man aber in Splitter, so
and in splinters go Went one however in splinters so

sollte dieser häßliche Bürger da die Fahrt zur Hölle
should this ugly civilian there the ride to the hell

mitmachen ... »Schätze, Herr, daß hier bald dicke Luft sein
along make Deems sir that here soon fat air be
in participate

wird«, sagte der Cradock, »schätze, daß das Gefecht mit
becomes said the Cradock Deems that the battle with

dem Franzosen Sie interessieren wird ...«
the Frenchmen you interest will

»Gnade!« schrie Herr Samanon.
Mercy cried Mr Samanon

»Und daß Sie es gern an Bord meines Schiffes
And that you it gladly on board of my ship

mitmachen.« Der Bunkerdeckel flog auf, der Quartermeister
make along The bunker cover flew on the quartermaster
in participate

Jackson half nach. Der Direktor Samanon war bis auf
Jackson helped to The director Samanon was until on

weiteres außerstande, seiner diplomatischen Mission im
additional unable his diplomatic mission in the

Auftrage der Bank nachzukommen ...
assignment of the bank to comply

Er, der Cradock, ging auf die Brücke und suchte mit
He the Cradock went on the bridge and searched with

dem Glase den Horizont ab, suchte, runzelte die Stirn.
the glass the horizon off searched frowned the forehead

»Sehen Sie etwas, Williams?« Jawohl, auch der Leutnant
See you something williams? Yes also the lieutenant
Look

Williams konnte es nun sehen. Dampfersmok im
Williams could it now see Steam smoke in the

Südwesten. Dampfersmok scheinbar aus drei
southwest steam smoke apparently from three

Schornsteinen. Drei Schornsteine hatte der »Sadi Carnot«.
chimneys Three chimneys had the Sadi Carnot

Der Cradock spie aus und legte das Glas in den Kasten
The Cradock spat out and put the glass in the cupboard

zurück.
back

Er berechnete die Entfernung. Gut und gern noch
He calculated the distance Good and gladly still

fünfundzwanzig Meilen. Da der »Sadi Carnot« dreißig in
twenty five miles There the Sadi Carnot thirty in
Since

der Stunde lief, so hatte man noch fünfzig Minuten bis
the hour ran so had one still fifty minutes until

zur Katzbalgerei, und da sein kleines Schiff dem
to the catfighting and there his little ship the

großen Franzosen und seinem Zehnzollkaliber ja doch
large Frenchmen and his ten inch caliber yes indeed

nichts anhaben konnte, so waren diese fünfzig Minuten
nothing on-have could so were this fifty minutes
harm

eigentlich identisch mit derjenigen Frist, die ihn noch
actually identical with of that deadline which him still

vom Tode trennte. Er lächelte: Todesfurcht war das
from the death separated He smiled fear of death was it

wohl nicht ... das Leben hatte reichgedeckte Tafeln
well not the life had richly covered tables

präsentiert, und man hatte sich sattgegessen mit gutem
presented and one had himself eaten full with good

Appetit. Todesfurcht war es eigentlich nicht – es war wohl
apetite Fear of death was it actually not – it was well

mehr Überraschung und Erstaunen ...
more surprise and astonishment

Erstaunen, daß ihm, dem glückhaften Abenteurer, dieses
Astonishment that him the happy adventurer this

herrliche Leben überhaupt einmal in den Händen
lordly life at all once in the hands
great

zerbrechen konnte. Erstaunen, weil das Verhängnis
break could Astonishment because the doom

doch gestern noch gar nicht dagewesen war, und
indeed yesterday still at all not had been there was and

weil es nun so urplötzlich daherkam aus einer
because it now so all of a sudden came along from a

unbeachteten Ecke. Erstaunen, weil der Tod nun ihm,
disregarded corner Astonishment because the death now him

dem hundertprozentigen Manne, von einer Frau kommen
the hundred percent man from a woman come

mußte. Von einer Frau, die er vor vierundzwanzig
must From a woman who he before twenty four

Stunden noch gar nicht gekannt, von der er heute
hours still at all not known (had) from who he today

nacht im Dunkeln eben nur erraten hatte, daß sie
night in the dark just only guessed had that she

schön gewesen, und von ihr nichts geblieben war, als
beautiful been and from her nothing remained was as

an dem ominösen Tüllfetzen in seiner Rocktasche ein
on the ominous scraps of tulle in his skirt pocket a

leichter Duft ihres Parfüms. Er nahm noch einmal das
light fragrance of her perfume He took still once the

Glas, suchte noch einmal den Westhimmel ab. Drei
glass searched still once the west sky -off- Three
binoculars

feine Rauchsäulen und darunter mit Zehnzollkanonen
delicate columns of smoke and there-under with ten inch guns
under it

und Pikringranaten der Tod. Er pfiff durch die Zähne:
and pikringranaten the death He whistled through the teeth

sollte denn nun einmal gestorben sein, so sollte er dem
should then now once died his so should he the

satten Europa wenigstens in die Ohren gellen, der
satiated Europe at least in the ears yell the

Trauersalut für den langen Cradock. Er sah nach der Uhr,
funeral salute for the tall Cradock He saw to the hour

fand, daß es allerhöchste Zeit war, und ging zu seinen
found that it very highest time was and went to his

Kanonen ...
cannons

Er ging zu dem Elfzentimeter, das, mühselig
He went to the eleven centimeter (gun) that laboriously

erbettelt vom Labradorer Parlament, das einzig
begged off from the labradorer houses of parliament the only

halbwegs brauchbare Geschütz seines Schiffes darstellte. Er
halfway usable gun of his ship represented He

schob die Artilleristen beiseite, die nun schon seit einer
pushed the artillerymen to the side who now already since an

Stunde da herumstanden. Morgensonne beschien schon
hour there stood around (The) morning sun shone on already

die spiegelglatte Bucht und dieses Monte Carlo, das mit
the smooth as glass bay and this Monte Carlo that with

den weißen Häusern und den harten Schlagschatten wie
the white houses and the hard drop shadows as

ein totes Korallenriff aussah. Diesseits also war mit
a dead coral reef looked On this side thus was with

kühlem Metall und der sauberen Sachlichkeit von Kammer,
cool metal and the clean objectivity from room

Verschluß und Richtmaschine das Geschütz ... jenseits
closure and aiming device the gun On the other side

mit Erkern und Erkerchen, mit Türmen und
with bay windows and small bay windows with towers and

Türmchen und Stuckorgien und erlogenem Rokoko und der
turrets and stucco orgies and deceitful rococo and the

aufgeblähten Kuppel das Kasino: da regte sich in dem
bloated dome the Casino there moved himself in the

langen Cradock, als er dieses einem schlechten Öldruck
tall Cradock as he this a bad oil pressure

nicht unähnliche Bild sah, erst recht ein knabenhafter
not dissimilar picture saw first right a boyish

und von mir keineswegs gebilligter Zerstörertrieb ...
and from me in no way approved destroyer drive

Denn so ist es doch nun einmal mit Kindern und
Then so is it indeed now once with children and
unavoidable

Barbaren: sieht ein Sechsjähriger im Walde das Wunder
savages sees a six year old in the forest the miracle

eines schönen neugeborenen Fliegenpilzes, so wird er ihn
of a beautiful newborn fly mushroom so will he him

köpfen ... kommt an einen recht schönen klaren Quell ein
behead comes on a right beautiful clear source a
arrives truly

Barbar, so wird er im günstigsten Falle
barbarian so will he in the most advantageous case
best

hineinspucken ... tritt ein mit sieben Schnäpsen im Leibe
spit into it steps a with seven (drink) shots in the body

fröhlich von der Arbeit heimkehrender Landmann vor
merrily from the work returning home farmer before

einen großen Kristallspiegel, so wird er (wofern er ein
a large crystal mirror so will he what he an

unverbildeter, von Okkultismus, Theosophie und
uneducated from occultism theosophy and

Psychoanalyse unbeschwerter fröhlicher Landmann ist) den
psychoanalysis carefree happy farmer is the

Trieb fühlen, mitten in diesen Kristallspiegel hinein leere
drive feel middle in this crystal mirror inside empty
urge

Bierflaschen zu werfen. Was, bitte, erwarten Sie von
beer bottles to throw What please expect you from

einem Manne, wie der lange Cradock einer war? Es mußte
a man as the tall Cradock one was It must

in diesem Falle gerade die aufgeblähte Renaissancekuppel
in this case just the bloated renaissance dome

seinen Zorn erregen und seine Zerstörerinstinkte nur noch
his anger arouse and his destructive instincts only still

steigern: da lud er selbst und richtete.
increase there loaded he himself and aimed

Sechshundert Meter und Aufschlagzünder. Als er dann den
Six hundred meters and impact detonator As he then the

Zündstrick schon in der Hand hielt und eben abziehen
spark plug already in the hand held and just pull off

wollte, da griff das Schicksal zum zweiten Male ein.
wanted there grabbed the fate to the second time -in-
intervened

Der Leutnant Kries (jener von mir schon erwähnte
The lieutenant Kries that from me already mentioned

Ostpreuße, der Tischkanten abbeißen und
East Prussian who table edges bite off and

Fünfschillingstücke zerbrechen konnte): item, der Leutnant
five shilling pieces break could Also the lieutenant
(latin)

Kries kam gelaufen und riß seinem Kapitän in der
Kries came ran and ripped his Captain in the

letzten Sekunde noch den Strick aus der Hand. –
last second still the rope from the hand

Mit dieser Intervention aber hatte es folgende
With this intervention however had it following

Bewandtnis: in seiner Kammer oben hatte der Funker
explanation in his room above had the radio operator

Bengtson, während sein Kapitän mit dem Tode zuerst und
Bengtson while his Captain with the death first and

dann mit dem Kasino von Monte Carlo in der
then with the Casino from Monte Carlo in the

geschilderten Weise kokettierte, zuerst ein Telegramm und
described manner flirted first a telegram and

dann ein Telephonat des fürstlich labradorischen
then a phone of the princely Labrador

Konsulates in Monte Carlo aufgenommen. Beide Nachrichten
consulate in Monte Carlo taken up Both notices

waren einerseits dringlich, andererseits waren sie
were on the one hand urgent on the other hand were they

so, daß jede von ihnen den Kapitän (der doch schon
so that each from them the Captain who indeed already

seit fünf Uhr früh mit zehn Atmosphären Überdruck
since five hour early with ten atmosphere overpressure
o'clock

herumlief) zur Explosion bringen mußte. Mit einem
walked around to the explosion bring must With one

Wort: der Funker Bengtson (ein kleiner schwächlicher
word the radio operator Bengtson a little weak

Schwede aus Halmstatt) hatte es nicht gewagt, die beiden
Swede from Halmstatt had it not dared the both

Telegramme seinem Kapitän persönlich zu überbringen. Er
telegrams his Captain personally to deliver He

hatte den Leutnant Kries gebeten, diese Mission zu
had the lieutenant Kries asked this mission to

übernehmen – da war der Leutnant Kries
take over – there was the lieutenant Kries

gerade noch zur rechten Zeit gekommen. Maria,
just still at the right time come Maria

Fürstin-Witwe von Labrador, kam nicht erst heute abend,
princess-widow from Labrador came not first today evening

sondern schon heute früh an Bord: das stand im
but already today early on board that stood in the

Telegramm. Maria, Fürstin-Witwe von Labrador stand zur
telegram Maria princess-widow from Labrador stood at the

Stunde nebst Hofdame, Zofe und Lederkoffern auf der
hour next (to) court lady maid and leather cases on the

Landungsbrücke, war im Begriff, ins Motorboot zu
jetty was in the understanding in the motorboat to

steigen, würde in längstens zehn Minuten an Bord sein:
rise would in at the longest ten minutes on board be
mount

das war der Inhalt des vom Konsul übermittelten
that was the content of the from the consul transmitted

Telephonates. Der lange Cradock hätte, wenn der Leutnant
telephone call The tall Cradock had when the lieutenant

Kries nicht zur Zeit gekommen wäre, zugleich
Kries not at the time come would be at the same time

mit dem Kasino seine ehemalige Tänzerin, Reitkameradin
with the Casino his former dancer riding mate
dancepartner

und jetzige Landesherrin beschossen. –
and current sovereign shot at

Löwen, die einmal vorbeigesprungen sind, werden
Lions who once jumped over are become

bekanntlich unsicher. Löwen, die zum zweiten Male
as known unsure lions (they) who for the second time

vorbeispringen, bekommen (so wenigstens stelle ich's mir
jump past become so at least set I it myself
imagine

vor!) entweder schwere Depressionszustände oder hüllen
before either heavy states of depression or envelop

sich in die stoische Würde eines Löwen, gegen
themselves in the stoic worthyness of a lion against

den sich endgültig das Schicksal erklärt hat. Die
which himself finally the fate declared has The

Reaktion des Kapitäns, der sich zum zweiten Male
reaction of the captain who himself for the second time

gehemmt sah in seiner Schießfreudigkeit, war weit weniger
inhibited saw in his easy shooting was far less

stark, als Bengtson befürchtet hatte. Der Cradock las die
strong as Bengtson feared had The Cradock read the

beiden Zettel, steckte sie in den Ärmel und pfiff leise
both notes stuck them in the sleeves and whistled softly

vor sich hin. Er für sein Teil wußte ganz genau,
before himself away He for his part knew completely exactly

was hier noch zu tun war: da es dieser Witwe von
what here still to do was there it this widow from

Labrador nun einmal gefiel, zwölf Stunden früher an Bord
Labrador now once pleased twelve hours before on board

zu kommen, so konnte man nicht schießen, mußte ohne
to come so could one not shoot must without

Donner, Blitz und Herostratenruhm als simpler
thunder lightning and herostate glory as simpler

Defraudant ins Zuchthaus marschieren. Marschierte man
fraud in the penitentiary march Walked one

aber ins Zuchthaus, so wollte man es nicht als armer
however in the penitentiary so wanted one it not as poor

Sünder tun. Sondern so, daß ganz Europa über den
sinner do However so that complete Europe over the
                                    all of

Zuchthäusler Cradock lachte. Kurz und gut: der Kapitän,
prisoners Cradock laughed Short and good the Captain

der sich für diesen Fall seinen ganz bestimmten Plan
who himself for this case his complete determined plan

zurechtgelegt hatte, tobte nicht, sondern begann den
laid out had raved not but began the

Sussexmarsch zu pfeifen. Dann sagte er dem Leutnant
Sussex march to whistle Then said he (to) the lieutenant

Kries, daß er Williams rufen solle. –
Kries that he Williams call should

Der Leutnant Williams, der die ganze Zeit auf der Brücke
The lieutenant Williams who the whole time on the bridge

gestanden und die drei Rauchsäulen im Westen
stood and the three columns of smoke in the West

beobachtet hatte, wollte eben seinem Kapitän melden, daß
observed had wanted just his Captain report that

es tatsächlich der Franzose sei. Der kleine Williams, der
it indeed the Frenchman be The little Williams who
French ship was

auf diese Weise schon von Donner und Blitz, von
on this manner already from thunder and lightning from

Heldengröße und Nelsontod geträumt hatte, fiel aus allen
hero size and Nelson-death dreamed had fell from all

Himmeln, als er vor seinem Kapitän stand. Nach dem
heaven as he before his Captain stood To the

»Sadi Carnot« nämlich fragte der Cradock überhaupt nicht
Sadi Carnot namely asked the Cradock at all not

mehr – er sagte nur, daß Ihre Hoheit, die
(any)more – he said only that her highness the

Fürstin-Witwe, nebst Gräfin Hensbarrow und Zofe Susan
princess-widow next (to) countess Hensbarrow and maid Susan

schon heute früh an Bord käme. Der kleine Williams
already today early on board would come The little Williams

ließ den Kopf hängen. Kein Heldentod und kein
let the head hang No hero death and no

Nelsonruhm! Sondern nur drei Weiber und fünf
Nelson glory But only three women and five

Lederkoffer. »Bitte Sie sehr«, sagte der Cradock, »die
leather suitcases Ask you very (much) said the Cradock the

Damen am Fallreep zu empfangen.« »Werden wir«, sagte
ladies at the gangway to receive Will we said

der Cradock, »dafür sorgen, daß von der Mannschaft,
the Cradock therefor worry that from the team
take care

wenn die Damen kommen, niemand an Deck ist.« Und mit
when the ladies come nobody on deck is And with

diesem Befehl (der noch zweimal wiederholt wurde und
this order that still twice repeated became and

somit wohl sehr wichtig war) drehte sich der
consequently well very important was turned himself the

Kapitän um und ging, Hände in den Taschen und noch
Captain around and went Hands in the pockets and still

immer den Sussexmarsch pfeifend, in sein Logis. Er, der
always the Sussex march whistling In his cabin He the

lange Cradock, wußte natürlich sehr genau, weswegen er
tall Cradock knew of course very precisely For what he

auf alles pfiff, und was er sonst noch tat. Den
on everything whistled and what he otherwise still did The

armen Williams aber ließ er jedenfalls als gebrochenen
poor Williams however let he anyhow as broken

Mann und in dem festen Glauben zurück, daß der Kapitän
man and in the firm believe back that the Captain

plötzlich in geistige Umnachtung versunken sei ...
suddenly in spiritual night sunk be
derangement was

Die nächsten Minuten aber, sie fielen geradezu grausam
The next minutes however they fell almost horrible

her über die Nerven des armen Williams. Von Backbord
away over the nerves of the poor Williams From port

kam der »Sadi Carnot«, von Steuerbord kam die
came the Sadi Carnot from starboard came the

»grundgütige Landesmutter«, in der Mitte war ein Schiff,
ground-goody country mother in the middle was a ship
principal kind mother of the nation

dessen Kapitän plötzlich geisteskrank geworden, dessen
whose Captain suddenly insane become whose

Mannschaft um fünf Uhr mit Krieg und Kriegsgeschrei
team for five hour with war and war cries
at o'clock

aus dem Bett geholt war und nun begreiflicherweise nicht
from the bed fetched was and now understandably not

wußte, was das alles eigentlich sollte.
knew what that everything actually should (mean)

Inzwischen und ringsum pfiff, fluchte, schrie und
In the meantime and all around whistled swore cried and

fragte es. Auf der Back maulten sie, daß sie, die nun
asked it On the back moaned they that they who now

zwei Stunden herumgestanden waren und sich schon
two hours stood around were and themselves already

auf ein schönes Scharfschießen gefreut hatten, nun
on a beautiful sharpshooting look forward had now

mit einem Mal unter Deck hinter verblendete Fenster
with one turn under deck behind blinded windows
at once

sollten. Achtern gab es dieser Frage wegen zwischen
should (go) Aft gave it this question because of between

dem Maat Scott und den Leuten eine regelrechte Keilerei,
the mate Scott and the people a downright boating

auf dem Batteriedeck waren sie im Begriffe, die
on the battery cover were they in the understanding the

Kartuschen verkehrt zu verstauen, und als er eben diesem
cartridges wrong to stow away and as he just this

Unfug ein Ende gemacht hatte, da kam zu ihm auf
nonsense an end made had there came to him on

die Brücke eine Ordonnanz gelaufen und meldete, daß der
the bridge an orderly ran and reported that the

Direktor Samanon in seinem Gefängnis zu ersticken
director Samanon in his jail to suffocate

drohe und zu toben anfange. Der Leutnant Williams
threaten(ed) and to rage start(ed) The lieutenant Williams

(äußerlich noch ziemlich in Form, innerlich schon
outwardly still rather in form internally already

sanatoriumsreif) machte kurzen Prozeß und ließ dem
sanatorium-ready made short process and let the

Direktor Samanon bestellen, daß er ihn sofort in die
director Samanon order that he him immediately in the

Kesselfeuer werde stecken lassen, wenn er nicht Ruhe
boiler fire would stick let when he not rest quiet

gäbe. Und als auch dieser Zwischenfall erledigt war, da
gave was And as also this incident finished was there

kam etwas, was dem armen Jungen den Rest gab ...
came something what the poor boy the rest gave

Der Doktor Crofts kam auf die Brücke. Der Doktor hatte
The doctor Crofts came on the bridge The doctor had

auch jetzt, in diesem Irrenhausmilieu, die »Times« in
also now in this madhouse environment the Times in

der Hand und war überhaupt ein Mann, der sich für
the hand and was at all a man who himself for

diesen Hexenkessel nur so ganz beiläufig interessierte.
this witch cauldron only so completely casually interested

Ganz beiläufig sagte der Doktor, daß außenbords
Completely casually said the doctor that outboard

schon das Boot mit Ihrer Hoheit zu sehen sei, und daß
already the boat with her highness to see be was and that

es in spätestens drei Minuten unten am Fallreep sein
it in no later than three minutes under at the gangway be

werde. Da war der kleine Williams fertig, und da lief
would There was the little Williams ready and there ran

er   vor   das   Logis   des   Kapitäns   und   trommelte   gegen
he   before   the   cabin   of the   captain   and   drummed   against
       to

die   Tür   und   schrie,   daß   er   noch   verrückt   werde   auf
the   door   and   cried   that   he   still   crazy   became   on

diesem   Schiff   und   dringend   um   Ablösung   bitte.   Da   ging
this   ship   and   urgent   for   relieve   ask(ed)   There   went

die   Tür   auf,   und   der   Cradock   kam   heraus.
the   door   on   and   the   Cradock   came   out
       open

Daß   der   Kapitän   wirklich   verrückt   geworden   war,   daran
That   the   Captain   really   crazy   become   was   there-on
                                               had

konnte   nun   leider   nicht   mehr   gezweifelt   werden.
could   now   unfortunately   not   (any)more   doubted   become

Der   Kapitän   trug   jetzt   oben   den   ihm   zukommenden
The   Captain   carried   now   above   the   him   coming

goldbetreßten   Galazweispitz   und   unten   die   gleichfalls
gold-pressed   gala-two-tip (hat)   and   under   the   also

zum   Parade-Anzug   gehörenden   hohen   Lackstiefel.
to the   parade suit   belonging   high   patent leather boots

Was   aber   in   der   Mitte   saß,   das   war   ein   bis   zu   den
What   hoever   in   the   middle   sat   that   was   a   until   to   the

Knien   reichender   alter   Gummimantel;   und   was   gleich
knees   reaching   old   rubber jacket   and   what   immediately

unter   diesem   Gummimantel   zu   sehen   war,   als   ein
under   this   rubber jacket   to   see   was   as   an

indiskreter Windstoß ihn lüftete, das war einfach
indiscreet gust of wind him aired that was simply

unfaßbar. Kopfschuß und Katastrophe war es, und der
incomprehensible Headshot and catastrophe was it and the

Leutnant Williams, selbst schwer erschüttert in seinem
lieutenant Williams himself heavy shocked in his

Gleichgewicht, wußte nicht, ob er darüber lachen oder
balance knew not whether he about it laugh or

weinen sollte. In diesem Augenblick konnte man unten
cry should In this moment could one under

am Fallreep schon den Motor des anlegenden Bootes
at the gangway already the engine of the on-laying boat
                                              boarding

rumoren hören.
rumble hear

Der Cradock aber tat nun wirklich auch alles, um
The Cradock however did now really also everything for

die Diagnose »plötzlich verrückt geworden« sicherzustellen.
the diagnosis suddenly crazy become to ensure

»Schätze«, schrie der Cradock, »daß Sie, Williams, über
(I) guess cried the Cradock that you Williams over

alles unterrichtet sind ... hoffe, Sie verstehen, daß mir
everything informed are (I) hope you understand that me

jetzt alles gleichgültig ist, und daß Europa wenigstens
now everything indifferent is and that Europe at least

lachen soll.« Das schrie der Cradock.
laugh should That cried the Cradock

Setzte wohl voraus, daß der Leutnant Williams die
Set well in front that the lieutenant Williams the

Privilegien der Cradocks kannte ...
privileges of the Cradocks knew

Nichts kannte der Leutnant Williams. War über nichts
Nothing knew the lieutenant Williams Was about nothing

unterrichtet. Wußte nur, daß der Kapitän verrückt
informed Knew only that the Captain crazy

geworden war, hörte nun schon (und das hatte gerade
become was heard now already and that had just

noch gefehlt!) unten auf dem Fallreep eine Frauenstimme,
still missed under on the gangway a female voice

lugte über die Reling und sah eine einzelne Dame im
peeked over the railing and saw a single lady in the

Reisekleid heraufkommen.
travel dress come up

Maria, regierende Fürstin-Witwe von Labrador. Da
Maria ruling princess-widow from Labrador There

beschloß er, zu retirieren.
decided he to retire

Wie er sich aber umdrehte, da sah er noch den
As he himself but turned around there saw he still the

Kapitän zum Fallreep gehen, und wie der Cradock dort
Captain to the gangway go and as the Cradock there

sich aufstellte, war er schuld, daß der arme Williams
himself up-set was he guilty that the poor Williams
straightened up

in seinem Kampf zwischen Lachen und einer anderen
in his fight between laughing and an other

Gefühlsäußerung endgültig sich für einen Lachkrampf
expression of emotion finally himself for a laughing fit

entschied.
decided

Der Kapitän nämlich, wie er da am Fallreep stand,
The Captain namely as he there at the gangway stood

hatte nun den Gummimantel fallen lassen. Er stand und
had now the rubber jacket fall let He stood and

hatte oben einen goldbetreßten Schiffhut. Und unten lange
had above a gold-pressed ship hat and under long

Lackstiefel. Und in der Mitte nichts, als einen
patent leather boots And in the middle nothing as a

dunkelblau- und weißgestreiften Badeanzug.
dark blue and striped white swimsuit

Und über dem Badeanzug um den Leib einen langen
And over the swimsuit around the body a long

Schleppsäbel.
drag saber
saber

Der kleine Williams wußte wirklich nichts von dem alten,
The little Williams knew really nothing from the old

einst im Kampfe mit der Jungfrau von Orleans
once in the fight with the maiden from Orleans

erworbenen Privileg der Cradocks. Er wußte nichts
acquired privilege of the Cradocks He knew nothing

davon und saß nun hinter der Hütte auf einer
there-from and sat now behind the Hut on a

Schlauchwinde und lachte.
hose winch and laughed

Einen entsetzlichen Lachkrampf, der gar kein Ende
A terrible laughing fit which at all no end

nehmen wollte.
take wanted

Der Schleppsäbel zum Badeanzug: das war das
The drag saber to the swimsuit that was the
saber with the

Allerschlimmste gewesen ...
worst been

Kapitel VI

Von Maria, Fürstin von Labrador, habe ich nachträglich zu
Of Maria queen from Labrador have I afterwards to

berichten, daß sie seit der Trennung von Cradock nicht
report that she since the separation from Cradock not

gerade angenehme Stunden verlebt hatte.
just pleasant hours spent had

So nämlich stand es doch nun einmal, daß sie selbst
So namely stood it indeed now once that she self
was well

sich schuldig fühlen mußte.
herself guilty feel must

Sie war es gewesen, um derentwillen der Cradock sich
She was it been for whose sake the Cradock himself
had

in diese unmögliche Perlen- und Schiffskassenaffäre
in this impossible Pearls and ship cash affair

gestürzt hatte ... sie war es gewesen, die ihn aus
rushed had she was it been who him out (of)
had

verletzter Eitelkeit in sein wahnsinniges Spiel und in den
injured vanity in his insane play and in the

Konflikt mit der Bank gehetzt hatte. Schoß er aber
conflict with the bank rushed had Shot he however

wirklich, so war der internationale Skandal da, so war sie
really so was the international scandal there so was she

es, die (allem Schuldgefühl zum Trotz) ihren alten
it who all guilt -to the- despite her old

Freund fallen lassen mußte. Seit dem allerersten Licht
friend fall let must Since the very first light

hatte sie mit dem Fernglase am Fenster gestanden, hatte
had she with the binoculars at the window stood had

das kleine Schiff beobachtet und allerlei verzweifelte
the little ship observed and all kinds of despaired

Orakel befragt, ob alles am Ende noch gut
oracle questioned whether everything at the end still good

ausgehen könne. Es war wirklich keine angenehme
go out could It was really no pleasant

Viertelstunde gewesen, die sie an diesem Morgen
quarter of an hour been which she on this morning

gegen sieben Uhr erlebt hatte ...
against seven hour experienced had

Wirkliche Hoffnung aber war in ihr tapferes Herz erst
Real hope however was in her brave heart first

eingezogen, als sie – in der allerkritischsten Minute – das
moved in as she – in the most critical minute – the

Boot des Direktors Samanon gesehen hatte.
boat of the director Samanon seen had

255

Sofort   hatte   sie   (zu   einer   gänzlich   unmöglichen
Immediately had   she   to   a   completely impossible
                                   at

Stunde!) ihren Konsul herausgeklingelt, und   sofort   war
hour   her   consul rang out (of bed) and   immediately was

jenes Telephonat arrangiert worden, das dann der Leutnant
that   phone   arranged   become   that then the lieutenant

Kries gerade in der allerletzten Sekunde noch dem Kapitän
Kries just   in the very last   second   still the Captain

überbracht hatte. Dann war sie pleine chasse   zur
brought   had   Then was she full   hunt   to the
                                            quickly

Landungsbrücke gefahren, hatte (die alte Violet und die
jetty   driven   had   the   old   Violet and the

Zofe schliefen natürlich noch) das erste beste Motorboot
maid slept   of course still the first best   motorboat

genommen. Ohne Gepäck und nur mit einer Handtasche,
taken   Without bagage and only with a   handbag

in der   die Maske von   gestern   und das ominöse
in which the mask   from yesterday and the ominous

Perlenkollier lagen. Sieben Uhr   und dreiunddreißig Minuten
pearl necklace lay   Seven   hour and thirty three   minutes
                               o'clock

war es, als sie, auf das Schlimmste und Allertollste gefaßt,
was it   as   she   on   the worst   and very great   taken
                                                              prepared

das Fallreep ihres Schiffes betrat. –
the gangway   of her ship   entered

Bewohner des europäischen Kontinents werden es
Residents of the European continent become it

vielleicht ohne weiteres verstehen, daß und weswegen
perhaps without additional understand that and for what

der oben geschilderte, etwas kuriose Empfang durch
the above described somewhat curious reception through
by

ihren Kapitän der Mary nicht so überraschend kam.
her Captain the Mary not so surprised came
as a surprise

Es ist, wie es ist: wird in London der Leichtmatrose James
It is as it is will in London the light sailor James

Taylor wegen öffentlicher Trunkenheit zur Geldstrafe
Taylor because of public drunkenness to the fine

von anderthalb Guineen verurteilt, so trägt bekanntlich
from one and a half guineas sentenced so carries as known

der das Urteil verkündende Richter eine Allongeperücke.
the the judgement proclaiming judge a lengthened wig

Will ich … etwa in einer leidlich modernen englischen
Want I somewhat in a tolerable modern English

Stadt wie Capetown … ein Taxi haben, so fährt jene »Cab«
city as capetown a taxi have so drives that cab

genannte, auf Räder gesetzte Rokokosänfte vor. Und
called on wheels set rococo-softness before And

wenn das Oberhaus dem
when the upper house the

Unterhaus Akten über Braugerstenzölle zuschickt, so
house files over malting barley tariffs sends so

überbringt nach jahrhundertealtem Brauch diese Akten ein
delivers after century old usage these files a

rotbefrackter Diener in Perücke und Degen, fragt vorher
red-stained servant in wig and sword asks before

bei dem Pförtner des Unterhauses an, ob er
at the usher of the house on whether he

eintreten dürfe, fragt und erhält seinen Bescheid
in-step might asks and receives his information
occur

vorgeschriebenerweise in einem Englisch, das zur Zeit
mandatory in an English that at the time

Richards III. schon so geklungen haben mag, wie heute
(of) Richard III already so sounded have may as today

unseren Ohren das Wessobrunner Gebet oder die
our ears the Wessobrunner prayer or the

Merseburger Zaubersprüche klingen würden.
Merseburger spells sound would

England ist eben konservativer als der Kontinent. Und
England is just more conservative as the continent And
than

alte Privilegien (gingen sie selbst um eine Audienz in
old privileges went they even for a audience in
were

Unterhosen) sind für ein englisches Hirn niemals Chimären.
underpants are for an English brain never chimeras

Außerdem aber hatte im vorliegenden Fall ja schon
In addition however had in the present case yes already

die alte Violet warnend an das alte Recht der Cradocks
the old Violet warning on the old right of the Cradocks

erinnert. Und drittens war einem Manne, der in einem
reminded And thirdly was a man who in a

siamesischen Tempel mit Baldriantropfen heilige Katzen
siamese temple with valerian drops holy cats

närrisch gemacht hatte, alles zuzutrauen. Item: die
foolish made had everything to entrust Also the
(latin)

Hoheit von Labrador war gar nicht so überrascht. Sie
highness from Labrador was at all not so surprised She

war eben auf alles gefaßt und war, was ja nur
was just on everything taken and was what yes only
for prepared

gebilligt werden kann, ihrerseits entschlossen, ihre
approved become can in turn decided her

Würde zu wahren. –
worthiness to keep
respect

Und nun war es so weit. Sie war die Ruhe selbst – der
And now was it so far She was the rest herself – the
calmness

Cradock, in Badeanzug, Lackstiefeln und Galahut
Cradock in swimsuit lacquered leather boots and gala hat

vor seiner ehemaligen Tänzerin stehend,
before his former dancer standing
dancepartner

stutzte. Die Frau, die da gekommen war, war eine
stopped short The woman who there come was was a

schöne und blühende Frau … war alles andere als
beautiful and flowering woman was everything other as

»grundgütige Landesmutter« und »freudlose Witwe«, und
ground-goody / principal kind country mother / mother of the nation and joyless widow and

merkwürdig bekannt waren ihm Figur und Stimme, und
strange known were him figure and voice and

seltsame Gedanken wollten kommen und ihn verwirren
strange thoughts wanted come and him confuse

im entscheidenden Augenblick. Daß hier Haltung und
in the decisive moment That here stature and

Frechheit seine einzigen Waffen waren, wußte er natürlich,
impudence his single weapons were knew he of course

und legte die Hand an den Hut und meldete, daß die
and put the hand on the hat and reported that the

ganze Mannschaft unter Deck sei. Dann begann er für sein
whole team under deck be Then began he for his

Leben zu fechten …
life to fight

»Mache«, sagte der Cradock, »wenn ich in diesem Anzug
Make said the Cradock if I in this suit

vor Ew. Hoheit erscheine, von einem verbrieften
before et. highness appear from a securitized
(ewige: eternal)

und Ew. Hoheit wohl bekannten Privileg
and et. (ewige: eternal) highness well acquaintances privilege

Gebrauch ...«
use

»Sparen Sie sich das!«
Save you yourself that

»Bitte unter dieser Voraussetzung Ew. Hoheit um
Sorry under this requirement et. (ewige: eternal) highness for

Gnade. Habe die Kasse dieses Schiffes unterschlagen.
mercy Have the cash register of this ship embezzled

Habe sie gebraucht, um einen Perlenschmuck für eine
Have it used for a pearl jewelry for a

hübsche Kokotte ...« –
pretty flirt

»Hübsche Kokotte?«
Pretty flirt

»Hübsche Kokotte zu kaufen.« So weit war es. Der
Pretty flirt to buy So far was it The

entscheidende Augenblick. Da nahm sie aus der Tasche
decisive moment There took she from the pocket

das Perlenhalsband. »Die Kokotte, Kapitän Cradock, gibt
the pearl collar The flirt Captain Cradock gives

Ihnen das Kollier zurück.« Dann nahm sie die Maske.
you the necklace back Then took she the mask

»Guten Tag, Kapitän Cradock.« Da war es, als das große
Good day Captain Cradock There was it as the great

Erkennen über ihn gekommen war, geschehen um seine
recognizing over him come was happened for his
done with

kühle Frechheit und um den Plan, Europa zum Lachen zu
cool impudence and for the plan Europe to the laughing to

bringen ...
bring

Aufgebaut hatte er diesen Plan auf der stillschweigenden
Built up had he this plan on the tacit

Voraussetzung, daß wirklich eine verbitterte Frau, eine
requirement that really an embittered woman a

»freudlose Witwe« (böser ältlicher Mann in Weiberröcken
joyless widow angry elderly man in women skirts

sozusagen ...) an Bord kommen werde.
so to speak on board come will

Gekommen war statt dessen eine schöne Frau, die man
Come was instead of that a beautiful woman who one

vor drei Stunden noch geküßt hatte; und man kann
before three hours still kissed had and one can

sich als Mann (wofern man unverbildete Instinkte hat)
himself as man in so far one uneducated instinct has

nicht lächerlich machen vor einer Frau, die man vor
not ridiculous make before a woman the one before

drei Stunden noch geküßt hat. Da man aber ein
three hours still kissed has There one however a

ritterlicher und wohlerzogener Mann war und diese
chivalrous and educated man was and this

Ritterlichkeit ihm jedes Erwähnen dieser Küsse für diesen
chivalry him each mention of these kisses for this

Augenblick verbot, so war für ihn eben das Spiel
moment prohibited so was for him just the play

verloren: Zusammenbruch, Blamage, Vernichtung.
lost Collapse embarrassment destruction

Er nahm seinen Gummimantel und legte die Hand an den
He took his rubber jacket and put the hand on the

Hut und bat um die Erlaubnis, sich entfernen zu
hat and bade for the permission himself distance to

dürfen.
may

Sie sah ihn streng an. Nichts mehr von
She saw him strict on Nothing (any)more from
   looked   in the face

»Madame« und »Domino«. Daß er sich als arretiert zu
madame and domino That he himself as locked to

betrachten und alles weitere in seiner Kabine zu
regard and everything further in his cabin to

erwarten habe, sagte die Hoheit von Labrador. Damit
expect have said the highness from Labrador There-with

drehte sie sich ungnädig ab und entließ ihn.
turned she herself merciless off and let go him

Dann freilich, als sie allein war, fühlte sie, daß es zu Ende
Then indeed as she alone was felt she that it to end

ging mit ihren Kräften. Sie setzte sich nieder, stützte
went with her powers She set himself down supported

den Kopf in die Hand, hätte am liebsten weinen mögen.
the head in the hand had at the ratherest cry may

Sie weinte nicht. Sie war nur eben sehr ratlos. Sie hörte
She cried not She was only just much at a loss She heard

wieder Schritte kommen und bemühte sich um gute
again steps come and occupied himself for good

Haltung. Als sie aber die Augen aufhob, da war
stature As she however the eyes picked up there was

jemand gekommen, der in diesem Falle wohl als rettender
someone come who in this case well as saving

Engel angesehen werden konnte. Der Doktor Crofts kam.
angel watched become could The doctor Crofts came

Regierende Häupter, soviel ihrer noch existieren in
Ruling heads so much of them still exist in

Europa, haben in den letzten zehn Jahren ziemlich seltsame
Europe have in the last ten years rather strange

Audienzen erteilt – ich glaube, daß diese
audiences granted – I believe that this

Begegnung zwischen der Fürstin-Witwe von Labrador und
encounter between the princess-widow from Labrador and

dem Doktor Crofts doch so ziemlich die seltsamste
the doctor Crofts indeed so rather the strangest

gewesen ist. Er war ein alter schottischer Herr mit
been is He was an old scottish gentleman with
had

ewiger Angst vor Erkältungen, hatte sich eben frisch
everlasting fear before colds had himself just freshly

rasiert und hatte nun (auf diese Begegnung war er
shaved and had now on this encounter was he

vorläufig wohl nicht gefaßt gewesen) zum Schutz gegen
for now well not taken been to the protection against

die Morgenbrise ein rotes Tuch um den Kopf gebunden.
the morning breeze a red cloth for the head bound

Er sah somit wie eine alte Frau aus, hustete, daß
He saw consequently as an old woman -out- coughed that
looked

es wie ein Eisenbahnunglück klang, und man kann ja
it like a railway accident sounded and one can yes
indeed

wohl auch sonst von ihm sagen, daß er die typische
well also otherwise from him say that he the typical

Ritterlichkeit des Briten alter Observanz unter ziemlich
chivalry of the British old observance under rather

rauhen Formen verbarg.
rough forms hid

Das aber hatte die Mary schon am Tage zuvor
That however had the Mary already at the day before

erkannt: daß er, der alte einsame Schiffsdoktor, seinen
recognized that he the old lonely ship doctor his

etwas leicht konstruierten Kapitän im Grunde als
somewhat easy constructed Captain in the ground as

verlorenen Sohn behandelte. Daß man gut aufgehoben sein
lost son treated That one good lifted up be

mußte, wenn man sein Herz ausschütten konnte bei dem
must when one his heart pour out could at the

alten Crofts. Item: was sich hier abspielte, das war nicht
old Crofts Also what himself here played that was not
(latin)

eine Unterredung von Hoheit und Untertan. Es war eine
a conversation from highness and subject It was a

Unterredung zwischen Beichtvater und Beichtkind. Nicht
conversation between confessor and confessing person Not

in den Formen der katholischen Kirche. Sondern in den
in the forms of the catholic church But in the

Formen eines alten Mannes, der keine Kinder hat und
forms of an old man who no children has and

manchmal doch so tut, als habe er welche: ja, aber ich
sometimes indeed so does as has he some yes but I
acts

will den Dingen nicht vorgreifen.
want the things not anticipate

»Doktor ...«
Doctor

»Ihre Hoheit ...«
Your highness

Es ging ihr so, wie es einem immer geht, wenn man in
It went her so as it one always goes when one in

schwieriger Situation sich recht zusammengenommen hat
(a) difficult situation oneself right really taken together has

und dann mit einem Male Rettung kommen sieht: die
and then with one time rescue come sees the
at

Nerven begannen zu versagen und trieben ihr die Tränen
nerves began to fail and drove her the tears

in die Augen.
in the eyes

Er seinerseits sagte sich, daß ein Schiffsdeck kein
He in turn said himself that a ship deck no

passender Aufenthaltsort ist für weinende Fürstinnen, und
appropriate abode is for crying princesses and

reichte ihr den Arm. Gleich darauf saß dann die
reached her the arm Immediately thereupon sat then the
handed

regierende Fürstin-Witwe Maria von Labrador in der
ruling princess-widow Maria from Labrador in the

Kabine des Marinearztes erster Klasse Wilbour Crofts. In
cabin of the marine doctor first class Wilbour Crofts In

einem Raum, den seit mindestens einem Jahrzehnt keine
a space that since at least a decade no

Frau betreten hatte. Auf einem Sofa, gegen das die
woman entered had On a sofa against which the

Granitplatten des Sinaigebirges schwellende Polster sein
granite slabs of the sinai mountains swelling pads be
hills

mochten. Zwischen Sammlungen von indianischen Totems
might Between collections from native american totems

und Negerfetischen, deren Anblick für Damenaugen nicht
and negro fetishes whose sight for lady eyes not

durchweg schicklich war. Unter der Photographie einer
throughout chic was Under the photograph a
always

noch in Aberdeen lebenden alten und schon ganz
still in Aberdeen living old and already completely

vertrockneten Crofts-Schwester, die so ziemlich die einzige
dried up Crofts sister who so rather the only

menschliche Brücke zwischen dem alten einsamen Herrn
human bridge between the old lonely gentleman

und dem Leben darstellte.
and the life represented

Von ihrer Seite aber begann es so, wie es beginnen
From her side however began it so as it begin

mußte. Mit Selbstanklagen und mit der notwendigerweise
must with self-accusation and with the necessarily

dazugehörenden Vorgeschichte. Daß sie Cradock doch
associated *prehistory* *That* *she* *Cradock* *indeed*

schon in London vor ihrer Ehe gekannt, daß sie
already *in* *London* *before* *her* *marriage* *known* *that* *she*

damals ... (das weitere brauchte, da der alte Herr einen
back then *the* *further* *needed* *there* *the* *old* *Mr* *a*

furchtbaren Hustenanfall bekam, nicht gesagt zu werden) ...
terrible *coughing attack* *got* *not* *said* *to* *become*

Daß sie Cradock volle zehn Jahre nicht gesehen, daß sie
That *she* *Cradock* *(a) full* *ten* *years* *not* *seen (had)* *that* *she*

sich unbändig gefreut habe auf dieses
herself *overwhelmingly* *looked forward* *have* *on* *this*
had

Wiedersehen, und daß sie es dann gewesen sei, die ihn
seeing again *and* *that* *she* *it* *then* *been* *be* *that* *him*
had

hineingehetzt habe in alle diese Wirrnisse.
rushed in *have* *in* *all* *this* *confusion*
had

In diesen unmöglichen Perlenkauf.
In *this* *impossible* *pearl purchase*

In dieses noch unmöglichere Spiel.
In *this* *still* *more impossible* *play*

Aus verletzter Eitelkeit.
From *injured* *vanity*

Weil es unerträglich war, daß ein Mann so rasch
Because *it* *unbearable* *was* *that* *a* *man* *so* *quickly*

vergessen konnte. Weil man doch nicht »freudlose
forget could Because one indeed not joyless

Witwe« sagte zu einer einst geliebten Frau. Weil man
widow said to a once beloved woman Because one

doch geschenkte Brautschleier nicht als Glückstalismane in
indeed given bridal veils not as lucky talismans in

den linken Schuh steckte ...
the left shoe stuck

Deswegen.
Because of that

Durch ihre Schuld.
Through her guilt

Ein internationaler Skandal.
An international scandal

Eine Situation, die sie jetzt womöglich nur durch die
A situation that she now possibly only through the

Bestrafung desjenigen Mannes lösen könne, den sie selbst
punishment of that man solve could that she herself

hineingehetzt habe. Eine Situation, in der sie sofortige
rushed in have A situation in which she instant
had

Hilfe brauche. An dieser Stelle wurden sie, da draußen
help need On this spot became she there outside
needed since

jemand stark an die Tür pochte, unterbrochen.
someone strong on the door knocked interrupted
loud

Der Leutnant Williams stand draußen und fragte nach dem
The lieutenant Williams stood outside and asked after the
                                                    for

Kapitän. Der Doktor hinter der Tür antwortete, daß der
Captain The doctor behind the door answered that the

Kapitän leider verstorben sei und eben begraben
Captain unfortunately deceased be and just buried
                            was

werde. Der Leutnant Williams sagte, daß er eine wichtige
became The lieutenant Williams said that he an important

Meldung habe vom »Sadi Carnot«. Der Doktor schrie,
notice have from the Sadi Carnot The doctor cried
       had

daß er nichts wisse vom »Sadi Carnot«. Daß der
that he nothing knew from the Sadi Carnot That the

Leutnant Williams mit oder ohne »Sadi Carnot« in die
lieutenant Williams with or without Sadi Carnot in the

Hölle fahren solle. Daß er, Crofts, eigenhändig jeden
hell drive should That he Crofts with his own hands everyone

erschießen werde, der noch einmal vom »Sadi Carnot«
shoot will who still once from the Sadi Carnot

rede. Mit diesem Bescheide entfernte sich der Leutnant
speak With this decision withdrew himself the lieutenant

Williams. Und schlimm war nur, daß jetzt die Hoheit nun
Williams And bad was only that now the highness now

durchaus wissen wollte, wer dieser »Sadi Carnot« war ...
throughout know wanted who this Sadi Carnot was
at all

Es	hatte	ja	doch	keinen	Sinn,	ihr	die	Wahrheit
It	had	yes	indeed	no	use	her	the	truth

vorzuenthalten.	Er	sagte	ihr	alles.		Daß	die	Bank	den
to withhold	He	told	her	everything		That	the	bank	the

Franzosen	gerufen	hatte.	Daß	der	Franzose	unterwegs	war,
Frenchman	called	had	That	the	Franchman	on the way	was

daß	der	Direktor	Samanon	im	Kohlenbunker	saß.	Daß
that	the	director	Samanon	in the	coal bunker	sat	That

alles,	auch	für	sie	selbst,	noch	viel,	viel	schlimmer
everything	also	for	her	self	still	much	much	worse

stand,	als	sie's	geglaubt	hatte.	Da	sprang	sie	auf.
stood	as	she it	believed	had	There	jumped	she	up

Es	gibt,	wenn	die	Fürsten	Frauen	sind,	solch	plötzliche
It	gives	when	the	royals	women	are	such	sudden

Temperaturstürze.	Sie	wußte	plötzlich	nichts	mehr	von
drops in temperature	She	knew	suddenly	nothing	(any)more	of

eigener	Schuld	und	Selbstbezichtigung.	Sie	war	mit	einem
own	guilt	and	self-accusation	She	was	with	one

Male	eine	kleine	Renaissancefürstin,	die	unbedenklich	ihre
time	a	little	renaissance princess	who	without thought	her

Freunde	opferte,	wenn	die	Freunde	Gefahr	brachten	über
friends	sacrificed	when	the	friends	danger	brought	over

den	Staat.
the	country

»Sie werden«, sagte Maria, die Fürstin-Witwe von Labrador,
You will said Maria the princess-widow from Labrador

»sofort den Ersten Offizier rufen und den Kapitän
right away the first officer call and the Captain

Cradock verhaften lassen.«
Cradock arrest let

»Es gibt«, sagte nachdenklich der Doktor Crofts, »im
It gives said thoughtful the doctor Crofts in the

Pazifik auf den Weihnachtsinseln gewisse Stämme, wo die
pacific on the Christmas islands certain tribes where the

Häuptlinge Weiber sind ...«
chiefs women are

»Sind Sie wahnsinnig?« schrie die Hoheit.
Are you insane cried the highness

»O nein«, sagte ernst der alte Doktor, »sie sind nicht
Oh no said serious the old doctor you are not

weiter wahnsinnig. Es sind nur sehr herrschsüchtige
further insane It/They are only very domineering

Weiber, die ihre Freunde zuerst zu Ministern machen und
women who her friends first to ministers make and

dann hinrichten lassen.« Da war es vorbei mit
then execute let There was it past with

Renaissance und Machiavell. Sie schob wie ein Kind die
renaissance and Machiavell She pushed as a child the

Unterlippe vor und fing bitterlich zu weinen an. So
bottom lip before and caught bitterly to cry -on- So
started

tat der alte Doktor das, was hier das Nächstliegende war.
did the old doctor that what here the closest was

Ging zu ihr und strich ihr über das Haar. »Aber«, sagte
Went to her and brushed her over the hair But said

etwas rätselhaft Wilbour Crofts, »es ist nicht so
something enigmatic Wilbour Crofts it is not so

schlimm damit. Es geht manchmal auch ohne
bad there-with It goes sometimes also without

Hinrichtung ab.« Und mit diesem etwas dunklen
execution off And with this somewhat dark

Trost ließ er sie vorerst einmal allein.
consolation let he her before first once alone
first

Wußte, daß er augenblicklich der einzige vernünftige
(He) knew that he immediately the only reasonable

Mann an Bord war. Wußte, daß die Pflicht zu helfen auf
man on board was (He) knew that the duty to help on

ihm lag. Ging hinaus und drehte ganz leise, um sie
him lay (He) went out and turned completely softly for her

nicht zu kränken, den Schlüssel um. Hatte so das
not to offend the key around (He) had so the

Gefühl eines Vogelzüchters, dem bis auf einen alle seine
feeling of a bird breeder who until on one all his

Vögel ausgekommen sind, und der nun wenigstens den
birds come out are and who now at least the
have

schönen bunten Wellensittich in Sicherheit hat.
beautiful colorful budgie in security has

Kapitel VII

Was das aber nun werden und wie es noch
What that however now become (would) and how it still

abgehen sollte ohne Zuchthaus, Thronerschütterung und
downgo should without penitentiary throne falling down and

europäischen Skandal, das wußte er selbst nicht. Er saß,
European scandal that knew he himself not. He sat

anzusehen mit seinem Kopftuch wie ein altes, verhutzeltes
to look at with his headscarf like an old confused

Marktweib, auf dem Kasten des Reserveruders, fühlte in
market woman on the cabinet of the spare rudder felt in

seinen alten, brüchigen Knochen die Gicht, stopfte sich,
his old fragile bones the gout stuffed himself

ratlos, wie er war, eine Pfeife und verpestete weithin
at a loss as he was a pipe and poisoned widely

Gottes Morgen mit seinen Rauchwolken: nun, nun ... die
God's morning with his clouds of smoke now now the

Götter schicken bekanntlich immer eine Hilfe oder doch
gods to send as known always a help or indeed

wenigstens eine Erleuchtung, solange es in einer solchen
at least an enlightenment as long (as) it in a such

Situation auch nur einen Mann gibt, der den Kopf nicht
situation also only a man gives that the head not

verliert und sich helfen lassen will. Schritte waren zu
loses and himself help let wants Steps were to

hören, und der alte Schiffsdoktor merkte, daß es keine
hear and the old ship doctor noticed that it no

Seemannsschritte waren. Unten über das menschenleere
sailor steps were Under over the deserted

Hauptdeck lief der Direktor Samanon.
main deck ran the director Samanon

Befreit hatte ihn aus seinem Prison jener Leutnant Kries,
Freed had him from his prison that lieutenant Kries

der Tischkanten abbeißen konnte, die Beschießung von
who table edges bite off could who bombardment from

Monte Carlo verhindert hatte und auch sonst ein
Monte Carlo prevented had and also otherwise a

vernünftiger Junge war und es im vorliegenden Falle
more reasonable boy was and it in the present case

höchst überflüssig fand, daß dieser unglückselige
most high superfluous found that this unfortunate
most

Ambassadeur der Bank von Monte Carlo nutzlos in seinem
Ambassador the bank from Monte Carlo useless in his

Gefängnis ersticken sollte ...
jail suffocate should

Er sah nun wenig repräsentabel aus mit besudeltem
He looked now little presentable -out- with defiled

Anzug, besudeltem Gesicht und den Gebärden eines
suit defiled face and the sign of a

Mannes, der vom Amoklaufen nicht mehr so weit
man who from the crazy-running not (any)more so far
going mad

entfernt ist. »Können Sie mir sagen, wie man wieder
removed is Can you me say how one again

fortkommt von diesem Höllenschiff?« schrie von unten der
gets away from this hellship cried from under the

Direktor Samanon. »Können Sie mir sagen, wie ein
director Samanon Can you me say how a

assyrischer Flügelochse auf den Sirius fliegen kann?«
more assyrian wing ox on the Sirius fly can

brummte böse und mißgelaunt der Doktor. »Zahle im
growled evil and moody the doctor (I) pay in the

Notfalle auch die Zweitausend«, schrie der Direktor
emergency also the two thousand cried the director

Samanon und gab erst jetzt preis, daß er für den
Samanon and gave first now prize that he for the
known

alleräußersten Notfall, um das Schlimmste zu verhüten,
most extreme emergency for the worst to prevent

das Geld mitbekommen hatte und in seiner Brusttasche
the money along gotten had and in his chest pocket

trug. Da sagte der alte Crofts gar nichts, sondern
carried There said the old Crofts at all nothing but

pfiff nur wie eine Spitzmaus durch die defekten Zähne.
whistled only as a shrew through the defective teeth

Wenn nämlich die drüben zum Zahlen bereit waren,
When namely the ones over there to the paying ready were
willing

so waren sie zu einem kostenlosen Arrangement
so were they to a free arrangement

vermutlich erst recht bereit: ganz fern am Horizont
probably first right ready completely far at the horizon
willing

sah der alte Herr das auftauchen, was die
saw the old gentleman that duck up what the
appear

Diplomatensprache des zwanzigsten Jahrhunderts einen
diplomatic language of the twentieth century a

Silberstreifen genannt hat. Er sagte Herrn
silver stripes called has He said (to the) gentleman

Samanon, daß man über alles weitere wohl reden,
Samanon that one over everything further well talk (would)

daß aber bei den Verhandlungen ein männlicher
that however at the negotiations a more masculine

Whisky nichts schaden könne. Er kletterte die Treppe
whiskey nothing harm could He climbed the stairs

hinunter und nahm den Direktor Samanon beim Arm. Beide
down and took the director Samanon at the arm Both

Herren gingen in die Messe hinunter.
gentlemen went in the mess(hall) down

Zuerst hatten sie sich aus der Pantry die
First had they themselves from the pantry the

Whisky-Flasche geholt, dann hatte der alte Crofts den
whiskey bottle fetched then had the old Crofts the

andern das Geld aufzählen lassen, und dann hatten sie
other the money count let and then had they

sich ... die Banknoten auf neutralem Boden in der
themselves the banknotes on neutral ground in the

Mitte ... einander gegenüber gesetzt an den langen
middle each other opposite set on the long

Mitteltisch.
middle table

Natürlich ist man rachsüchtig, wenn man für eine volle
Of course is one vindictive when one for a full

Stunde in einen Kohlenbunker gesperrt worden ist, und so
hour in a coal bunker blocked become is and so

führte der erste Waffengang zu keinem Resultat. »Wären
led the first gun walk to no result Would
negotiation

Sie zu einem gütlichen Arrangement gegen Rückgabe der
you to an amicable arrangement against return of the

Summe bereit?« fragte der Doktor und legte die Hand auf
sum ready asked the doctor and put the hand on

das Geld. »Sie fürchten, wenn ich mich nicht täusche, die
the money You fear when I myself not deceive the

unausbleiblichen völkerrechtlichen Folgen?« sagte böse
inevitable international law consequences said evil angry

auf der anderen Seite der Direktor Samanon und faßte
on the other side the director Samanon and grasped

seinerseits nach den Banknoten. Da mußte sich der
in turn to the banknotes There must himself the

alte Doktor sagen, daß mit Überrumpelung hier nichts
old doctor say that with surprise here nothing

auszurichten war und daß Hilfe herbeigeholt werden
to achieve was and that help brought here become

mußte. So ließ er also die Banknoten liegen, wo sie
must So let he thus the banknotes lie where they

lagen, und erbat sich zehn Minuten Bedenkzeit und
lay and begged for himself ten minutes time to think and

ging.
went

Den Kabinenschlüssel drehte er auch dieses Mal so leise,
The cabin key turned he also this once so softly

daß sie nichts merkte. Sie hatte sich nun ausgeweint
that she nothing noticed She had herself now cried out

und saß still in der Sofaecke und streckte ihm in ihrer
and sat quiet in the sofa corner and extended him in her

Hilflosigkeit nur die Hände entgegen. »Guten Tag, kleine
helplessness only the hands towards Good day little

Hoheit«, sagte sanft der alte Doktor und sagte das so, daß
highness said softly the old doctor and said that so that

ihr wieder ein ganz klein wenig die Sonne
(for) her again a completely little few the sun
bit

scheinen wollte. Dann setzte er sich neben sie auf das
shine would Then set he himself beside her on the

Plüschsofa und schilderte ihr die Situation und gab ihr die
plush sofa and described her the situation and gave her the

nötigen Instruktionen.
necessary instructions

Erstens: Königinnen dürfen beileibe nicht geweint
First (of all) queens may by all means not cried

haben, wenn sie sich an den Verhandlungstisch
have when they themselves on the negotiating table

setzen. Zunächst also mußten einmal gründlichst die
set Then thus must once most thoroughly the

Tränen aus dem Gesicht gewaschen werden, und der alte
tears from the face washed become and the old

Herr brachte selbst die kärglichen Kosmetika seiner
gentleman brought himself the scanty cosmetics of his

Toilette, und sie tat das Nötige mit dem Eifer eines
toilet and she did the necessary with the zeal of a

kleinen Schulmädchens, dem der alte Onkel zeigt, wie man,
small schoolgirl who the old uncle shows how one

ehe die Mutter es sieht, den garstigen Tintenklecks
before the mother it sees the nasty inkblot

entfernt aus dem neuen Kleid ...
removed from the new dress

Zweitens: man mußte, wenn man die Bank zu einem
Second one must when one the bank to a

anständigen Arrangement bringen wollte, sofort wieder
decent arrangement bring wanted immediately again

die regierende Fürstin sein. Eine Fürstin, die es
the ruling queen be A queen who it

einerseits einsieht, daß es eine Ungehörigkeit ist, wenn
on the one hand sees in that it a impropriety is when
admits

einer ihrer Offiziere die Bank von Monte Carlo mit
one (of) her officers the bank from Monte Carlo with

Bomben bedroht und dann den Direktor in einen Bunker
bombs threatens and then the director in a bunker

sperrt. Eine große Dame aber auch, die es im
locks A great lady but also who it in the

entscheidenden Augenblick einfach nicht versteht, daß
decisive moment simply not understands that

man einer schönen Frau deswegen ernstliche
one a beautiful woman because of that serious

Unannehmlichkeiten bereiten will ...
inconveniences prepare wants

Eine Fürstin, die empört ist, wenn man einen
A queen who outraged is when one a

Karnevalsstreich aufblasen will zu einer internationalen
carnival prank blow up wants to an international

Affäre. Eine Fürstin, die über den Orden Sixtus des
affair A queen who over the medal Sixtus of the

Großmütigen verfügt und ältere französische Herren,
magnanimous disposes and older French gentlemen

wenn sie artig sind, beglücken kann, Ihre Hoheit ...
when they good are delight can your highness

So war das. Er war ein alter asthmatischer Großvater, der
So was that He was an old asthmatic grandfather who

ächzend seiner erwachsenen Enkelin eine Lektion über
groaning his adult granddaughter a lesson over

den Umgang mit störrischen Männern gibt. Und in fünf
the dealing with stubborn men gives And in five

Minuten hatte er sie so weit, daß sie wieder die kleine
minutes had he her so far that she again the little

Mary war mit dem jungenhaften Lachen und dem
Mary was with the boyish laugh and the

unverzagten tapferen Herzen. Da gingen sie denn zu
undaunted brave heart There went they then to

Herrn Samanon in die Messe hinunter.
Mr. Samanon in the mess away-under
down under

Daß sie vor zehn Minuten noch bitterlich geweint hatte,
That she before ten minutes still bitterly cried had

konnte man ihr nun wirklich nicht ansehen: sie kam
could one her now really not on-see she came
see of

hineingerauscht wie in ihren jungen Jahren die selige
rustled into it as in her young years the blessed
deceased

Königin Viktoria in eine Parlamentseröffnung. Er seinerseits
queen Victoria in an opening of parliament He in turn

– der Direktor Samanon nämlich – mochte ja nun
– the director Samanon namely – might yes now
indeed

wirklich etwas erstaunt sein über die sozusagen vom
really somewhat astonished be over the so to speak from the

Himmel gefallene Monarchin; fand aber (ältere
sky fallen monarch found however older

französische Herren verstehen das immer ganz
french gentlemen understand that always completely

ausgezeichnet) sofort allem Groll zum Trotz die
excellent immediately all resentment to the despite the

Geste des Mannes, der weiß, was er einer großen
gesture of the man who knows what he a great

Dame schuldig ist. Item, es gab ohne besondere Etikette
lady owing is Also it gave without special etiquette
(latin)

und Zeremonie eine hübsche Begrüßungsszene. Der alte
and ceremony a pretty welcome scene The old

Regisseur goß sich hinter dem Rücken der beiden
director poured himself behind the back of the both

Akteure rasch einen zweiten Whisky ein.
actors quickly a second whiskey in

So glatt freilich sollten diese Verhandlungen nicht
So smooth freely should these negotiations not
        indeed

verlaufen. Daß sie alles und ganz besonders
run their course That she everything and completely particularly

das dem Direktor Samanon widerfahrene Ungemach auf
that the director Samanon happened inconvenience on

das allerlebhafteste bedaure, sagte sie ...
the most lively deplore said she

Daß ihm in der Tat eine schwere Kränkung widerfahren
That him in -the- deed a heavy insult happen
            great

sei, sagte der Direktor Samanon.
be said the director Samanon

Daß sie zu jedweder Genugtuung bereit sei, sagte die
That she to any satisfaction ready be said the

Hoheit von Labrador.
highness from Labrador

Daß er diese Güte zu schätzen wisse, sagte der Direktor
That he this quality to estimate knew said the director
                esteemed

Samanon. Daß man aber die völkerrechtlichen Folgen
Samanon that one however the international law follow

nun einmal nicht außer acht lassen könne.
now once not out of guard let could
the eye

In dieser Gefechtsphase, wo das Kleingewehrfeuer zu
In this battle phase where the small gun fire to

prasseln begann, wurde sie wieder die streitbare Hoheit.
patter began became she again the controversial highness

Ob er sich überlegt habe, daß gestern so
Whether he himself considered have that yesterday so

etwas wie Karneval gewesen sei in Monte Carlo?
something as carnival been be in Monte Carlo

Ob man an dieser azurnen Küste sich noch erinnere,
Whether one on this azure coast himself still remember

daß mitunter absonderliche Dinge geschähen in
that every now and then strange things happen in

Karnevalsnächten?
carnival nights

Ob man in Monte Carlo nicht wisse, daß der Kapitän
Whether one in Monte Carlo not knew that the Captain

Cradock ein Mann sei, über dessen Streiche schon ganz
Cradock a man be over whose prank already complete

Europa gelacht, und der zum mindesten den Vorzug
Europe laughed and who at the least the preference

habe, daß er immerhin etwas Leben zu bringen pflege in
have that he after all some life to bring used to in

die trübselige Atmosphäre des ehedem weltberühmten,
the gloomy atmosphere of the before world famous

nun aber aus der Mode gekommenen Spielkasinos?
now however out (of) the fashion come casino

Ob man hierzulande eigentlich den letzten Rest von
Whether one in this country actually the last rest of

Humor verloren habe und ob man, wenn man schon
humor lost have and whether one when one already

durchaus Rache nehmen wolle, diese Rache durchaus
throughout revenge take wanted this revenge throughout
at all at all

nehmen müsse an ihr? An ihr, die in diesem Falle als
take must on her On her who in this case as

Staatsoberhaupt die Verantwortliche und Leidtragende sei?
head of state the responsible (one) and guiding (person) be

An ihr, die bislang immer an altfranzösische Ritterlichkeit
On her who so far always on old French chivalry

geglaubt habe ...
believed have
had

Und mit dieser letzten Frage hatte sie denn wirklich die
And with this last question had she then really the

ganz große Kanone abgefeuert gegen die feindliche
completely great canon fired against the enemy

Stellung. Daß auch ihm dies alles mehr als schmerzlich sei,
position That also him this all more as painful be

beteuerte der Direktor Samanon. Daß er gern jedes auch
asserted the director Samanon That he gladly each also

nur halbwegs annehmbare Arrangement eingehen wolle.
only halfway acceptable arrangement enter wanted

Daß er freilich selbst nicht wisse, wie die in Cap
That he indeed himself not knew how the in Cap

d'Antibes nun einmal unternommenen Schritte rückgängig
of Antibes now once undertaken steps undone

zu machen seien ... hier wurde der Direktor Samanon
to make be here became the director Samanon

unterbrochen. Der Leutnant Williams war gekommen.
interrupted The lieutenant Williams was come
                                         had

Er hatte den seelischen Kräften des Leutnants Williams
He had the emotional powers of the lieutenant Williams

zuviel zugemutet, dieser Morgen. Zuerst war Krieg
too much expected of this morning First was war
                                         had

ausgebrochen zwischen Labrador und Monaco, dann war
broken out between Labrador and Monaco then was
                                                   had

der Kapitän verrückt geworden, dann war die »grundgütige
the Captain crazy become then was the ground-goody
                                            principal kind

Landesmutter« gekommen. Dann hatte man dieses
country mother come Then had one this
mother of the nation

Telegramm aufgefangen, das zum dritten Mal an diesem
telegram caught up that for the third time on this

Tage alles auf den Kopf stellte ..., hatte den Kapitän
day everything on the head put had the Captain

gesucht, war überall auf verrammelte Türen gestoßen,
sought was everywhere on barricaded doors bumped halted

ward überall mit Flüchen fortgeschickt, fand endlich
became everywhere with curses sent away found finally

die Hoheit hier. In dieser unaufgeräumten Messe, wo es
the Highness here In this untidy mess where it

nach muffigem Plüsch und kaltem Zigarettenqualm roch ...
to musty plush and cold cigarette smoke smelled

In Gesellschaft des Herrn Samanon, der frisch aus
In company of the gentleman Samanon who fresh from

dem Kohlenbunker kam. In Gesellschaft des Doktor Crofts,
the coal bunker came In company of the doctor Crofts

der in Gegenwart Ihrer Hoheit Whisky trank und ein
who in presence of her Highness whiskey drank and a

rotes Tuch um den Kopf gebunden hatte. Etwas
red cloth for the head bound had Somewhat

überrascht, ja ... er stotterte und konnte das, was er zu
surprised yes he stuttered and could that what he to

sagen hatte, nicht recht so aufbauen, daß die anderen es
say   had   not right so build up that the others it

verstanden ...
understood had

Täuschung beim Beobachten. Drei Schornsteine, ähnliche
Mistake   at the observing Three chimneys   similar

Silhouette, große Entfernung. Gar nicht der »Sadi Carnot«.
silhouette great distance At all not the Sadi   Carnot

Sondern ein friedlicher Indienfahrer. Der P. & O. Liner
But   a   peaceful   India-goer   The P. & O. liner

»Bornemouth«. Und dann dies hier ... ein Telegramm, das
Bornemouth   And then this here   a telegram   that

alles über den Haufen warf ... der Doktor hatte es ihm
everything over the heap threw   the doctor had it him
          upside down

schon aus der Hand gerissen.
already from the hand ripped

In Cap d'Antibes hatte, wie erinnerlich, der französische
In Cap d'Antibes had as remembered the   French

Admiral Constance nicht recht schlafen können in dieser
admiral Constance not right sleep been able in this

Nacht. Er hatte für die letzte Entscheidung über den
night He had for the last decision   over the

telegraphischen Hilferuf Monte Carlos die Rückkehr
telegraphic cry for help (of) Monte Carlo the return

seines Adjutanten abgewartet ... Beide Herren hatten
of his adjutants waited Both gentlemen had

zunächst einmal das internationale Flottenhandbuch
first once the international fleet manual

vorgenommen und hatten festgestellt, daß der labradorische
taken in front and had determined that the Labrador

Kreuzer »Persimon« mit seinen alten Donnerbüchsen
cruiser Persimon with his old thunderbusses
warship

wirklich nicht viel mehr Gefechtswert besaß als ein
really not much (any)more fightable possessed as a

ausrangierter verbeulter Petroleum-Tin.
discarded dented petroleum tin

Beide Herren waren sich klar darüber, daß sie, um
Both gentlemen were themselves clear about it that they for

diese Kriegsmacht niederzukämpfen, mit dem modernsten
this war power to fight down with the most modern

Kriegsschiff Europas angebraust kommen würden. Daß
warship (of) Europe brewed come would That

ihnen also die Gefahr der Lächerlichkeit drohte und
them thus the danger of the ridiculous threatened and

daß ... von allen diesen Dingen abgesehen ... das Telegramm
that from all this things off-seen the telegram
aside

des Kasinos wie ein übler Karnevalsscherz aussah.
of the casino as a bad carnival joke out-saw
looked

Seeoffiziere, wenn sie sich ohne diplomatische
Naval officers when they themselves without diplomatic

Anweisung des eigenen Staates in internationale
instruction of the own state in international

Zwistigkeiten einmischen, laufen bekanntlich immer Gefahr,
quarrels interfere run as known always danger

müssen mit der Möglichkeit von üblen Komplikationen und
must with the possibility from foul complications and

Kammerdebatten rechnen und lassen sich in
chamber debates count and let themselves in

Zweifelsfällen von ihren Adjutanten gern überzeugen, daß
cases of doubt from her adjutants gladly convince that

eine Intervention gut und heldenhaft, daß aber
an intervention good and heroic that however

Abwarten besser ist. Item: auf dem »Sadi Carnot« hatte
off-wait better is Also on the Sadi Carnot had
to await (latin)

der Adjutant noch eine Weile am Bette des
the adjutant still a while at the bed of the

gichtleidenden Chefs gesessen, beide Herren hatten die
suffering from gout boss sat both gentlemen had the

Angelegenheit provisorisch mit einem Whisky-Soda erledigt.
matter provisionally with a whiskey soda finished

Folgende Antwort war also am Morgen hinausgeknattert
Following answer was thus at the morning rattled out

aus der Funkstation des »Sadi Carnot«, hatte nicht nur
from the radio station of the Sadi Carnot had not only

die Antennen des Kasinos, sondern auch die der
the antennas of the casino but also those of the

»Persimon« erreicht, und war dann so zu jenem Telegramm
Persimon reached and was then so to that telegram

geworden, mit dem der Leutnant Williams zwanzig
become with which the lieutenant Williams twenty

Minuten lang vergeblich durch das ganze Schiff gelaufen
minutes long in vain through the whole ship ran

war.
was
had

»Der Flottenchef der Station von Cap d'Antibes betrachtet
The fleet chief of the station of Cap of Antibes considered

die Meldung der Bank von Monte Carlo, daß ein
the notice of the bank from Monte Carlo that a

labradorischer Kreuzer die Bank mit Artilleriefeuer bedrohe,
Labrador cruiser the bank with artillery fire threaten
warship

für einen unangemessenen Karnevalsscherz, den er sich
for an inappropriate carnival joke which he himself

dringend verbittet. Eventuelle Ruhestörungen in Monte
urgently forbade Any rest disorders in Monte

Carlo unterliegen als innere Angelegenheit der dortigen
Carlo underlay as inner matter the there (present)
are subject to

Staatsexekutive. Unterzeichnet: Constance, Vizeadmiral.«
state executive   Undersigned   Constance   vice admiral.

So war der Wortlaut. Katastrophe. Schwerste Niederlage
So was the text   Catastrophe   Heaviest   defeat

der Bank. Der Direktor Samanon war in sich
of the bank The director Samanon was in himself

zusammengebrochen, sah aus, als sei er plötzlich zwanzig
collapsed   saw out as be he suddenly twenty
                   looked

Jahre älter geworden … ich glaube nicht, daß Napoleon
years older become   I believe not   that Napolean

nach Waterloo sehr viel anders ausgesehen haben kann.
after waterloo very much different looked   have can

»Glaube, daß meine Mission hier beendet ist«, sagte tief
(I) believe that my mission here finished is said deeply

gebrochen der Direktor Samanon. »Glaube, daß diese
broken   the director Samanon. (I) believe that this

Mission eben erst beginnt«, sagte die Hoheit von
mission just first starts   said the highness from

Labrador. Und was sie dann in Szene setzte, das war
Labrador and what she then in scene set   that was

schlechthin ein Meisterstück weiblicher Diplomatie …
par excellence a masterpiece of feminine diplomacy

»Wollen wir auf Deck gehen?« fragte sie und wechselte
Want   we on deck   go   asked she and exchanged

mit dem Doktor einen Blick. »Wollen Sie die Güte haben,
with the doctor a glance Want you the quality have

mich zu führen«, fragte sie Herrn Samanon und hing
me to lead asked she Mr. Samanon and hung

sich in seinen Arm ein. Ach ja, es tut gut, eine
herself in his arm in Oh yes it does good a

schöne Frau durch die Morgenbrise der Côte d'Azur
beautiful woman through the morning breeze of the coast of Azure

zu führen ... es tut doppelt gut, wenn man die Fünfzig
to lead it does double good when one the fifty (years)

hinter sich hat und wenn die schöne Frau eine
behind himself has and when the beautiful woman a

regierende Fürstin ist ...
ruling queen is

Sie promenierten zu zweit ... der Doktor hatte sich
They promenaded to second ... the doctor had himself

beurlaubt, saß vor seinem Logis und hatte mit einem
on leave sat before his cabin and had with one

Male eine ganz dringende Schreibarbeit zu erledigen ...
time a completely urgent paperwork to take care of

Sie promenierten zu zweit. Arm in Arm. Dreimal um
They promenaded to second Arm in arm Three times around

das Hauptdeck. Das aber war das diplomatische
the main deck That however was the diplomatic

Meisterwerk der kleinen Mary, daß sie den auf der
masterpiece of the little Mary that she the on the

ganzen Linie geschlagenen Direktor Samanon so behandelte,
whole line hit director Samanon so treated

als sei nicht er, sondern sie die Geschlagene, die
as be not he but she the struck (one) the

Hilfsbedürftige, die auf die Ritterlichkeit ihres Partners
needy who on the chivalry of her partners

Angewiesene. »Internationaler Skandal« ... das blieb auch
instructed (one) International scandal that remained also

nach diesem Telegramm bestehen. »Ganz persönliche
after this telegram exist All personal

Verpflichtung, der Bank und ihrem Direktor Genugtuung zu
obligation the bank and her director satisfaction to

geben« ... das blieb ebenfalls bestehen. Und was doppelt
give that remained likewise exist And what double

und dreifach bestehen blieb, das war ihre Bedrängnis als
and triple exist remained that was her distress as

verantwortliches Staatsoberhaupt und als hilfsbedürftige
responsible head of state and as needy

Frau.
woman

»Arrangement«, sagte schließlich, als sie nach
Arrangement said finally as she after

viertelstündiger Deckpromenade zum zwanzigsten Male bei
quarter of an hour   deck promenade   at the   twentieth   time   at

dem Logis des Doktors vorbeikamen, die Hoheit.
the   cabin of the   doctor   went past   the highness

»Was in den Kräften eines Mannes steht, der   Ew.
What in the powers of a   man   stands who   et.
                                                (ewige: eternal)

Hoheit sich ganz persönlich verpflichtet fühlt«, sagte
highness himself completely personally   obliged   feels   said

Herr Samanon.
Mr   Samanon

»Habe da inzwischen etwas entworfen«, sagte der
Have there In the meantime something   designed   said   the

Doktor und hatte inzwischen Williams' Füllfederhalter
doctor and had In the meantime Williams   fountain pen

ruiniert und ein halbes Dutzend Bleistifte abgebrochen,
ruined and a half   dozen   pencils   broken off

»wofern es beliebt, kleine Hoheit.«
what   it pleases little   highness

Es waren zwei Entwürfe. Ein amtliches Kommuniqué der
It were two   drafts   One   official   communiqué of the

Bank und eine inspirierte Notiz für die gesamte Presse der
bank and an   inspired notice for the entire   press the

Côte d'Azur. Unangemessener Karnevalsscherz eines in
coast of Azure   Inappropriate   carnival joke   of one in

dieser Richtung international bekannten Seeoffiziers ...
this direction international acquaintances naval officers

durchaus nicht (wofür der Bank hinreichende Beweise
throughout not for which the bank adequate proofs
at all

gegeben seien) ernst zu nehmen. Peinlicher Vorfall,
given are serious to take Painful incident
had Embarrassing

durchaus zu mißbilligendes Benehmen des Kapitäns ... in
throughout to disapprove behavior of the captain in
at all

Wirklichkeit aber durchaus keine schlimme Absicht.
reality however throughout no bad intention
at all

Keinerlei Attentate auf die Bank. Keine geladenen Kanonen.
None at all attacks on the bank No loaded cannons

Keine Ursache zur Beunruhigung ...
No root cause to the alarm

Summa summarum: nichts, als ein schlimmer Streich, für
Sum of all nothing than a bad prank for
(latin) (latin)

den die Regierung des einschlägigen Staates (der Name
which the government of the relevant state the name

wurde nicht genannt!) angemessene Bestrafung des
became not named appropriate punishment of the

betreffenden Offiziers zugesagt habe. »Fünf Tage
concerned officer promised have Five days

Stubenarrest«, proponierte der Doktor.
house arrest proposed the doctor

»Drei … um der Form zu genügen«, sagte Herr Samanon.
Three … for the form to satisfy said Mr Samanon

»Vierzehn Tage, bei ebensolanger Enthebung vom
Fourteen days at just as long removal from the

Kommando«, entschied streng und klug die oberste
command decided strict and sensibly the top

Kriegsherrin von Labrador. Nach außen machte sie
warlord from Labrador To (the) outside made she

dabei das Gesicht der großen Katharina, als sie ihren
there-by the face of the great Catherine as she her

ehemaligen Freund Menschikow nach Sibirien schickte.
former friend Menshikov to Siberia sent

Innerlich war sie in der Stimmung eines Mannes, der
Internally was she in the mood of a man who

im Traum seine Tante geschlachtet hat und hingerichtet
in the dream her Aunt slaughtered has and executed

werden soll und aufwachend erkennt, daß alles
become should and waking up recognizes that everything

eben nur ein Traum und der etwas fette Räucheraal
just only a dream and the something fat smoked eel

von gestern abend gewesen ist.
from yesterday evening been is

So war das. Reinschrift und Unterzeichnung so
So was that Beautiful writing and signing as
(Official version of the letter)

bald wie möglich. Ein kleines nettes Kommuniqué, das den
soon as possible A little nice communiqué that the

beiden Partnern nicht wehe tat. Das schöne Erklärungen
both partners not harm did That beautiful explanations

gab, Beruhigung schuf und die Schädigung der Hotels
gave calm created and the damage to the hotels

nach drei Tagen schon wieder gutgemacht haben würde
after three days already again well done have would

durch die Auswirkung einer hübschen Propaganda für
through the impact of a pretty propaganda for

dieses ein wenig aus der Mode gekommene Monte Carlo.
this a little out of the fashion come Monte Carlo

Durch das Aufhorchen der Welt. Durch die Sensation.
Through the listen up of the world Through the sensation
Because of listening Because of

Durch die Aussicht für Chicagoer Industriewitwen und
Through the out-view for (from) Chicago industrial widows and
Because of expectation

New-Yorker Shopkeepertöchter, in Monte Carlo gelegentlich
New Yorker shopkeeper-daughters in Monte Carlo occasionally

einen netten kleinen Nervenkitzel erleben zu können.
a nice small nerve tickle live to see to can
(thrill) experience be able

Einen Nervenkitzel, den Cannes und Nizza und San
A nerve tickle that Cannes and Nice and San
(thrill)

Sebastian bisher nicht hatten bieten können ...
Sebastian until-here not had offer been able
until now

So war das also. Aufatmen. Befreiung. Am Himmel der
So was that thus Up-breathe Liberation at the sky the
    Exhale

rosige Schein, den der Direktor Samanon sah, der kam
rosy shine which the director Samanon saw which came

vielleicht von dem fürstlich-labradorischen Großkreuz Sixtus
perhaps from the princely Labradorian grand cross Sixtus

des Großmütigen her ...
of the magnanimous forth

»Und nun ...« sagte die Hoheit.
And now said the Highness

»Und nun Frühstück«, sagte der Doktor Crofts. Und dann
And now breakfast said the doctor Crofts and then

sagte er noch, daß man die ganze Menschheit einteilen
said he still that one the whole mankind in-part
                                                    divide

könne in böse Menschen, die morgens eine trockene
could in bad people who in the morning a dry

Semmel herunterwürgen ... und in gute, die um sechs
roll choke down and in good who around six

Uhr früh schon den Appetit einer Riesenschlange haben.
hour early already the apetite of a giant snake have
o'clock

Ein liebes nettes kleines Frühstück. Frugal aber nett. Eier,
A dear nice little breakfast Frugal but nice Eggs

Zunge, Schinken, Lachs, Kaviar, Langusten, Birkhuhn,
tongue ham salmon caviar crawfish black grouse

Roastbeef, Honig, Butter, Jams, Schwarzbrot, Kognak. Das
roast beef honey butter yams black bread cognac That

sagte der Doktor Crofts. Dann gab sie dem Leutnant
said the doctor Crofts Then gave they the lieutenant

Williams (als dem in Behinderung des Kapitäns
Williams as the in disability of the captain

Rangältesten) die nötigen Anweisungen, äußerte die
rank-eldest the necessary instructions uttered the
most senior (said)

Vermutung, daß die Herren jetzt ja wohl das Bedürfnis
suspicion that the gentlemen now yes well the desire
indeed

haben würden, sich umzukleiden, und daß (bei der
have would himself to change and that at the

Ähnlichkeit beider Staturen) der Frühstücksdreß des
similarity of both statures the breakfast of the
sizes

Direktors Samanon am besten wohl aus der
director Samanon at the best well from the

Zivilgarderobe des Doktor Crofts bestritten werden könne.
civil wardrobe of the doctor Crofts contested become could

Das sagte die Hoheit. Dann sagte sie noch, daß vielleicht
That said the Highness Then said she still that perhaps

noch ein fünfter Gast – der verlorene Sohn nämlich – an
still a fifth guest – the lost son namely – on

der Frühstückstafel teilnehmen werde. Und dann,
the breakfast bar take part will And then

nachdem die Herren entlassen waren, befahl sie, den
after the gentlemen dismissed were ordered she the

Kapitän Cradock zu rufen. –
Captain Cradock to call

Eine ganze Weile verging, bis er kam. Sie war allein. Sie
A whole while passed until he came She was alone She

lehnte an der Reling, sah nach Monte Carlo hinüber. Sonne
leaned on the railing saw to Monte Carlo over Sun

und das satte Grün der Hänge ... fernes Rufen und das
and the full green the hang distant call and the
cliff

Farbenspiel der bunten Wagen auf der Straße nach
play of colors of the colorful cars on the street to

Cannes. Leben, das erwachte.
Cannes Life that woke up

Sie dachte nach. Leben war gut. Leben war heilig. Was
She thought after Life was good Life was holy What
pondered

aber da in dem verlogenen Bau mit seiner
however there in the lying construction with his

verlogenen Stuckfassade sich Nacht für Nacht gebärdete,
lying stucco facade himself night for night gestured

das war das Leben nicht.
that was the life not

War Formlosigkeit und Verwesung. Geschrei und
(That) was informality and decay Shouting and

Getöse eines Geschlechtes, das auch zur Lasterhaftigkeit
roar of a lineage that also for the viciousness

längst zu müde war ...
long to tired was
already

Sie runzelte die Stirn. Ihr eigenes Leben war freudlos
She frowned the forehead Her own life was joyless
had

gewesen. Streng und kalt und leidlich sauber. Es sollte so
been Strict and cold and tolerable clean It should so

bleiben.
stay

Sie ging auf und nieder auf dem leeren Deck. Der Mann,
She went up and down on the empty deck The man

den man geliebt hatte in zehn öden Jahren, war ein
who one loved had in ten barren years was a

Mann. Aber ein schönes, ungezähmtes Tier zugleich ...
man But a beautiful untamed animal at the same time

Ein Abenteurer, der Verwirrung stiften konnte. Es sollte
An adventurer who confusion raise could It should

nicht so sein, daß er ihr Leben verwirrte. Es sollte nicht
not so be that he her life confused It should not

so sein. Sauber und stark und klar sollte es bleiben. Wie
so be Clean and strong and clear should it stay As

bisher. Sie nahm den Spiegel und ordnete sorgfältig ihr
until-here She took the mirror and ordered carefully her
until now

Haar. Da hörte sie Schritte. Der Cradock war gekommen.
hair There heard she steps The Cradock was come
had

Da stand er. Ein Mann, der in einem etwas
There stood he A man who in a somewhat

verwegenen Salto das Genick gebrochen hatte und
daring somersault the neck broken had and

sich keine Illusionen machte über die Folgen. Ein
himself no illusions made over the consequences A

Mann, der gewillt war, die Folgen auf sich zu
man who willing was the consequences on himself to

nehmen.
take

Da standen sie also. »Haben Sie mir nichts zu sagen,
There stood she also Have you me nothing to say

Kapitän Cradock?«
Captain Cradock

Er schwieg. Er sah auf seinen Degen, den er vorhin
He was silent He looked at his sword which he a while ago

bei seinem Abgang fortgeworfen hatte und der dort
at his departure thrown away had and which there

noch immer lag. Es gab nun keinen Kapitän Cradock
still always lay It gave now no Captain Cradock

mehr. Er schwieg. Da half sie ihm.
(any)more He was silent There helped she him

Sie sah sich um. Das Deck war leer. »Komm«, sagte
She saw herself around The deck was empty Come said

die kleine Mary. Sie gingen an die Reling.
the little Mary They went to the railing

Sie nahm die Perlen aus der Tasche. Perlen, die einmal
She took the Pearls from the pocket Pearls which once

einer unglücklichen Frau gehört hatten. »Du wolltest
an unhappy woman belonged to had You wanted

mir eine Freude machen?« sagte die kleine Mary.
me a joy make said the little Mary

Er nickte stumm.
he nodded mutely

»Sie haben uns nicht viel Glück gebracht, Frederic
You have us not much fortune brought Frederic

William.« Wieder nickte er. Da nahm sie das Kollier
William Again nodded he There took she the necklace

und warf es ins Wasser. »Es ist wohl besser so für uns
and threw it in the water It is well better so for us

beide«, sagte sie. Da nahm er plötzlich ihre Hand und
both said she There took he suddenly her hand and

küßte sie. »Verzeih du mir«, sagte der Cradock und
kissed her Forgive you me said the Cradock and

begriff, daß da noch etwas anderes über Bord
understanding that there still something else over board

geworfen worden war als ein Schmuck. »Verzeih.«
thrown become was as than a jewel Forgive (me)

Da drehte sie sich rasch um und hatte wohl
There turned she herself quickly around and had well

etwas an ihrem Haar zu ordnen. »Oh, kein Grund
something on her hair to order Oh no reason

mehr, Frederic William«, sagte die kleine Mary und
(any)more Frederic William said the little Mary and

machte ein trotziges und tapferes Jungengesicht. »Kein
made a defiant and brave boy face No

Grund.« Dann ging sie dorthin, wo der Degen lag.
reason Then went she there-to where the sword lay

»Willst du ihn wieder haben?«
Want you him it again have

Er schüttelte stumm den Kopf. Er hatte sie schwer
He shook mutely the head He had her heavy

kompromittiert – es war in der Ordnung, daß sie ihn
compromised – it was in the order that she him

fallen ließ. »Habe dir zuviel Ungelegenheiten gemacht.«
fall let (I) have you too many inconveniences made

Da sagte sie ihm alles.
There told she him everything

Daß kein »Sadi Carnot« kam. Daß kein internationaler
That no Sadi Carnot came That no international

Skandal	da	war.	Daß	kein	Direktor	mehr	im
scandal	there	was	That	no	director	(any)more	in the

Kohlenbunker	saß.	Daß	der	Direktor	Samanon	gegenwärtig
coal bunker	sat	That	the	director	Samanon	currently

Frühstückstoilette	machte.	Daß	alles	gut	war,	daß	nur
breakfast toilet	made	That	everything	good	was	that	only

ein	paar	Tage	Stubenarrest	übriggeblieben	waren ...	ihr
a	few	days	house arrest	over-remained	were	her

zuliebe ...	sonst	nichts ...
for the sake of	otherwise	nothing

Er	nahm	den	Degen.	Er	küßte	wieder	ihre	Hand.	Dann
He	took	the	sword	He	kissed	again	her	hand	Then

sah	er	traurig	vor	sich	hin.
saw	he	sad	before	himself	away

»Willst	du	mir	dein	Wort	geben,	daß	du	nicht	mehr
Want	you	me	your	word	give	that	you	not	(any)more

spielst?«	fragte	sie.
play	asked	she
gamble		

Er	nickte.
He	nodded

»Nie	mehr?«
Never	(any)more

Er	nickte.	Ganz	leicht	war	das	nicht.	Mußte	aber
He	nodded	Completely	easy	was	that	not	Must	however

sein einer gütigen Frau zuliebe. »Mein Wort.«
his a kind woman for the sake of My word

»Und dann das andere. Daß du nie mehr Kriege
And then the other That you never (any)more war

erklärst ohne meinen Willen? An die europäische
declare without my will On the European

Zivilisation?«
civilization

Da lächelte er. »Solange ich in Ew. Hoheit
There smiled he As long as I in et. Highness
(ewige: eternal)

Diensten bin.«
service am

»Immer, Cradock!«
Always Cradock

Da schüttelte er traurig den Kopf. Ein Mann war ein
There shook he sad the head A man was a

Mann. Mußte so sein, wie Gott ihn erschaffen hatte.
man Must so be as God him created had

Ein Abenteurer war ein Abenteurer. Mußte so sein, wie
An adventurer was an adventurer Must so be as

Gott ihn erschaffen hatte.
God him created had

Ein Komet war ein Komet. Mußte ruhelos durch das
A comet was a comet Must restless through the

Weltall sausen, Unfug stiften, bis er irgendwo
space zoom nonsense raise until he somewhere

zerspellte ...
shattered

Es mußte wohl so sein. Er schüttelte den Kopf. »Solange
It must well so be He shook the head As long as

ich in deinen Diensten bin.«
I in your serve am

»Immer!«
Always

»Nein.«
No

Es war wohl besser so für sie und für ihn. Er konnte
It was well better so for her and for him He could

dieses Schiff führen ... noch ein halbes Jahr. Des
this ship lead still a half year of the

Anstandes halber. Der Form wegen, die gewahrt werden
decency half The form because of which observed become

mußte. Dann wollte er gehen.
must Then wanted he go

»Wohin?«
Where

Er sah sie stumm an, machte eine etwas müde
He looked her mutely at made a somewhat tired

Handbewegung.
hand movement

»Cradock, wohin gehst du?«
Cradock where-to go you

Er lächelte ein wenig und schwieg. Abenteurer wissen
He smiled a little and was silent Adventurers know

nicht, wohin sie gehen. Da nickte sie stumm. Es war
not where-to they go There nodded she mutely It was

so. Es mußte wohl so sein. Und daß es nun ein sauberer,
so It must well so be And that it now a cleaner

scharfer Schnitt war – das war wohl das Gute
sharper cut was – that was well the good (thing)

daran.
there-on
about it

Sie standen zusammen an der Reling. Ein Boot kam.
They stood together on the railing A boat came

»Meine alte Violet.« Sie lachte.
My old violet. « She laughed

Ein Windstoß fuhr über die Bucht, der böse Husten
A gust of wind drove over the bay the evil coughing

kam wieder. Er sah sie erschrocken an.
came again He saw her frightened on

»Und du?«
And you

Sie lächelte nur. Sie hatte ihr tapferes Knabengesicht.
She smiled only She had her brave boy's face

»Du bist leidend?«
You are suffering

»Oh, nicht der Rede wert.«
Oh not the speech worth

»Und gehst nun nicht dorthin«, er machte mit dem Kopf
And go now not there he made with the head

eine Bewegung dorthin, wo hinter Meeresbläue und
a movement there-to where behind sea blue and

Sonnenfeuer Ägypten lag. »Und gehst nicht dorthin ...
sunfire Egypt lay And go not there

meinetwegen?«
because of me

Da lachte sie. »Die Kohlengelder, mein Herr Kapitän,
There laughed she The coal money my Mr Captain

liegen dort, wo die Perlen liegen.« Da senkte er den
lie there where the Pearls lie There lowered he the

Kopf. Sehr tief beschämt. Er war ein ritterlicher Cradock.
head Very deeply ashamed He was a chivalrous Cradock

Daß sie etwas, was ihr zukam, entbehren sollte
That she something what her came to dispense with should

seinetwegen: das war die bitterste Lektion.
because of him that was the bitterest lesson

»Ich werde keine Kriege mehr erklären ohne dich.«
I will no War (any)more declare without you

Da sah sie sich um auf dem menschenleeren Deck,
There saw she herself around on the deserted deck

vergewisserte sich, daß es niemand sah. Ging zu ihm und
assured herself that it nobody saw Went to him and

strich ihm beruhigend über das Haar, in dem wirklich
brushed him soothing over the hair in which really

noch kein Grau zu finden war. »Alter, dummer Junge!«
still no grey to find was Old stupid boy

sagte die kleine Mary.
said the little Mary

Unten am Fallreep brummte schon der Motor. Violet
Under at the gangway growled already the engine Violet

Gräfin Hensbarrow, Zofe Susan und fünf nun etwas
countess Hensbarrow maid Susan and five now somewhat

deplazierte Lederkoffer.
misplaced leather suitcases

»Nun wird es wohl ein Ende haben mit uns beiden«,
Now will it well an end have with us both

sagte die kleine Mary.
said the little Mary

»Nun muß es wohl sein.«
Now must it well be

Sie sahen sich an. Nein, keine Vertraulichkeiten.
They looked each other at No no confidentialities

Scharfer, sauberer Schnitt und tapfere Herzen. Sie gaben
Sharper cleaner cut and brave heart They gave

sich die Hand.
each other the hand

»Du.«
You

»Du.«
You

»Und vergibst mir?«
And (you) forgive me

»Dummer Junge!«
Stupid boy

Die anderen, sie hatten nun ihre Frühstückstoilette
The others they had now their breakfast toilet

beendet. In goldbetreßtem Gala-Zweispitz und funkelnden
finished In gold-pressed gala bicorn and sparkling

Lackstiefeln ein frisch aus dem Ei geschälter
lacquered leather boots a fresh from the egg peeled

Marineleutnant Fennimore Williams.
naval lieutenant Fennimore Williams

In etwas abgetragener Uniform ein alter, dicker,
In somewhat more worn uniform an old more thick

asthmatischer Schiffsdoktor Wilbour Crofts.
more asthmatic   ship doctor   Wilbour   Crofts

In einem ausgeliehenen, aber angesichts der gleichen
In a   borrowed   but   in face   of the (the) same

Staturen leidlich sitzenden Cutaway ein nun wieder
stature   tolerable sitting   cutaway   a   now again
size

sauberer und stattlicher Direktor Samanon.
clean   and stately   director   Samanon

In einem würdigen, leicht nach Kampfer duftenden und
In an   dignified easy   to   honeysuckle smelling and

mit Hilfe der Zofe Susan glücklich zugehakten Reisekleid
with help of the maid Susan happy   hooked up   travel dress

eine ältliche, auf Zucht und gute Sitte haltende Hofdame,
an   elderly   on   breed and good habit holding   court lady
                                                minding

Violet Hensbarrow.
Violet Hensbarrow

Vorstellung und Tischordnung und zu allem ein tapferes
Presentation and table arrangement and to all   a   brave

Weiberherz, das sein Inneres nicht offenbart.
woman heart that her inner (thoughts) not disclosed

Eine angemessene Tischordnung.
An   appropriate   table arrangement

Die Hoheit von Labrador und der Repräsentant der
The Highness from Labrador and the representative of the

Bank von Monte Carlo.
bank from Monte Carlo

Die Gräfin Hensbarrow und der Doktor Crofts.
The countess Hensbarrow and the doctor Crofts

Kleine Flottenleutnants bekommen noch keine Tischdame.
Little fleet lieutenants become still no table lady

Und der verlorene Sohn namens Cradock sitzt zur Linken
And the lost son name Cradock sits to the left

der Hoheit von Labrador.
of the Highness from Labrador

Bomben auf Monte Carlo sind gut. Aber zu Tisch gehen
Bombs on Monte Carlo are good But to table go

ist besser. Und alle die bösen Menschen haben
is better And all the bad people have

morgens keinen Appetit, und alle die guten Menschen
in the morning no apetite and all the good people

haben um sechs Uhr früh schon einen Hunger wie eine
have at six hour early already a hunger as a
o'clock

Riesenschlange. Ein nettes, liebes, kleines Frühstück. Frugal
giant snake A nice dear little breakfast Frugal

aber nett. Eier, Zunge, Schinken, Lachs, Kaviar, Langusten,
but nice Eggs tongue ham salmon caviar crawfish

Birkhuhn, Roastbeef, Honig, Butter, Jams, Schwarzbrot,
black grouse roast beef honey butter yams black bread

Kognak. So, und nicht anders …
cognac So and not different

Am Abend aber, als die Hoheit von Labrador sich
At the evening however as the Highness from Labrador herself

von dem Direktor Samanon noch nach der Corniche
from the director Samanon still to the corniche

führen ließ, war da unter dicken, mit dem letzten
lead let was there under thick with the last

Kohlenschutt gespeisten Rauchwolken ein kleines Schiffchen
coal debris fed clouds of smoke a little boat

zu sehen, das in Savona Gelder für neue Kohlen vorfinden
to see that in Savona funds for new coals find
                                                  are found

sollte.
should

Ein kleiner silbriger Kreuzer, der Kurs nach Osten
A little silvery cruiser which course to (the) east
                     warship

nahm.
took

Der Herr Direktor Samanon fragte, wohin er ginge.
The Mr. director Samanon asked where-to he went

Die Hoheit an seiner Seite überhörte die Frage und
The Highness on his side ignored the question and

antwortete nicht.
answered not

Abenteurer kennen ihren Weg nicht.
Adventurers know their way not

Und nie steigt ein Mann höher, als wenn er nicht weiß,
And never rises a man higher as when he not knows

wohin er geht.
where-to he goes

www.ingramcontent.com/pod-product-compliance
Lightning Source LLC
Chambersburg PA
CBHW071407090426
42737CB00011B/1380